D0442568

Music, Madness, and the Unworking of Language

COLUMBIA THEMES IN PHILOSOPHY, SOCIAL CRITICISM, AND THE ARTS

JOHN T. HAMILTON

Music, Madness, and
the Unworking of Language

Columbia University Press / New York

Columbia University Press
Publishers Since 1893
New York   Chichester, West Sussex
Copyright © 2008 Columbia University Press
All rights reserved

Library of Congress Cataloging-in-Publication Data

Hamilton, John T.
   Music, madness, and the unworking of language / John T. Hamilton.
      p. cm. — (Columbia themes in philosophy, social criticism, and
the arts)
   Includes bibliographical references and index.
   ISBN 978-0-231-14220-5 (cloth : alk. paper)—ISBN 978-0-231-51254-1
(e-book)   1. Music—Philosophy and aesthetics—History.   2. Music
and language.   3. Music—Psychological aspects—History.   I. Title.
II. Series.

   ML3800.H246   2008
   780.1—dc22   2007036012

Columbia University Press books are printed on permanent
   and durable acid-free paper.
This book is printed on paper with recycled content.

Printed in the United States of America
c 10 9 8 7 6 5 4 3 2 1
Designed by Lisa Hamm

References to Internet Web sites (URLs) were accurate at the time
of writing. Neither the author nor Columbia University Press is
responsible for URLs that may have expired or changed since the
manuscript was prepared.

For Jasper and Henry—

avant toute chose

Split the Lark—and you'll find the Music—

—Emily Dickinson

Contents

A Note on Translations and Abbreviations

I REFER THROUGHOUT to the original texts and, when available, offer standard English translations, supplying a second page reference. In general, these translations have been modified toward greater literalness. Unless otherwise noted, all other translations are my own.

Spelling in the primary sources has not been modernized. For collected editions, volume number is followed by the page reference or, where relevant, a book number and then a page reference. References to the Weimarer Ausgabe of Goethe's *Werke* are to section, volume, and page.

Concerning ancient Greek, I have chosen to transliterate single words for the sake of comparison, while retaining the original alphabet for longer phrases and citations.

References to Plato's works are from John Burnet's edition (*Platonis Opera*, 5 vols. [Oxford: Clarendon, 1972–76]). In translating into English, I have consulted the *Complete Works*, ed. John M. Cooper (Indianapolis: Hackett, 1997). For the convenience of the reader with different translations, I have simply marked each citation with the conventional manuscript number.

The following abbreviations are used for frequently cited editions:

EH   Friedrich Nietzsche. *The Antichrist, Ecce Homo, Twilight of the Idols, and Other Writings*. Trans. Judith Norman. Cambridge: Cambridge University Press, 2005.

HMW   *E. T. A. Hoffmann's Musical Writings*. Ed. David Charlton. Cambridge: Cambridge University Press, 1989.

HW   E. T. A. Hoffmann. *Sämtliche Werke*. 6 vols. Ed. Hartmut Steinecke. Frankfurt: Deutscher Klassiker, 1993. (Note that the second volume is further divided into two subvolumes.)

KM   E. T. A. Hoffmann. *The Life and Opinions of the Tomcat Murr.* Trans. Anthea Bell. New York: Penguin, 1999.

KSW   Heinrich von Kleist. *Sämtliche Werke und Briefe.* 2 vols. Ed. Helmut Sembdner. Munich: Deutscher Taschenbuch, 2001.

KU   Immanuel Kant. *Kritik der Urteilskraft.* Vol. 5 of *Gesammelte Schriften*, 24 vols. Ed. Royal Prussian Academy of Sciences. Berlin: de Gruyter, 1969. *Critique of the Power of Judgment.* Trans. Paul Guyer and Eric Matthews. Cambridge: Cambridge University Press, 2000.

NR   Denis Diderot. *Le neveu de Rameau.* Ed. Jean Fabre. Geneva: Droz, 1963. *Rameau's Nephew and d'Alembert's Dream.* Trans. Leonard Tancock. New York: Penguin, 1966.

NW   Friedrich Nietzsche. *Sämtliche Werke: Kritische Studienausgabe.* 15 vols. Ed. Giorgio Colli and Mazzino Montinari. Munich: Deutscher Taschenbuch, 1988.

PG   G. W. F. Hegel. *Phänomenologie des Geistes.* Vol. 3 of *Werke*, 20 vols. Ed. Eva Moldenhauer and Karl Markus Michel. Frankfurt: Suhrkamp, 1986. *Phenomenology of Spirit.* Trans. Andrew Miller. Oxford: Oxford University Press, 1977.

ROC   Jean-Jacques Rousseau. *Œuvres complètes.* 5 vols. Ed. Bernard Gagnebin and Marcel Raymond. Paris: Gallimard, Bibliothèque de la Pléiade, 1959–95. *The Confessions.* Trans. J. M. Cohen. New York: Penguin, 1954.

WW   Wilhelm Heinrich Wackenroder. *Sämtliche Werke und Briefe: Historisch-kritische Ausgabe.* 2 vols. Ed. Silvio Vietta and Richard Littlejohns. Heidelberg: Carl Winter, 1991. *Wilhelm Heinrich Wackenroder's Confessions and Fantasies.* Trans. Mary H. Schubert. University Park: Pennsylvania State University Press, 1971 (translations from the *Herzensergießungen* and the *Phantasien über die Kunst*).

Hors d'œuvre I

What then is madness, in its most general but most concrete form, for anyone who immediately challenges any hold that knowledge might have upon it? In all probability, nothing other than the absence of work ["l'absence de l'œuvre"].

—MICHEL FOUCAULT, *HISTORY OF MADNESS*

I N 1989 the Stadtmuseum of Nürtingen published a handsome catalog to mark the opening of a new standing exhibit honoring one of the city's most famous sons, Friedrich Hölderlin. The volume features twelve letters selected from the museum's archive, written between 1828 and 1832 by Hölderlin's warden, the master carpenter Ernst Zimmer. Reproduced on color plates, Zimmer's reports promised a privileged glimpse of the poet who since 1807, upon being judged insane by family, friends, and local authorities, was consigned to the tower room above the carpenter's house in Tübingen. The correspondence, however, graciously transcribed by the editors, Thomas Scheuffelen and Angela Wagner-Gnan, in fact contributes nothing new to Hölderlin's fateful biography (Friedrich Beißner had already included a transcription of them in his critical edition). The scanty testimony, moreover, hardly offers a vivid portrait of the man. Still, something is communicated, or rather *related*, namely, the fact— perfectly obvious and terribly simple—that this unique, nonrepeatable life had existed. The faded sepia lines, together with the official governmental stamps, enhance the documentary quality of the pages. The life of the poet, now gone, is thereby displayed, suspended in epistolary formal- dehyde, disinfected and preserved for posterity. This concrete evidence, al- though barely illuminating the author's life and even less his work, points nonetheless to the poet's singularity, to the person extrinsic to and therefore in excess of the work.

What is most striking, above all, is the collection's title. Quoted from one of Zimmer's last letters, it is as directive as it is descriptive and charged with especial significance:

« . . . die Winter Tage
bringt Er meistens am Forte Piano zu . . . »

(". . . he usually spends the winter days at the pianoforte . . .")

The words, doubly protected by quotation marks and ellipsis points, provocatively conjure the image of the mad musician. The citation-cum-title comes across as an invitation to consider the solitary life that followed a poetic career emphatically as musical. The figure of the neurotically tempered pianist begs the passerby to listen for the music that accompanied the sad downfall. Introduced into the silence of the *nox mentis* are the sounds of improvisations, the precise nature of which one can only guess: Some incomprehensible, shapeless melody? A phrase recalled from childhood? The aimless modulation of triads? Or perhaps an uncanny threnody vainly reaching out for an absent god? Whatever it may have been, the sound was lost upon emission. Hölderlin's *moments musicaux* bear no opus number.

Among the many issues that make this anecdote pertinent is the dogged tenacity—as late as 1989—of the wholly romantic coupling of music and madness. The portrait of Hölderlin presented here could be conflated with a host of figures, historical and fictional, who share a similar fate. One is reminded, for example, of that other tragic hero of the nineteenth century, Friedrich Nietzsche, who, according to his many hagiographers, spent his last days in Turin alone at the piano, lost in frenzied meandering. We are thus asked to consider Hölderlin's derangement overall ("meistens") as a fall—or an ascent, which here amounts to the same—to music. The case of Nietzsche—*der Fall Nietzsche*—reinforces the implication, namely, that after the word has been exhausted—be it the *logos* of philosophical inquiry or the verse of lyric poetry—there is only madness and music. The image of Hölderlin at the piano, speechlessly looking out at the frozen waters of the Neckar, suggests that language had run its course. As if words no longer worked. As if writing had become impossible.

When Hölderlin does write—and, according to Zimmer and other witnesses, the occasions across these three decades are decidedly few—he writes in fragments, in a language that is broken into pieces, disarticulated, and obscure. Now and then, however, he pens brief, relatively coherent poems devoted to the seasons. Reminiscent of children's songs, the lines appear to reintroduce music to language.

Wenn aus der Tiefe kommt der Frühling in das Leben,
Es wundert sich der Mensch, und neue Worte streben

Aus Geistigkeit, die Freude kehret wieder
Und festlich machen sich Gesang und Lieder.

Das Leben findet sich aus Harmonie der Zeiten,
Daß immerdar den Sinn Natur und Geist geleiten,
Und die Vollkommenheit ist Eines in dem Geiste,
So findet vieles sich, und aus Natur das meiste.

     d. 24 Mai 1758
     Mit Unterthänigkeit Scardanelli

(When from the depth spring comes into life
Mankind marvels, and new words strive
Out of intellect, joy turns round
And festively there appear song and sound.

Life is to be found in the harmony of the seasons,
So that evermore nature and spirit escort sense,
And perfection is one in the spirit,
Thus much is to be found, and from nature the most.

     24 May 1758
     Your humble servant, Scardanelli)

The evocation of vitality and wonder, novelty and song, expresses an experience of breakthrough, starkly opposed to the madly musical winter of
Hölderlin's discontent. The poem, with its gently musical end rhymes—
one thinks of a lullaby—literally "strives" for "new words," which would
wrest themselves free of intellection ("aus Geistigkeit") and break into a
music ("Lieder und Gesang"), redeeming life from a language turned cold.
Indeed, the lines seem to realize the beloved Rousseau's dream of returning to the (Mediterranean) origin of language, where word and song
reveled in unison, where an authentic accent underscored the speaking
subject's immediate presence.

What contradicts this optimism, however, is the date and signature
that Hölderlin appends to the poem. Rather than accurately designating
the poem's source, both the date—1758, some fourteen years before
Hölderlin's birth—and the hauntingly Italianate, quasi-musical name of
Scardanelli bring about a referential disorientation or derangement. If
writing is still possible, it is so only as something anachronistic and
pseudonymous. To be sure, music ("Lieder und Gesang") is figured as
authentic, yet precisely as a figure, it bespeaks expropriation. The subject
of inscription has been radically displaced. The signature disrupts.
Theories of expression, representation, and intention—of the mimetic

figuration of words—underlie a working of language whereby something is lost.

Personal subjectivity as a fixed entity, capable of grounding discourse, becomes something suspect. The Hölderlinian subject of writing, who marks the text as out-of-date and authored by another, reveals the alienating function of this work. (Rousseau of course is no stranger to this.) Hölderlin's attested incapacity or unwillingness to enter into verbal communication with visitors and old friends may be further symptoms of this fear of self-betrayal. Writing and speaking appear to equal self-loss, as though the referential mechanism of words—and especially the word "I"—fails to coincide with a feeling of selfhood. The pseudonymity and anachronism of Hölderlin's mad signature—Scardanelli, 1758—redefine the gesture of authorial signing itself as an abandonment to language, literally as subordinating oneself ("mit Unterthänigkeit") to programs of convention. Rather than legitimizing the work as a mark from the outside, the signature here operates from within. It becomes yet another signifier among others, a subject that is subject to play, a possible victim of misinterpretation or abuse. The author's name, which should stand as the transcendental origin of the poem, is thereby implicated and indicted. That which should be situated at a validating position outside the text loses its own validity. The subject of writing—this *parergon*, both "beside" and "contrary to" (*para-*) the "work" (*ergon*)—can only remain outside the œuvre by virtue of being within it. The signature, which should promote the writer to the status of authority and authorship (*auctoritas*), here signals instead that the writer, by writing, has auctioned himself off.

And so Hölderlin "usually spends the winter days at the pianoforte." The man who once worked out a poetics of alternating tones and discussed representation in terms of rhythm has now himself become a poem: a magnum opus of solitude and silence, of madness and music. Still, as Heidegger would note, something may be disclosed in this withdrawal, a truth that would be all the truer insofar as it could not be made to fit into the production of sense—a truth, radically singular and frighteningly evanescent, that would resist subscription to any concept. Would this something, then, not be better understood as a nothing, that which has being purely by being lost?

The following study does not primarily take into account poets who become poems. Instead, it deals with writers who attempt to appropriate the unworking effects of music and madness as a technique for retrieving—Orphically, one could say—that which is already gone. Through metaphors of music and madness, they attempt to bring to the light of day this Eurydicean point of selfhood that, according to the very law of metaphor, must return to the dark. The point, timeless and spaceless, can neither be held nor be beheld. Likewise, the subject of writing persists only in the work that marks its absence. That said, this nothing may only be taken as not something provided one stays in a working system that divides being from nonbeing. Outside this work, the nothing may indeed be not nothing. The hopelessness of the law is the condition of possibility for hope. If Hölderlin and his piano are conjured in this hors d'œuvre, it is only because, at the very least, his insane rhapsodies serve as a resonating figure of what Blanchot has called, in direct reference to the Orpheus myth, *désœuvrement*. Whether there was method in it or not, Hölderlin's musical benightedness motivates thinking about the unworking of language. Given the ambiguity of the genitive (subjective and objective), the unworking of language begins to point to the way music and madness may disarticulate representational discourse as well as the means by which language can always disable the devices designed to evade it. The texts below, which all turn to the theme of music and madness, reverberate with Hölderlin's concerts for no one: evanescent soundings that are "in all probability" nothing. In the end, it may be "nothing other than the absence of the work," which is to say—perhaps after the end (or before the beginning)—everything.

I owe an immense debt of gratitude to the staff and colleagues at the Wissenschaftskolleg zu Berlin where, as a resident fellow in 2005–2006, I was able to complete the majority of my manuscript. Many thanks also to Lydia Goehr for her kind encouragement and support throughout. I would also like to express my fondest appreciation to all those who read portions of the work in various drafts and offered indispensable comments: Daniel Albright, Marshall Brown, Thomas Christensen, Peter Fenves, Judit Frigyesi, Eileen Gillooly, Christopher Hasty, Jennifer Hui Bon Hoa, Irad Kimhi, Reinhart Meyer-Kalkus, Eyal Peretz, Alexander Rehding, Timothy Reiss, Thomas Schestag, Marc Shell, William Todd, and Hans Zender. Thanks also to Glenn Most and to my dear friends in the Leibnizkreis, which continues to provide an exceptional forum for presenting my work in progress: Manuel Baumbach, Barbara Borg, Bettina Full, Dag-Nikolaus Haase, Martin Holtermann, Helga Köhler, Martin Korenjak, Stefan Rebenich, Adrian Stähli, Martin Vöhler, and Antje Wessels. Earlier versions of some chapters were first presented as talks at Johns Hopkins University, the University of Chicago, New York University, the Rheinische

Music, Madness, and the Unworking of Language

Introduction

THE SUBJECT OF MUSIC AND MADNESS

Kreisler stood there shaken to the depths, unable to utter a word. He had always been obsessed with the idea that madness lay in wait for him like a wild beast slavering for prey, and one day would suddenly tear him to pieces.

—E. T. A. HOFFMANN, *LEBENSANSICHTEN DES KATERS MURR*

MUSIC'S PROXIMITY to madness is a theme dear to German romanticism. Hoffmann's Kreisler—the eccentric if not altogether deranged composer—is but one of many examples that populate not only this writer's fiction but also the literature around 1800. Alongside Hoffmann's retinue of characters who actively wield or passively submit to the irresistible force of music stand analogous figures in the works of the period's most prolific authors. Kreisler, the "mad musician par excellence" (*HW* 2.1.370), together with Ritter Gluck and Donna Anna, Theodor of "Die Fermate" and the baroness of "Das Majorat," Rat Krespel and his daughter, Antonie, are all paradigmatic for the era.

The inclination to associate mental disturbance with the realm of sound proceeds almost effortlessly. "So much lies merely in the mischief [*Spuk*] that my notes create," Kreisler confesses. "They often come to life and jump up from the white pages like little black many-tailed imps. They whirl me along in their senseless spinning . . . but a single tone, shooting its ray from the holy glow, will still the tumult" (*HW* 2.1.369/*HMW* 131). Kreisler's problem, caught between the spooky taunts of mischievous notes and the redemptive tone of the numinous, between madness as heightened consciousness and as utter dementia, continually crops up in an age assured of music's power but uncertain of where it might lead.

The trend—provocatively intermingling literary and clinical discourses, pathology and aesthetics, art and psychology—is strikingly persistent. It features a repertoire of conceptions and motifs shared among writers whose dispositions and purported intentions are otherwise quite divergent. Thus the late, brooding walks in the *Nachtwachten des Bonaventura* (1803), which expose a musically charged dark side of the workaday world, presages in a different key the strange events of Kleist's

Heilige Cäcilie (1811), where four brothers are struck insane upon hearing an oratorio at High Mass. The senility of Goethe's harpist in *Wilhelm Meisters Lehrjahre* (1795–96) serves both as complement and contrast to the naïveté of Florio, the young man who is induced to mad hallucinations by sound and music in Eichendorff's *Das Marmorbild* (1819). Countless examples can be accumulated, from Karl Philipp Moritz and Jean Paul Richter to Novalis, Ludwig Tieck, and Clemens Brentano. Indeed, a cursory reading of the period would readily demonstrate, despite great diversity, a common tendency to link musical production and reception with descriptions of mad experience.

To be sure, the writers who are here loosely grouped under the term "romantic" did not invent the idea of music's strong influence on states of the soul. Nor did such conceptions vanish in a later age. There existed a long classical tradition devoted to the so-called power of music. This widely held idea, based on a belief in music's incomparably strong effect on the character and emotions of listeners, on the ethos and pathos of the citizenry, could be viewed in either a positive or a negative light, as pathogenic or therapeutic. The ambiguities are pervasive. Orpheus's ability to appease the Furies is matched by his cruel death at the hands of the frenzied Maenads. The deeply felt nostalgia that overcomes Odysseus before Demodocus's harp modulates to fright in encountering the Sirens, whose song would put an end to any hope for a return home. Plato's fear that musical mimesis might lead to hysteria among the guardians of his ideal city is eased by the philosopher's appreciation, expressed in the *Timaeus*, of the musical relationships that underlie and maintain a sound cosmic order. Timotheus's legendary lyre—recorded by Plutarch, Suidas, and Boethius and then celebrated by Renaissance theorists such as Franchino Gafurrio and Gioseffo Zarlino—was said to have been capable of inciting Alexander to murder as well as escorting him back to sanity. Music's power is matched only by its ambivalence.

Music's influence on the passions, its direct bearing on the *affectus animi*, epitomized by the figure of Timotheus, was considered universal, as is evident in both classical and Christian traditions.[1] For example, in his *Musica demonstrata* (1496), Jacques Lefèvre d'Étaples correlated the story of Timotheus to the Old Testament account of David (1 Samuel 16:23), whose psalms exorcised the demons that attacked the melancholic King Saul.[2] The early eighteenth century found its own Timotheus in Carlo Farinelli, the famous castrato who sang the same four arias every evening for twenty years to the Bourbon king Philip V of Spain in order to cure the sovereign of his manic fits. Elsewhere, the theme abounded in treatises on so-called musical magic and in folklore. It was perpetuated in the myriad examples of the indomitable strength of music, from pied pipers to Apulian tales of tarantism, from treatises on the efficacy of religious hymns to Agrippa's *De occulta philosophia* (published in 1533), which describes in detail the manipulation of celestial powers by means of sounds, tones, and melodic phrases.[3]

The notion that musical art affected psychological processes survived in the literature that basked in romanticism's long shadow, even when romantic tendencies were critically reassessed or disavowed, for example, in the series of bizarre or maddening violinists of the nineteenth century, from Heine's *Florentinische Nächte* (1837) and Lenau's *Faust* (1836) to Grillparzer's *Der arme Spielmann* (1848) and Keller's *Romeo und Julia auf dem Dorfe* (1855). Paganini's mesmerizing hold over his audiences was corroborated by many accounts of Mephistophelean virtuosi in the literature from Biedermeier on.[4] The general theme would later receive fresh impetus in Wagnerism and could be witnessed in the work (and life) of Friedrich Nietzsche, a musical madman in his own right. Spurred by Schopenhauer, he aligned tonal art to Dionysos *mainomenos*, the mad god, and thereby reevaluated philosophical aesthetics on the basis of irrational impulse. In the Nietzschean aftermath, the figure of the deranged composer saw its greatest and most abysmal illustration in Thomas Mann's *Doktor Faustus*, where romantic energy rose to a fevered pitch before consuming itself in the catastrophic *Götterdämmerung* of 1945.

To close the history of the mad musician with Mann's Faustian Leverkühn is not to suggest that this figure does not continue to shape the German cultural and literary imagination. Madly musical protagonists may be found in many post-1945 literary works, for example, in the novels of Thomas Bernhard and Elfriede Jelinek, who both consciously engage in the tradition at hand. Add to that the countless publications of musical biographies, from Haydn to Schumann, from Beethoven to Wagner, from Mahler to Hugo Wolf, so replete with descriptions of mental illness that they often read like psychopathological case studies. One need only consult Franz Franken's four-volume study *The Maladies of Great Composers* to ascertain to what extent psychoses and neuroses still color German conceptions of musical production.[5]

That said, it would nonetheless be imprudent to ascribe this theme exclusively to some Teutonic imaginary. There are countless representations of unhinged composers, overly impassioned instrumentalists, and dangerously affected listeners in practically all major literatures. One thinks, for example, of Balzac's *Gambara* (1837), Tolstoy's *Kreutzer Sonata* (1890), or D'Annunzio's *Trionfo della morte* (1894). The trend predictably continues in film and the visual arts. Popular as well as so-called serious music are consistently represented as experiences that border on something irrational, ravishing, or provocatively fascinating. The power of music—beneficial or detrimental, from the mother's lullaby to the fascist broadcast—names music's undeniably strong influence, its overwhelming emotional force, its capacity to seize and overtake, its elemental energy difficult to master. The subject's loss of rational control in musical experience, the rise of unexpected passions or the sudden welling-up of tears, is hardly the province of a precise epoch or ethos but rather is a transcultural, transhistorical phenomenon.

From another perspective, the recurrent topic belongs to the even broader stereotype of the tortured genius, which derives from the Aristotelian problem (30.1) linking melancholia and giftedness. To this line of thought belongs Seneca's famous pronouncement that "there is no genius without a mixture of dementia" ("nullum ingenium sine mixtura dementiae," *De tranquilitate animi*). Both observations are again modulations of the entire tradition of inspiration or enthusiasm that since Plato's *Ion* and *Phaedrus* falls beneath the banner of divine madness.[6] To this day, in the popular and academic press, clinical psychologists as well as neuroscientists continue to be intrigued by the relation of creativity and mental illness. Works on the imagination's indebtedness to bipolar disorder, autism, or brain physiology are legion.[7]

It is not, however, my intention to deal directly with these issues. Instead, I have chosen to look into the complex ways music and madness are treated in a specifically romantic tradition. I have therefore restricted my examination to a period of European history that, in my view, represents the deepest and most prolonged reflection on specific issues raised by the coupling of music and madness. The scope stretches from the latter half of the eighteenth century to the first decades of the nineteenth, from Diderot's *Neveu de Rameau*, with emphasized focus on this text's reception and appropriation by the German romantics, to the work of E. T. A. Hoffmann. As shall become evident, however, these historical borders cannot be respected. The astounding persistence of the problems under investigation requires a broader view so as to include both the ancient sources, which instigate the central challenges, and their rich afterlife in recent formulations of literary criticism, aesthetic theory, and the philosophy of language.

The sheer preponderance of this literary practice immediately raises key questions. Why, first of all, *music* and madness? What does a highly refined art form have to do with mental disorders? How do these two heterogeneous experiences relate? And what distinguishes the specifically romantic appropriation of this convergence?

Some initial, highly general responses may be ventured here, in anticipation of a more elaborate, critical investigation below. For example, it would appear that music and madness need to be related through the third term of language. Considered romantically as spheres that challenge the norms of denotation and signification, music and madness may be said to define the upper and lower limits of language, respectively. In the epigraph cited above, Kreisler's inability to "utter a word" ("keines Wortes mächtig") can signal either a verbal failure or a sublime affect. Both mark out a conceptual border beyond which language cannot reach. On the one hand, if the rational working of language is what distinguishes mankind from beast, then Kreisler's speechlessness may be taken as a symptom of an imminent insanity, of a psychically disturbed state, explicitly described as savage, that would tear his individual identity into pieces. Language—understood, say, as self-representation, communication, or expression—works by means of an intentionality that is grounded in a stable, unified subject, and it is that subjective ground that madness threatens to undo. On the other hand, the composer's muteness may be interpreted as a transcendent move into areas of meaning that words cannot touch. If in the first case madness reduces man to the status of beast, to hunted prey—as in the classical examples of the madly driven Orestes, Ajax, and Pentheus—in the second case music constitutes a spiritual remedy to an existential wound we all share, bound to a symbolic logic that abstracts our relation to the world. Whereas madness as the lower limit to language dissolves the boundaries between mankind and savagery, music as the upper limit overrides the division that separates humanity from the divine. In purely linguistic terms, music frees us from the reductive powers of conceptualization. Certainly, this topos of ineffability underpins much of the tradition.[8]

It was in fact romantic theory that first exploited the irrational (or suprarational) force of purely instrumental music. What would eventually come to be known as absolute music—music liberated or absolved from all verbal discourse—was proffered as being capable of presenting human truths that evaded the rigid definitions and concepts of the lexicon and verbal syntax. Hoffmann himself was largely responsible for promoting music's reevaluation as an autonomous rather than ancillary art form. In his famous review of Beethoven's Fifth Symphony (1810), he writes: "Music discloses to man an unknown realm ["ein unbekanntes Reich"], a world that has nothing to do with the outer sensual world surrounding him, a world in which he leaves behind all feelings ascertainable by concepts in order to devote himself to the inexpressible ["dem Unaussprechlichen"]"

(*HW* 1.532/*HMW* 236). Music's transcendence is based on a series of negations—"unknown," "inexpressible"—and thereby moves beyond the positivism of human perception and cognition. Although this transcendence is generally presumed to be an ascent toward a divine sphere, it could just as well mark a descent into feral nature. The norm of subjective humanity, which is soberly distinct both from gods and beasts, blocks the approach to this musical experience, whose abnormality is based on a withdrawal from or a renunciation of the quotidian.

From another angle, one could say that music is not necessarily a medium more perfect than language but rather one that is qualitatively different. It could be taken as presenting its contents with an immediacy that is lost to the reflective mechanism of verbal communication. Here, music and madness truly belong together, occupying the same sphere. That is to say, they are not joined simply by sharing a capacity to limit language from either side of symbolization; they do not mark out the upper and lower limits to language but rather constitute a realm entirely removed from language use. Kierkegaard, one of romanticism's greatest readers and harshest critics, follows this logic when he has his aesthete (author A of *Either/Or*) reappraise the "apparent poverty of language" as its "wealth": "The immediate is really the indeterminate, and therefore language cannot apprehend it; but the fact that it is indeterminate is not its perfection but an imperfection."[9] Kierkegaard essentially replaces the notion of the infinite with the problem of the indefinite. Here especially we can see how notions of ineffability can easily yield space to the threat of madness. It is not gratuitous that Kierkegaard, in an earlier passage from the same text—the celebrated reading of Mozart's *Don Giovanni*—ecstatically thanks the composer for "the loss of [his] reason" (47).

Two distinct scenarios can therefore be specified: (1) music and madness limit language from two opposing sides, from above or below the subjective norm; or (2) music and madness limit language from a shared position, from the sphere or stage of immediacy as opposed to the mediation of reflection. In either case, music and madness seem to constitute an origin of language that by definition is not comprehended by language. If this origin—illogical, insofar as it falls outside the *logos*—were appropriated by literature, it would represent literature's striving toward something beyond language, something beyond or incompatible with the literary work itself. Music and madness, then, would unwork language by occupying spaces outside the work of language, moments of nonrepresentability that occur within the linear movement of representation, spaces that reside as the inaccessible kernel of the work. In this sense, music and madness would comprise the work's own internal interruption.

For these reasons, music promises the poet liberation, the means for escaping the diminution and restrictions that invariably occur in verbalization, but like madness it also threatens complete incommunicability. In his essay "Silence and the Poet" (1967), George Steiner reflects on this ambivalence by turning to the myths of full poetic (musical) expression, where mortals vie with the gods and therefore arouse their jealous violence. The dismemberment of Orpheus, the flaying of Marsyas, and the cutting of Tamyris's tongue demonstrate the outrage that shadows the careers of the transgressive artist. From one perspective, one finds the idealization of music that begins with German romanticism and goes on to nourish later European poetics from French symbolism on, where music's attraction lies in its promise to free the poet from one kind of language by opening up new dimensions of the word. In a formulation reminiscent of Novalis, Steiner writes: "By a gradual loosening or transcendence of its own forms, the poem strives to escape from the linear, denotative, logically determined bonds of linguistic syntax into what the poet takes to be the simultaneities, immediacies, and free play of musical form."[10] Yet, from another, darker perspective, this kind of reaching out beyond the limits of reflective, rational language can result in a dangerous overreaching. The same impulse that drove the poet toward the "free play of musical form," may well end up causing him to lose his mind, like Hölderlin in his tower.

These provisional remarks occlude many important complications, which will motivate the closer readings below. Here, I shall restrict my comments to a few main points. First, there is hardly a vaguer term than "madness." Hoffmann, for example, who was conversant with the latest psychological literature, had an entire nomenclature of pathologies and conditions at his disposal—dementia, amentia, insania, delirium, vesania, melancholia, mania, and so forth—each with its own particular sets of manifestations, which could be interpreted from many different perspectives, say, as a somatic or spiritual problem, temporary or chronic, inherited or traumatically caused. Although, in the epigraph given above, Hoffmann's *Wahnsinn* alludes to a decidedly negative ordeal, colored in by the typically romantic sickness of tornness, or *Zerrissenheit*, we can readily find instances where the author describes mental derangement as a blessing that promises higher states of consciousness, related to the classical notions of the Platonic *theia mania* (divine madness) or its latter-day development into the *furor poeticus*, the inspirational gift that transformed the Renaissance artist into "another God," an *alter Deus*. Cyprian, one of the members of Hoffmann's Serapion Brothers, who regularly meet to investigate the *Wahnsinn* that "lies deep in human nature," states his belief that nature "grants abnormal people glimpses into its most gruesome depths," yielding "intimations and images that strengthen and animate the spirit in an especially uplifting manner" (*Die Serapions-Brüder*, HW 4.37). Like a trance, madness, for those who are able to return from it and reflect on it, broadens the subject's experience rather than tearing it to pieces. It represents the defamiliarization necessary for the process of psychic expansion. If this psychedelism redefines eccentricity as a godsend, then it would be the world left behind that should be portrayed as truly mad. Plato's allegory of the cave is a case in point. Those deemed insane would then be the only ones who were not.

Second, notwithstanding Hoffmann's contributions to the elaboration of the idea of absolute music, music's autonomy should certainly not be taken for granted. In fact, as a Kapellmeister, Kreisler is primarily a composer of vocal music. The first decades of the nineteenth century still grappled with the musico-aesthetic debates of the centuries before, which all presupposed music's inseparable relation to language. To be sure, arguments concerning song were often based on charges of madness. The properties of tone, accent, and rhythm were singled out as formidably comprising the force of a passage without contributing to the lexical meaning of the text. Melismatic passages and polyphony were especially feared as verging on irrationality, insofar as these techniques weakened the communicative power of the word and therefore blurred music's association to discursive clarity. Yet here the potential madness was still verbal—bestial, perhaps, but not entirely inhuman.

The third complication is neither psychopathological ("what is madness?") nor aesthetic ("what is music?") but rather cultural. Why, we may ask, with occasional exceptions, are we dealing with a particularly German theme? If we agree with the thesis of Pamela Potter, that "music represented a mode of artistic expression in which all Germans could share," that it served to "overcome a long history of political fragmentation and regional differences,"[11] then why has this musical legacy been allied with madness, with a mental state that is ambiguous at best? Bypassing for a moment the dangerously essentialist presumptions implicit in Potter's remark—is there, after all, such a thing as "the Germans"!—it would be worthwhile to consider precisely how the two themes were deployed toward the definition of a personal or national identity. Is there something theoretically important, something obtainable for philosophy or cultural history, at work here?

The focus on literary works brings me to yet another complication, namely, the problem of metaphor, which leads to the study's core. The present project is *about* music and madness in the strictest terms: not as tonal art and mental states as such but rather as specialized metaphorical strategies deployed in or constituting works of literature. Although scholars are in the main cognizant of this figurative status, the large number of attempts to investigate the correlation of literature to mental illness or to musical experience has foundered precisely on this point. What Calvin Brown dubbed "musico-literary studies" in his seminal *Music and Literature* (1948) generally remain content to identify literary instances of music or musicality as metaphors of greater or lesser appropriateness, without considering their particular semiotic and semantic consequences. As Eric Prieto has recently argued, such critics "mistake the effect (metaphors) for the cause (the irreducible heterogeneity of music and literature)."[12] In this regard, literary treatments of the effects of madness have fared much better. Foucault's groundbreaking *Histoire de la folie* (1961) and the many studies published in its wake, above all the work of Shoshona Felman, should be lauded for paying attention to the specificity of represented madness and its philosophical implications rather than generalizing its force simply as one metaphor among other possibilities.[13]

The problem of metaphor once again demonstrates that the issue of music's relation to madness is best investigated in relation to language. If we take music to be the nonsemantic elements of song or a purely instrumental piece and then declare that music "speaks," then it is not, *stricto sensu*, music but rather music transformed (or metaphorized) into rational discourse, into something extramusical. Judging music to be somehow linguistic, as many aestheticians have done, often strives to interpret auditory experience by nonauditory means. The musicologist Carolyn Abbate therefore regards all writing on music as prosopopoeia, as giving language to that which itself has none. Radically considered, writing on music assigns the rights of subjectivity to language alone, while music abides, paradoxically, as a mute object, as a nonthinking *res extensa*. In concentrating, then, on the tropological nature of music criticism, Abbate implicitly reserves a space for music to remain as such, to sneak past the pull of reductively distorted verbalization: "Music may thus escape philosophical critiques of language, perhaps even escape language entirely."[14]

Abbate's remarks concerning music find a telling analogue in Derrida's main problem with Foucault's project concerning madness. In general, Derrida chides the *Histoire de la folie* for failing to escape the pitfalls that inevitably frustrate any desire to restore madness to language.[15] Foucault's self-styled "archaeology of silence" sought to discover a new language or to use "words without language," as a way of saying madness, instead of speaking about it, in a writing that would not reinforce the so-called Cartesian great confinement. Nonetheless, Derrida detects the same prosopopoeiac gesture that troubles Abbate's reflection on musicology. "Foucault," Derrida writes, "wanted madness to be the *subject* of his book in every sense of the word: its theme and its first-person narrator, its author, madness speaking about itself" (39; emphasis in original). He therefore questions the feasibility of such a project: "Would not the archaeology of silence be the most efficacious and subtle restoration, the *repetition*, the act perpetrated against madness—and be so at the very moment when this act is denounced?" (41).

The problem is of course irresolvable. The desire to bring music and madness into rational language as well as the hesitation to do so both require a division that maintains a fundamental difference. In the first instance, the division produces the ground for translation, for finding terms of equivalence on either side of the divide; in the second instance, the division is upheld so as to protect the nonsemantic from the crime of symbolization. Preserving madness and music from discursive formulation underscores the very same separation that encourages translation.

Literary cases of the mad and the musical therefore harbor a dual threat: either language fails to accomplish what it set out to do or language succeeds and thereby strips music and madness of the power to remain musical and mad. Concerning music, the desire to explicate melodies or harmonies rests on the decision to allow acoustic material to be supplanted with a syntax, grammar, and lexicon that are qualitatively different. If, however, music resists definition, then we witness how language ultimately breaks down before that which it cannot grasp. Projects of bringing madness to language lead to the same alternative. Either one or the other must suffer destruction. To write about madness is to cause the incommunicable to communicate, to let the incomprehensible be comprehended, and therefore to make madness no longer mad. Language's achievement depends on transforming madness into something rationally explicative— something communicative and comprehensible—as we do when we say that madness is pathological, symptomatic of unconscious desires, or a clever method for deception. But if madness holds out as that which defies all understanding, then rational language must yield and forgo its designs to impose sense. Every linguistic encounter with either music or madness thus seems poised on the brink of two abysses: the emptiness of the abstract concept or the awed silence before the ineffable.

Although the last few decades have seen much scholarship on the isolated topics of music *or* madness in relation to language—say, on music and literature or on literature and madness—surprisingly little attention has been paid to the specific association of music *and* madness in literature and its ramifications for theories of aesthetics, representation, and linguistics.[16] It is this deficit that my book hopes to address.

When the topic of music and madness crops up in scholarship, it is usually discussed in reference to the operatic tradition. Analyses tend to concentrate on notions of exclusion or insubordination or subversion, often with a focus on the acoustic properties of the voice as opposed to sense-laden properties of the word. In the history of opera, the tension is perhaps most evident in the eighteenth-century division between the recitatives, which traditionally communicate the dramatic plot, and the arias, which constitute a break in the action or a suspension of narrative information. Accordingly, Mladen Dolar writes: "The aria could present the voice beyond meaning, the object of fascination beyond content; it could aim at enjoyment beyond the signifier, at the immediate fascination with a senseless object."[17] From a physiological point of view, one can recognize how beautiful singing, which requires an open, unobstructed passage from throat to mouth, consequently renders the text less intelligible. The softening of the consonants, of the occlusives, precipitates a general derationalization—or maddening, if you will—of speech. Michel Poizat, too, focuses on this "enjoyment beyond the signifier," on this *jouissance*, which for him results not from listening to unintelligible speech but rather from perceiving the process of the dissolution of sense.[18] Jouissance consists in hearing how a working (communicative, informative) language comes to be unworked by senseless sound. To borrow Lacan's pun, *j'ouïs sens*: "I heard meaning," and now I am open to the senselessness that drives unbounded desire. Wagner's endless melody, which he derived from Gluck's blurring of the aria/recitative distinction, plunges the listener into an oceanic continuity that, according to Poizat, "tends to corrode or erode the signifying scansion of language" (75). The result is maddening.

As purely phonic resonance, the voice could indeed be said to function in conflict with the word. The simple emission of sound, the material substrate of every signifier, obstructs the operative efficacy of the word, which ultimately articulates sense on a symbolic, that is, immaterial plane. Julia Kristeva's well-known psycholinguistic distinction between the symbolic (conscious, rational) and the semiotic (libidinal, pleasurable) speaks precisely to this division of labor, with the latter frequently associated with an idea of musicality.[19] The rational working of verbal language must essentially channel this phonematic resource, this "semiotic chora," and repress its more intractable elements in order to ensure the proper formulation of sense. Nonetheless, like Freud's return of the repressed, sonority, rhythm, and timbre—remnants of a preverbal, lost sphere of pleasure—continue to press upon the symbolic process of signification and thereby threaten to destabilize the very ground of subjectivity, namely, the systematic functioning of language that produces the subject.[20] Again, the voice as such opens the door onto irrationality or regression. Thus Roland Barthes, who comes to associate the "pleasure of the text" explicitly with the "grain of the voice," turns the linguistic act of reading into an experience better understood beneath a series of psychoanalytic rubrics: "neurosis," "fetishism," "obsession," "paranoia," and "hysteria."[21]

The tension between the rationalizing force of the word and the maddening subversion of the voice certainly appears to course through German romantic literature, especially in its flirtations with irrationalism. The texts studied below, however, were not destined for the living voice or the theatrical stage but rather for the sphere of publication and private readership. If the voice plays a role, it is not the piercing cry of the soprano but the silent voice of the written page. But what is this voice? To whom does it belong? What I would like to suggest is that, above all, the nonsemantic, fascinating voice of romanticism's mad music is the voice of the author or rather the voice of the living person who is to become an author, who is about to ascribe his or her voice to a system that will work it into sense and thereby work it off. For these writers, this voice can never be adequately or fully captured by representational language. It resists entrance into the same and even withdraws from the assignation of difference, which only serves to reinforce the notion of sameness. Irreducible to any concept, outside every system (for example, the system of identity and difference), the voice's singularity is what evanesces into the work—be it the book itself or the identity of authorship. The work's discursiveness, its capacity to circulate in a meaningful language (meaningful for others and for oneself), is premised on the negation of this uniqueness. That is to say, the voice is the Eurydicean point that retracts from the production of meaning. Thus—in anticipation of a detailed analysis—music and madness, insofar as they confound this regime of semantic clarity, hold out the hope, however tenuous, that what has been silenced may be heard, that the self, which has disappeared into the work, may be recognized. The metaphorical strategy is Orphic to the extreme, insofar as it allows the self to be seen, it allows the voice to be heard, but only at the moment of fatal evanescence. In the end, the reader does not see anything at all save disappearance itself.

For the writers around 1800, self-inscription was an especially acute problem, more or less directly instigated by Rousseau's autobiographical projects and anxieties.[22] This theoretician of immediate expression and singular accents fell into a writing career that he would always feel had betrayed him. As he famously recounts in his *Confessions*, it was in the "excessively hot" summer of 1749, during a visit to his friend Diderot, who had been placed under house arrest in Vincennes, that the young man "fell upon" (*tombai*) the notice from the Dijon Academy announcing the essay competition that would launch his writing career: "Has the progress of the sciences and arts done more to corrupt morals or improve them?" "The moment I read this I beheld another universe and became another man [*un autre homme*]" (ROC 1.351/327). The alienating effect of this event leads to a reflection on personal memory and music lost: "Once I have written a thing down, I entirely cease to remember it. . . . Before I studied [music] I knew great numbers of songs by heart; but since I learned to sing from written music, I have been unable to remember any of them." The fall into writing—into its concomitant alienation and amnesia—consequently marks a new period of near madness: "I was in a state of agitation bordering on delirium. Diderot noticed it. . . . He encouraged me to give my ideas wings and compete for the prize. I did so, and from that moment I was lost. All the rest of my life and of my misfortunes followed inevitably as a result of that moment's madness" (1.351/328). According to the apologist, then, Diderot's exhortation led directly to exposure and terrifying misprision. In the *Confessions'* subsequent chapters, Rousseau goes on to stress the distorting effects that writing had on his identity: "I was truly transformed; my friends and acquaintances no longer recognized me" (1.416–17/388). The *Confessions* ask to be read as a story of a series of disfigurements caused by culture, a narrative of misrecognition, which is here to be set straight. As the so-called Neuchâtel preface points out, contrary to Montaigne, who merely offered a dissimulating profile, Rousseau promises to present himself in his entirety and in perfect transparency (1.11/49–50). Nonetheless, the paranoiac fear of expropriation and self-oblivion would eventually haunt the exculpatory, self-justifying *Confessions* themselves. Hence we have the subsequent autobiographical supplements of the *Dialogues* and the *Rêveries du promeneur solitaire*. The project of self-introspection and self-formation leads to a frightful repetition compulsion, the need to write over and over again. They are all in a sense fruitless attempts to reappropriate in writing what has been lost in writing.

Rousseau thereby sets the key for a later age obsessed with notions of selfhood. Here identity—one's manifest appearance to others—came to be regarded as a falsification, a terribly constraining, oppressive, mortifying construct. The failed correspondence between lived experience and representation motivated attempts to have the self emerge in the literary work without allowing it to be distorted by that work. And this task, I believe, is what the romantic tradition of music and madness ultimately addresses. To put it in the simplest of terms (and this of course remains to be demonstrated): as metaphors of nonrepresentability, music and madness could introduce into a text the nonrepresentability of the self. They could open up, within representational language, a new dimension that exceeds or eludes representation. Still, as in the case of Rousseau, precisely because we are dealing with a literary tradition, this hope for reappropriation—however clever or secretive—is always accompanied by the possibility of further expropriations.

A quick glance at the major texts treated below would reveal a high frequency of self- or quasi-self-representation: for example, Diderot's Moi in *Le neveu*, Wackenroder's Berglinger, and Hoffmann's Kreisler. The project may be formulated in terms of a first, second, or third person. It may involve a narrator's personal, unnerving encounter, as in Rochlitz's "Besuch im Irrenhause" or Hoffmann's "Ritter Gluck." It may even be diffracted among multiple personalities, for example, in the series of anonymous characters that surface in Kleist's *Heilige Cäcilie*. One might go so far as to include Hegel's *Geist*—that uncanny double of the philosopher who courses through the *Phänomenologie*, the book that nearly drove its author insane (so he confessed to Schelling).

To qualify the tradition of music and madness as an autobiographical project is not to say that the generic terms of the "autobiographical pact," as defined by Philippe Lejeune, are fully respected. Rather, the proposed identification of the narrator or character with the proper name that signs the book is precisely what is being called into question.[23] Nothing could be more improper here, for we are dealing throughout not with the stabilization of identities but rather with a typically romantic critique of identity. Philippe Lacoue-Labarthe and Jean-Luc Nancy locate the singular work of romanticism precisely in this critique of identity, which aims, on the one hand, to create a sensible presentation (*Darstellung*) of the free, absolute subject while, on the other hand, destabilizing the ground for this presentation. For this reason, they resort to Maurice Blanchot in order to redefine romanticism: "Within the romantic work, there is interruption and dissemination of the romantic work, and this in fact is not readable in the work itself.... Rather... it is readable in the unworking [*désœuvrement*], never named and still less thought, that insinuates itself throughout the interstices of the romantic work."[24] *Désœuvrement*—this unnamable, unthinkable something, this *aliquid* that disables sense, that disengages from the production of meaning—constitutes for Lacoue-Labarthe and Nancy the force of romanticism. Although the authors of *The Literary Absolute* specifically have the *Athenaeum*'s mode of fragmentary writing in mind, this failure of thought (which is less thought's negation than its impossibility) rhymes well with Hoffmann's allusion to music's "unknown realm ["unbekanntes Reich"]." It is, indeed, not fortuitous that music and madness frequently emerge as an unnamable, unthinkable, and hence unknowable character of the texts studied below.[25]

Lacoue-Labarthe's and Nancy's allusion to Blanchot brings this issue of the unnamable and the unthinkable back to the theme of the voice. In *L'espace littéraire* (1955), Blanchot evokes the myth of Orpheus, specifically the fated gaze, to open literature to that which is outside the work. Looking back at Eurydice ruins the singer's work, not in terms of a failure but rather in terms of a necessary movement that "carries the work beyond what assures it."[26] It is a sacrifice that "consecrates the song" (232/176). In a later text, discussing the writings of Novalis—with the clearly Orphic overtones that are very much fitting for this poet—Blanchot remarks: "One can indeed say that in these texts we find expressed the non-romantic essence of romanticism, as well as all the principal questions that the night of language will contribute to producing the light of day: that to write is to make (of) speech (a) work [*œuvre*], but that this work is an unworking [*désœuvrement*]; that to speak poetically is to make possible a non-transitive speech whose task is not to say things (not to disappear in what it signifies), but to say (itself) in letting (itself) say."[27] This nontransitive speech is nothing other than the voice, that which says nothing but itself. And this is precisely how the voice is enlisted into the service of music and madness, whose work is to unwork. The contradiction is intended. Regarded either as language's upper and lower limits (savage muteness and mystical transcendence) or as an immediacy qualitatively distinct from the reflective work of verbalization, music and madness can resist the reductive nature of representational discourse; they can allow the subject to evade the mimetic double that threatens to rob one of one's self—but only as tropes, that is, only by reinserting and thereby losing the subject in the work.

Before closing this introduction, it will be helpful to circle back to my starting point, to the eminently circular figure of Hoffmann's Kreisler. Hoffmann's *Fantasiestücke*, as published in the definitive edition of 1819, feature two series of texts whose authorship is attributed to the fictional

Kapellmeister. Hoffmann plays the role of an editor who presents the writings of the mysterious man, described as someone on the verge of madness. That Kreisler is a strongly autobiographical figure is apparent throughout Hoffmann's writing career. There is evidence that he planned at many points to write an entire "musical novel" in the guise of a biography of his imagined composer.[28] There is mention of a collection of "Lucid Periods of a Mad Musician" ("Lichte Stunden eines wahnsinnigen Musikers").

Autobiography seems to convert a life into a static form, into a work, and it is precisely this formatting that Hoffmann's writing resists. Paul de Man's well-known definition of autobiography as "defacement" underlines the predicament. De Man's emphasis on the "privative" function of "language as trope" reveals the referential crisis that confronts the would-be autobiographer—the written I is never adequate to the writing I. In challenging the commonsensical understanding of autobiography as employing "a simpler mode of referentiality" (say, in comparison with so-called fictional works), de Man writes: "We assume that life *produces* the autobiography as an act produces its consequences, but can we not suggest, with equal justice, that the autobiographical project may itself produce and determine the life and that whatever the writer *does* is in fact governed by the technical demands of self-portraiture and thus determined, in all its aspects, by the resources of his medium?"[29] Consequently, the autobiographer who desires to write himself writes himself away. The author auctions himself off. He gives himself a shape that betrays the experience of a life that is fuller, uncontainable—excessive. The autobiographical form invariably deforms.

Hoffmann tackles the problem in his incomplete novel, the *Lebensansichten des Katers Murr* (1820–21). Here the autobiographical task falls to a writing cat and thereby introduces multiple layers of irony. To begin, the book merges the human with the bestial—a typical ironic technique that Hoffmann derived from the engravings of Jacques Callot. In the text entitled "Jacques Callot," the head piece to his *Fantasiestücke*, Hoffmann writes: "Irony, in that it sets man and animal in conflict, derides man with his paltry works and endeavors ["mit seinem ärmlichen Tun und Treiben"]; it resides only in a profound soul, and Callot's grotesque forms, created out of animal and man, reveal to the serious [*ernsten*], deeper-seeing observer all the hidden meanings that lie beneath the cloak of the scurrilous [*Skurrilität*]" (HW 2.1.18/HMW 76).

The irony of the *Lebensansichten* satirizes the idea of forming in general, for the tomcat Murr is conventionally "educated" (*gebildet*) and blatantly "forms" (*bildet*) his life in the style of the popular *Bildungsroman*. Furthermore, Murr uncaringly tears out sheets of his master's printed copy of

Kreisler's biography to be used as a blotting paper for his own *ouvrage*. The work that contains the formed life of the composer is literally unworked and consigned to the status of "waste paper" (*Makulatur-Blatt*). When the manuscript is delivered to the publisher, the Kreisler pages are accidentally printed along with the feline autobiography. The ironic conflict is therefore very real for the novel's reader, who must work through alternating stories, interruptions, and gaping lacunae.

Hoffmann confided to his friends that he hoped this book would finally show his authentic self ("What I now am and can be").[30] But how in fact does that authenticity manifest itself? Where is Hoffmann to be heard as "he is and can be"? I would like to offer a conjecture, however playful. In a letter to his Bamberg friend, Dr. Speyer, Hoffmann seems to joke with his own first name, Ernst, by employing the Callotian terms of "seriousness" (*das Ernste*) and "the scurrilous" (*Skurrilität*) that had marked the *Fantasiestücke*: it was "the highly wise and profound tomcat Murr . . . *a real cat* . . . [who] gave me the opportunity for this scurrilous [*skurrilen*] joke, which weaves through a truly very serious [*ernste*] book" (May 1, 1820, HW 5.913; emphasis in original). Is it the writing self—a self that would only be betrayed by an inadequate literary act of self-representation—that peeps out from beneath "the cloak of the scurrilous"? Is the encryption of the name Ernst, intended or not, where the self slips into the work without being subsumed or sublimated by it? If so, *das Ernste* enters the text precisely by remaining outside it, or rather it is in the text by virtue of being its outside, located in the work indeed as a kind of crypt.

The doubling of the autobiographical project, split between a cat and a mad musician, blatantly frustrates the gestures of simple identification ordained by Lejeune's autobiographical pact. The line of every represented life, which runs from a beginning to an end (from a birth to a death, metaphorical or physical), is broken, falsified, wasted. It is in this break that Hoffmann could show what he truly is, but only as that which always retreats, as that which resists every form. Capturing the authentic self in representation is impossible. In a particularly telling passage, Kreisler comments on the impossibility of giving his true name. Alluding to Tieck's *Ritter Blaubart*, Kreisler confesses, "I once had a most excellent name, but over the course of time I have almost forgotten it, and can recollect it only dimly now" (HW 5.77/KM 50). Although Madame Benzon pleads with Johannes to pronounce his other name, he refuses: "It is impossible, and I half suspect that where my name as passport through life for my outer form ["meine äußere Gestalt"] is concerned, my dim memory of my former self derives from that agreeable time when I was really not yet born ["da ich eigentlich noch gar nicht geboren"]" (HW 5.77/KM 50). In contrast to the name of Kreisler, explicitly attached to his "outer form" ("äußere Gestalt"), there is another secret name—barely remembered and unspeakable—that belongs to a sphere beyond or before this form, before his birth, before the beginning. This anterior time, which marks the utopia when one was "not yet born," can only appear in the postnatal realm as that which has been negated: "It is impossible." As for his present "appearance, complexion, and physiognomy," nothing is more perfect than the name that he now uses and that others use to address him. In other words, the name Kreisler is what *works*—"Turn it upside down, dissect it with the anatomical knife of grammar, and its internal content will prove better and better" (*HW* 5.77–78/*KM* 50).

This description of a self engaged in societal communication stands in stark contrast to a barely remembered self, which throughout the *Lebens-ansichten* is coded as something musical and mad. It is this latter self that proves to be an object of frustration for Kreisler's biographer. Although the man may be given a form—to be inverted or dissected at will—the essence of the subject eludes grasp: "Nothing more tiresome for an historian or a biographer than when, as if riding a wild colt, he must cavort this way and that, over stocks and stones, up hill and down dale, always searching for trodden paths and never finding them. Such is the case of the man who has undertaken to set down for your benefit, gentle reader, what he knows of the bizarre life ["von dem wunderlichen Leben"] of Kapellmeister Johannes Kreisler" (*HW* 5.58/*KM* 37).

To offer a brief, provisional summary: the turn to music and madness seems to promise that the self may be spared the inversions and perversions of verbal formation. As a metaphor of nonrepresentability, musical madness can enter into representation while pointing to what exceeds the form in which it appears. Consequently, the broken lines of the life stories contained in Hoffmann's *Lebensansichten* raise form itself to the status of metaphor. In this way, the very idea of form comes to be interrogated.

Certainly, this problematization is no simple affair. Language can only be unworked by language itself. There is indeed an explicit antiverbalism that courses through Hoffmann's works and continues straight to Nietzsche. Words are suspect, because they reduce or generalize that which is presumably irreducible. Nietzsche writes at the end of his career: "Our true experiences are not garrulous ["nicht geschwätzig"]. They could not be communicated even if they wanted to be. . . . The things we have words for are also the things we have already left behind. There is a grain of contempt

in all speech. . . . People vulgarize themselves when they speak a language"
(*Ecce Homo*, NW 6.128/*EH* 205). The obvious problem is that every statement
of the antiverbal position is formulated in the very verbal system under
attack. Here, as in Hoffmann, a concept of irony helps to weather the
logical disturbance, especially when raised to Schlegel's perpetual "irony
of irony." For Nietzsche, as well as for his predecessors, music and madness
together set up a limit toward which language aspires but never reaches.
The limit may be understood as an immanent realm of the body or a transcendent realm of the spirit, a dream world or a world of pain and despair.
It may simply mark the feeling of life itself—*ein Lebensgefühl*—which is
lost as soon as it is recognized. The assumption of something extratextual
is always accomplished by a new textualization. In part, the unworking of
language, for which music and madness are powerful metaphors, names
this impossible desire of giving mediated expression to the immediate.
However naive or ill-fated, however sophisticated or hopeless, it constitutes the energy of the texts below.

1

Hearing Voices

DIDEROT WROTE no autobiography. Unlike Rousseau, he left no confessions, no reveries. There was never any promise to offer the world a complete "work [*ouvrage*] unique and unparalleled in its truthfulness ["par une veracité sans exemple"], so that for once at least the world might behold a man as he was within" (*Confessions*, ROC 1.516/478). To attempt a straightforward account of one's life, to present one's self in a form proffered as all-inclusive, presumes a faith in writing that Diderot ostensibly lacked. Rousseau, too, discovered the problems associated with writing, yet madly tried to remedy them by writing more, which only exacerbated his various crises. In his own judgment, this Genevan Icarus clearly went too far in following his surrogate father's advice—"[Diderot] exhorted me to give my ideas wings ["de donner l'essor à mes idées"].... I did so, and from that moment I was lost" (ROC 1.351/328). In retrospect, Rousseau realized that he had written a *monumentum*—an act of remembrance, a public work, but also a tombstone. Like Horace, he could boast that he would "not die entirely" (*non omnis moriar* [*Odes* 3.30.6]), which implies, needless to say, that part of him already had. Hence Rousseau referred to having fallen into writing ("je tombai"), deliriously believing that by writing more, he could emerge from this *tombeau*.

The Daedalian Diderot would fly more cautiously, which is not to say that he did not endeavor to represent himself in his texts. Deployed across his writing career are a number of first-person narrators, all endowed with multiple, unambiguous details that readily refer to the author's life. Yet two major aspects differentiate Diderot's personae from Rousseau's. First, Diderot generally provides but a limited portrayal, allowing only enough of his character to be seen in order to situate the views put forward. Second, this character rarely appears alone. Instead, he is placed in relation to another personage, who is set up as an agent of qualification, prepared to challenge and interrogate the first-person standpoint. Where Rousseau aspires to produce a total, reappropriated form—however faulty or vulnerable or scandalous—Diderot prefers to dramatize vulnerability itself, namely, by staging the breakdown of form through dialogue.[1]

Among other intentions (didactic, scientific, moral, and so forth), Diderot's use of dialogue actively demonstrates the problem of self-representation. It does so by allowing voices to clash, by destabilizing held positions, especially those that one might deem philosophical. To be sure, dialogue has always been the genre of polyphony, but in Diderot's hands this multiplication of voices occurs not simply between interlocutors but also within them. The polyphony is both inter- and intrasubjective. More often than not it most strongly affects the speaker who says "I." If the auto-biographical project depends on some idea of constancy—at the very least, on some feeling of self-identity over time—Diderot's texts expose the un-steadiness, and therefore the fragility, of any subjectivity that might ground this sense of selfhood.

Rousseau, it should be recalled, disdained polyphony precisely because it concealed the emotive communication of an individual soul. For him, the primacy of melody lay in its original capacity to "imitate the in-flections of the voice, to express its complaints, its cries of pain or joy, its threats, its whimpers [gémissements]." In this sense, one can say that melody "not only imitates, it speaks" (Essai sur l'origine des langues, ROC 5.416). For Rousseau, the subsequent development of harmony and the in-vention of polyphony in European music history are marks of a degen-eration, whereby music becomes divorced from verbal expression and the voice of the individual speaker is lost. The enunciation of meaning, or even truth, is only possible in self-expression, in letting the accents of speech imitate intimate passions. For Diderot, on the contrary, meaning tends to elude this ego position. As Jean Starobinski and others have ob-served, for the majority of Diderot's texts, this privilege of communi-cation, of expressing one's singularity, belongs rather to the other, not to the first-person writer, who himself lacks the necessary coherence.[2] Only by transferring the word to another voice, only by way of alterity, can Diderot be said—paradoxically—to speak. A biographical detail makes the case. In handing over a manuscript to his publisher, Jacques-André Naigeon, Diderot writes: "Set my work [travail] as you wish ["comme il vous plaira"]; you have the authority ["vous êtes le maître"] to approve, to contradict, to add, to remove."[3] Authorization, so to speak, lies not in the author's hands but rather in the hands of the addressee, who reads "as it pleases"—"comme il vous plaira." Finding one's voice requires hearing the other's voice. Rousseau's narcissism is countered by Diderot's echo. This, at any rate, is true until the writer himself suffers the greatest alienation of all. Starobinski cites from Diderot's late *Essai sur les règnes de Claude et de Néron*: "One only thinks, one only speaks forcefully from the depths of one's tomb ["du fond de son tombeau"]; it is there that one must place oneself, it is from there that one must address mankind."[4] Personal identity and the right to speak may only be obtained post mortem. Although Starobinski convincingly concludes that it is this position of imagined posterity that energizes Diderot's writing, it is also possible to say that dialogue, by depriving the speaker of an identifiable, stable voice, also guards him from the grave, from the fatal eloquence of the monumentum.

Doubtless the most well-known example of polyphonic disruption is *Le neveu de Rameau*, which Diderot developed over a period of some time and which was, incidentally, only published posthumously. Here the author imparts to a first-person narrator (Moi) many of the attributes that the present-day reader can recognize as having belonged to the philosophe. The antagonist, set in the third-person (Lui), clearly plays the role of Starobinski's "autre," who enables Moi to light upon his own stance—"he is the speck of yeast that leavens the whole and restores to each of us a portion of his natural individuality" (*NR* 5/35). This process is carried out by causing every position pronounced by Moi to be tested, ridiculed, and shaken. Through the course of the dialogue, the first-person interlocutor finds himself unable to assume an unequivocal sense of who he is. Self-representation therefore takes place only in order to reveal its difficulties, if not its impossibility. It is certainly not gratuitous that Lui is a mad musician—at least as musical and perhaps as mad as Rousseau himself—for both music and madness, from the point of view of the French eighteenth century, turn the idea of representation, including self-representation or self-expression, into a problem. As this chapter will show, the encounter—or, better, the confrontation—between the philosopher and the musical madman inevitably turns on issues of selfhood and otherness, on identity and difference, on form and formlessness. To put it in terms that touch on the broader concerns of this study, the force of music and madness in *Le neveu* challenges the viability of perceiving one's life as an *ouvrage*, of speaking exclusively *du fond de son tombeau*.

SIRENS AT THE PALAIS ROYAL

How did they meet? By chance, like everybody. What were their names? It doesn't matter. Where did they come from? From the place most nearby. Where were they going? Does anyone really know where one goes?

—DIDEROT, *JACQUES LE FATALISTE*

There is a particular moment in *Le neveu de Rameau* that has consistently attracted Diderot's biographers. In short, it provides a telling portrait of the philosopher as a young man:

> LUI: Now, *monsieur le philosophe*, put your hand on your heart and tell the truth. There was a time when you weren't as well off [*cossu*] as you are today.
>
> MOI: I'm not all that well off even now.
>
> LUI: But you wouldn't still be going to the Luxembourg in summer, you remember . . .
>
> MOI: That'll do, yes, I remember.
>
> LUI: In a grey plush coat.
>
> MOI: Yes, yes.
>
> LUI: Threadbare on one side, with a frayed cuff, and black woolen stockings darned up the back with white thread.
>
> MOI: All right, all right, have it your own way [*tout comme il vous plaira*].
>
> LUI: What did you do in those days in the Allée des Soupirs?
>
> MOI: A rather sad picture.
>
> LUI: After that you used to trot along the road.
>
> MOI: Quite right.
>
> LUI: You used to give math lessons.
>
> MOI: Without knowing a word about it myself: isn't that what you're driving at?
>
> LUI: Exactly.

(NR 29/55)

This simple exchange is important for those concerned with Diderot's life story because it seems to provide access to a phase of his career that has otherwise left little trace. We know that he arrived in Paris as a sixteen-year-old bourgeois eager to complete his studies, and although conflicting reports place the young student among either the Jansenists at the Collège d'Harcourt or the Jesuits at Louis-le-Grand (or both), it is nonetheless clear that he received a master of arts at the Université de Paris in 1732, comfortably supported by an allowance from his father, an established cutler in the Gallic town of Langres. Subsequently, however, on being cut off from his father's resources—thanks to his obstinate refusal to enter any profession—little is known about the future philosophe until 1742, when he began to publish his first works. Before this entrance into authorship, a general obscurity prevails. Arthur Wilson, Diderot's English biographer, vividly expresses the chronicler's despair: "This period of [Diderot's] life is a documentary desert, filled with shimmering mirages of assertion and whimsy, with widely spaced waterholes of verifiable fact upon which the panting searcher stumbles when just about to expire."[5] He suggestively adds, "Diderot himself seldom spoke of [these years] and, indeed, seems almost intentionally inscrutable about this period." The reminiscences of Madame de Vandeul, Diderot's daughter, which otherwise serve as a rich and detailed source of information, have practically nothing to offer. For a man who was fond of relating anecdotes from his life, this lacuna is particularly striking. One is led to sense feelings of shame or embarrassment, a desire to conceal a time when somebody was simply nobody, and this indeed is the overall tone one finds in the passage cited above.

Here the biographer's speculation, based on fragments of documentary evidence, is supplemented by a self-representation from Diderot's own pen. The shame or embarrassment that one may surmise only from the philosopher's reticence concerning this early phase of his life is now openly admitted. The renowned writer, the ambitious Encyclopedist, the essayist and novelist, allows a glimpse of his precarious career beforehand. Yet, needless to say, this self-portrait is gravely compromised by a number of points. First, it comes not from the first-person narrator but rather from his interlocutor, the nephew of Rameau. The depiction is confirmed by the former, but only concessively, incidentally in nearly the same way Diderot addressed Naigeon above—"tout comme il vous plaira." Second, the validity of the nephew's words, like all his statements throughout the dialogue, is undermined by his penchant for hyperbole, distortion, and deception. Lui is no ordinary conversation partner but rather is represented as a madman, whose comments should always be taken *cum grano salis*. Nonetheless, Lui's portrayal of Moi's former state does elicit a strong reaction. The truth of what he says is not denied but simply quashed. The image of the philosopher as a penurious bohemian in a threadbare coat may merely be how he appeared to others, but this appearance is, so to speak, authorized.

It is not my intention to justify or discredit the use of literary material to contribute to an author's biography. Rather, I have chosen this example because it touches on one of the key contentions of this study, namely, that the literary treatments of music and madness here discussed, beginning with *Le neveu de Rameau*, persistently press on the division that separates life and work. Diderot's dialogue relates a chance encounter with a historical figure, the bizarre nephew of the famous composer Jean-Philippe Rameau. The afternoon's conversation proceeds digressively, moving across topics that range from aesthetics and science to education and morality. Although the centripetal force of Moi's enlightened method works hard to systematize the nephew's skewed thoughts, the latter's alienating perspective, punctuated by eccentric outbursts and frenzied musical performances, resists philosophy's gravitational pull. At stake is truth, or at least the representation of truth, including the representation of one's self. In staging the conjunction of musical and mad experience in the form of a dialogue, Diderot's text explicitly turns to the figure of the mad musician to broach problems of subjectivity, selfhood, and personal identity. As I have suggested throughout, the entire area of inquiry may be consolidated into a question of voice.

To return to the passage cited above, Moi's uneasy impatience is directly tied to the fact that he is now, to put it simply, a self—*un moi*.[6] Well before its appropriation by psychoanalytic discourse ("le Moi" translates Freud's "Ich" or "ego"), the term was established from the seventeenth century on as a means for discussing an idea of selfhood that was conscious of itself in its substantial uniqueness and indivisibility. "Le moi consiste dans ma pensée"—"The self consists in my thought," Pascal writes in the first book of his own *Pensées*.[7] Accordingly, throughout *Le neveu de Rameau*, Moi is at pains to present himself as an autonomous individual, one who feels secure in his integrity, confident in his learning, and proud of his accomplishments. Here, in this passage, his bold interlocutor dredges up the past, when this personal identity was not yet so firm. Without doubt, he hits a nerve. The exchange is even more poignant insofar as it reveals that Moi in former days uncannily resembled the nephew as he is here represented: leading a financially precarious life, scrounging for work, posing as an expert pedagogue, and so forth. *Le moi*—the self—is conversing in part with the him (*lui*) who he was or perhaps still is. Many scholars have pointed out how closely the nephew's dissertations on intellectual topics match Diderot's own published works.[8] The encounter with Lui could become an opportunity for Moi to establish his own identity across time; the debates might provide him the chance to discover or affirm a sense of selfhood: hence one aspect of the former's appeal. However, the nephew's madness (and, I would argue, his musicality) short-circuits again and again Moi's strategy. If, as Socrates suggested in Plato's *Republic*, the human soul might be compared to the stratified structure of the polis (2.368c–e), then Lui personifies serious attacks, ready to besiege the citadel, analogous to the role of *mousikê* in the ideal city, which the philosopher feels may bring the entire edifice down (4.424c–e).

In the opening pages, the narrator brilliantly sets up a program of self-identification by presenting a picture of himself as a paragon of self-sufficiency. "Come rain or shine ["Qu'il fasse beau, qu'il fasse laid"], my custom is to go for a stroll in the Palais Royal every afternoon at about five. I am always to be seen there alone ["C'est moi qu'on voit, toujours seul"], sitting on a seat in the Allée d'Argenson, meditating" (*NR* 3/33). Opposed to Lui's depiction of the narrator's once-bohemian ways, when the *collégien* aimlessly wandered through the left bank hoping to pick up some work, Moi places himself squarely in the gardens of the Palais Royal, on the *rive droite*, where he consistently and honorably philosophizes. "C'est *moi* qu'on voit," he asserts: always there, indifferent to the weather, indeed immune to any external contingencies that might disrupt a mind less constant. Others see him, but that hardly matters, for his existence stands without relation to anyone other than himself. His mental constancy is therefore matched by perfect self-containment: "I hold discussions with myself ["Je m'entretiens avec moi même"] on politics, love, taste or philosophy." Thus Moi "speaks" from a kind of crypt, sealed off from alterity, impregnable, practically *du fond de son tombeau*.

The capacity for learned soliloquy may initially come across as being eminently philosophical. One is reminded of Socrates' well-known definition of thinking (*dianoeisthai*) found in the *Theaetetus*: "Λόγον ὃν αὐτὴ πρὸς αὑτὴν ἡ ψυχὴ διεξέρχεται περὶ ὧν ἂν σκοπῇ. . . . οὐκ ἄλλο τι ἢ διαλέγεσθαι, αὐτὴ ἑαυτὴν ἐρωτῶσα καὶ ἀποκρινομένη"—Thinking is "a speech [*logos*] that the soul goes through with itself about the objects under consideration. . . . [It is] nothing other than carrying on a discussion [*dialegesthai*], which asks itself questions and answers them itself" (189e–190a). Yet this model for thinking—including the models it has helped to spawn, from incipient notions of self-consciousness in Descartes to the Husserlian ideal of autoaffection—is not without ambiguity.

On the one hand, the narrator's ability to hear his own utterances, to speak with himself, to enjoy a continuous circuit that internally links mouth to ear, is grounded in or grounds a site of origin, uncorrupted by mediation. By stressing the identity of speaker and listener, by locating the communicative poles within the mental confines of a single individual, the narrator furnishes himself with a subjectivity defined in isolation to everyone else. The silence of the discussion, moreover, in removing the speech (the *logos*) from the corporeal means of production, preserves it from the contingency conventionally ascribed to the body. As Descartes famously formulates it: the act of thinking "needs no place and depends on no material thing; so that this self ["ce moi"], that is to say the soul [*âme*] by which I am what I am ["par laquelle je suis ce que je suis"], is entirely distinct from the body, and moreover, that even if the body were not, it would not cease to be all that it is."[9] The narrator's indifference to the weather is therefore based on the incorporeal essence of thinking, which leads to a negation of difference itself. Listening to one's own voice arrives as the singular guarantee for remaining spontaneous, autonomous, and absolutely self-present.

On the other hand, however, this verbalization unfolds in a linear temporality, which should call attention to the basically evanescent quality of the voice. Pronounced or unpronounced, the voice evaporates on emission, dying within the moment of birth. With each word supplanting the one before, the conversation, despite its self-containment, turns out to be a rather poor candidate for maintaining presence. Far from securing the self's propriety, the voice could well be understood as that which escapes and thereby undermines the subject's position. Rather than assuring my autonomy, my voice—or better, *the* voice—may deliver me over to a kind of madness.[10]

Diderot appreciates these doubts by disclosing how the self-enclosed thinker in fact suffers breaches from within: "Je m'entretiens avec moi même"—"I hold discussions with myself on politics, love, taste or philosophy and let my thoughts wander in complete abandon ["à tout son libertinage"], leaving them free to follow the first wise or foolish [*folle*] idea that comes along, like the young rakes ["jeunes dissolus"] we see in the Allée de Foy who run after a giddy-looking little piece with a laughing face, sparkling eye and tip-tilted nose, only to leave her for another, accosting them all, but sticking to none. In my case my thoughts are my wenches" (NR 3/33). What this striking passage demonstrates is that, however confined within the limits of inwardness, Moi's thoughts expose him to an external space of contingency, dissolution, and even madness (*folie*). Consequently, the constancy, illustrated in the opening statement on his indifference to the weather, is now seriously disturbed. Entering into diverse intellectual pursuits, he falls into a digressiveness that eludes subjective control. The unforeseeable lines of chased thoughts translate into the transitory ("sticking to none"). The narrator continues: "If it is too cold or wet I take shelter in the Café de la Régence." The libertinism of his thinking reminds the narrator that he is not purely mind, that he has in fact a body exposed to the climate, that the edifice of self-consciousness is already leaking.

Faced with the fleetingness of the voice, the philosopher can only hope to gather its instants into a meaningful sequence, into an account or *logos*. The term "*logos*," it should be remembered, is derived from "*legein*," the Greek verb for gathering. The one who converses, even the one who converses with himself, in order to proceed rationally, strives to string each word, each phrase, into a linear chain of significance. Thought requires construction, piece by piece, ideally with a steady model in mind, the very steadiness of which, however, stands at risk of being severely compromised by the time necessary for meaningful production.

Another example from classical philosophy may be helpful. In Plato's *Sophist*, the Eleatic stranger provides a clear definition of speech (*logos*) with recourse to the construction metaphor. He begins by listing the building blocks, whose raw material consists of the voice (*phônê*). There are basically two kinds of vocal objects: nouns (or names, *onomata*) and verbs (*rhêmata*). The stranger then proceeds to explain the mode of putting them together. "No *logos* is formed only from names spoken in a row, or from verbs spoken without names" (262a). Mere contiguity is insufficient for the composition of speech. A *logos* cannot be accomplished simply by accumulating blocks of vocal utterances. An example is provided: "'walks runs sleeps,' and other verbs that signify actions. Even if somebody said all of them one after another, he would not produce [*apergazetai*] a *logos*" (262b). Speech production is literally work (*ap-ergazetai*), a bringing-to-completion by joining a name to an action, as in "man learns." The one who speaks accomplishes something by "weaving together" (*sumplekôn*) the basic components of language. "For this reason," the stranger concludes, "we said he speaks or gathers [*legein*]" (262d). Needless to say, not all "vocal signs" (τὰ τῆς φωνῆς αὖ σημεῖα) can be "joined together"—and here the stranger borrows a term from carpentry: *harmottei*. Rather, only those sounds that can be harmonized can "produce speech" (λόγον ἀπηργάσατο [262e]) in the proper sense. Like a craftsman, the speaker fits together the sounds at his disposal according to a unifying idea, in order to construct a work. To elaborate, the stranger insists that "*logos*, whenever it is, must be of something, and it is impossible not to be of something" (Λόγον ἀναγκαῖον, ὅτανπερ ᾖ, τινὸς εἶναι λόγον, μὴ δὲ τινὸς ἀδύνατον [262e]).

The sounds and speeches that surface in the mind of Diderot's narrator, precisely as "wenches," may not lead to productivity. Fundamentally digressive, these *catins* tend to unwork the work of *legein*, that is, they resist a unifying plan, which would lead to a fruitful gathering. The mere succession of thoughts, advancing in blind metonymy unhinged from paradigms of selection, cannot ensure that the self-addressed speaker is in fact a speaker in the proper, rational sense. On the contrary, the thoughts thus described border on irrationality, as that which evades the grasp that would collect them into an overarching concept. Striving to keep all verbalization within the borders of the psyche is an attempt to corral thinking into a chain of significance, which in turn would ground the subject as a subject of speech. By allowing his "thoughts to wander in complete abandon," Moi places himself in a particularly vulnerable position.

It is indeed in this state of insecurity that the narrator falls into an encounter with the mad nephew. There is an initial attempt to retrench in his self-isolation, to resist entering into a relation with anyone outside his consciousness, but the now-evident fragility of his autonomy readily gives him away. "There I was, watching a great deal but saying little and listening to as little as I could ["écoutant le moins que je pouvois"], when I was accosted [abordé] by one of the weirdest characters in this land of ours where God has not been sparing of them" (NR 4/33). The borders of the ego cogitans have been breached. The magic, apotropaic circle of intellectual narcissism has been broken. The moi will be compelled to enter into conversation with someone other than himself.

Whereas the narrator first attempted to define himself by negating difference, the nephew appears as an embodiment of difference itself. "He is composed of the highest and the lowest, good sense and madness [déraison]" (NR 4/33). One day "thin and gaunt," the next "sleek and plump," he is pure change, entirely without identity: "Nothing is less like him than himself ["Rien ne dissemble plus de lui que lui-même"]" (NR 4/34). Unlike the narrator, who purported to be indifferent to the weather, the nephew lets his behavior be dictated by the climate, for example: "If the weather is mild ["Si la saison est douce"], he walks up and down the Cours or the Champs-Elysées all night" (NR 5/34). He is a study in inconstancy, a man who adapts to his environment. Indeed, to follow the dialogue's Horatian epigraph, which astrologically places the nephew beneath the sign of the Vertumni, the Roman gods who ruled over the alternation of the seasons, one may say that change is his birthright.

I shall return in a later section to the epigraph from Horace and its context in the poet's Satire. For now, I want to stress that it is above all the nephew's voice that distinguishes him. Contrary to the narrator's silent soliloquy, Lui's utterances demand to be heard by the other; they incite rather than block a relation to the outside. The nephew's adaptability to the climate is symptomatic of his embodiedness, which, together with his loud speech and behavior, concretely define his relatedness to others around him. Thus, with "lung power quite out of the ordinary ["d'une vigueur de poumons peu commune"]," his voice is as sublimely irresistible as the Sirens'—"If you ever run into him and his originality does not hold your interest, you will either stuff your fingers into your ears or run away" (NR 4/34).

The allusion is noteworthy. Circe warned Odysseus that no one is able to withstand the allure of the Sirens' song, and despite the narrator's prophylactic attitude ("écoutant le moins que je pouvois"), he is fascinated. The Sirens' ability to captivate, it should be noted, lies in their promise to reveal complete knowledge—for they "know everything that has happened upon the nourishing earth" (*Odyssey* 12.191)—a more than sufficient enticement for the Encyclopedist. More specifically, to stay with Homer for a moment, the Sirens offer a knowledge that assures identification: "We know everything that has happened in wide Troy/How Argives and Trojans suffered by the will of the gods" (12.189–90). Odysseus of course, as an eye-witness, is already well aware of what took place on the battleground before Troy. He already knows how the Argives and the Trojans suffered. Whence, then, the attraction? Why enter into risk? Clearly, the overpowering desire to listen to the Sirens' song can only be a desire for the Same.

Likewise, as suggested above, Diderot's narrator initially opens his ears to the nephew's voice in order to return to himself. Accordingly, Moi immediately modifies his judgment on the nephew by subsuming his "originality" into a type. As the narrator continues his description, he shifts modes, defining the nephew not as an "original," but rather as a familiar "character," related to the countless buffoons that course through didactic literature from the Middle Ages on. In other words, the narrator, in the course of a single paragraph, forces the nephew's uniqueness to be understood in relation to the long tradition of didactic fools, perfectly recognizable in Sebastian Brant's *Narrenschiff* (1492), Erasmus's *Encomium Moriae* (1509), or Louise Labé's allegorical *Débat de folie et d'amour* (1555). It is in this sense that the fool can serve as the leavening in society (NR 5/35). The substitution of "character" for "original"—betraying, incidentally, Moi's own inconstancy—is symptomatic of an intellectual will to gather this experience into a narrative or *logos* that would reaffirm his subjective position. The narcissism has not been broken but simply projected. It explicitly robs the mad musician of his individuality in order to reassert the narrator's selfhood. Yet, as the dialogue unfolds, it turns out that the nephew, as pure otherness, is anything but a type. His uniqueness prevents the philosopher from being restored to himself. Tellingly, in Homer, although it is unclear whether the Sirens will grant the harvesting of knowledge of the Same—their call may only be an empty temptation—it is nonetheless perfectly clear, as Circe asserts, that by taking the bait one forfeits all chances of ever returning home.

At any rate, the narrator ignores the risk and attempts to domesticate his wild interlocutor, thereby creating the major tension that motivates the dialogue, namely, between the gathering energies of Moi, eager to discover the *logos* that would reestablish his subjectivity, and Lui's forces of disintegration, which threaten to shatter every endeavor to subsume his singularity.

On the broadest level, the means of appropriation are already arranged by Moi's dual function as a participant in the dialogue and a narrator. As the subject of the narration, Moi alone has the privilege of reducing the dialogue's proceedings into a story. The frequent parenthetical remarks, which are offered as descriptions of the nephew's eccentric pantomime behavior, are a sure sign of this privilege. The parentheses rhyme with the intellectual brackets that initially distinguished the narrator as an indifferent, isolated thinker. In the body of the dialogue proper, instead of dissolutely pursuing his own strumpet thoughts, Moi now stalks the digressions of the other, still with the intent of accumulating them into meaning and still exposing himself to hazard. Indeed, the parentheses often express a deep hermeneutic frustration: "I was listening to him ["Je l'écoutais"]; and as he was acting the scene of the pimp and the maiden he was procuring, I was torn between opposite impulses ["l'âme agitée de deux mouvements opposés"] and did not know whether to give in to laughter or furious imagination. I felt embarrassed ["Je souffrois"]. . . . I was dumbfounded ["J'étois confondu"] at such sagacity and such baseness, such alternately true and false notions, such absolute perversion of feeling and utter turpitude, and yet such uncommon candor. He noticed the conflict going on inside me ["en moi"] and said: What's the matter?" (NR 24/51). Rather than allow a consolidation of the self, the nephew's actions occasion an inward split resulting in confusion. The madman's capacity to alternate infects his observer, causing him to suffer from shifting points of view.

This power of alternation lies in the nephew's musicality, for music's temporal aspect, its potential for effecting change over time, is the source of fascination as well as the cause of confusion. Taking place in an irreversible flow, one could say that there is no true repetition in music, at least no repetition in the strict sense. Every reprise is at once equal and unequal to its preceding occurrence. Although all aesthetic experience admittedly participates in some kind of temporal unfolding—the time to read a poem or a novel, the time to scan a picture or circle around a sculpture—music's time is perfectly inherent. The temporality involved in the reception of the visual or literary arts is independent of the object; the reader or viewer brings his or her own subjective time to the aesthetic experience. With music it is different. Musical perception is necessarily coincident with the work's unfolding.[11] A specific portion of time fundamentally constitutes the music. Temporality belongs to the piece. As movement proceeding in a rigorously unidirectional line, music corporeally binds the listener, who must yield his or her personal time to the progression at hand. This compulsory bond between listening and unfolding, this submission of subjective time to the tempo of a musical piece, clarifies music's hold on the listener, its capacity to captivate or even bewitch.

Both the narrator and the nephew are irresistibly caught, the former in his fascination, the latter in being possessed. The dialogue takes place precisely because Moi relaxes his philosophical control, his rational autonomy, and lets himself to be taken in by the heteronomous pull of the madman's contagious music. The nepotic Siren exerts a powerful hold on the philosopher, who, succumbing to the alien tempo, becomes moved, overwhelmed, and altered. In staying, in leaving his ears unplugged, however bound to the mast of good sense, the Odyssean narrator chooses to undergo the musical-dialectical experience of becoming other.

BETWEEN THE INFINITE AND THE INFINITESIMAL

Moi searches for reconciliation, synthesis, and self-identity by collecting the nephew's singular instants that pile up in confusion ("He sang thirty tunes on top of each other and all mixed up ["Il entassoit et brouilloit ensemble trente airs"]" [NR 83/102]). Brashly vocal ("Outside, the café windows were thronged with passers-by who had stopped because of the noise" [ibid.]), the twinkling of each phrase dissipates into air. Mere contiguity. If the narrator is an allegory of selfhood, the nephew is an allegory of voice: unique and evanescent, communicating itself before it communicates any definitive sense. With his "thirty airs" the nephew entangles bits and pieces of French and Italian, tragic and comic opera: "Je suis un pauvre misérable . . . Monseigneur, Monseigneur, laissez-moi partir . . . O terre, reçois mon or, conserve bien mon trésor. . . . Mon âme, mon âme, ma vie! O terre! . . . Le voilà le petit ami, le voilà le petit ami!—Aspettare e non venire . . . A Zerbina penserete . . . Sempre in contrasti con te si sta . . ." (ibid.). This cento of eighteenth-century opera does nothing to hide the quilter's needle. The semantics of these phrases are inconsequential. Thus decontextualized, they are in fact to a large extent meaningless. In giving himself over to pure vocalization, the nephew fails to communicate sense for the ingathering narrator. Nonetheless, he certainly communicates himself, the simple fact that he is there, face to face, as someone who must be heard, without necessarily being understood. On this basis, Foucault sees in *Le neveu* a sustained "fascination with the immediate."[12]

If the narrator wants to collect the nephew's performed utterances and gestures into a stable meaning, if he wants to steady the coruscating promise of the madman's voice, he must do so in relation to a fixed, identifiable knowledge. In Greek, this knowledge is best designated by the term *epistêmê*, a standing in place, immovable and therefore timeless. In other words, the collecting (*legein*), which is thinking, moves from an axis of sequence to an eidetic space of simultaneity. The linear discursiveness of speech is translated into an object for contemplation, which serves as the guide for further organizing or correcting what is said. The history of metaphysics is for the most part constituted by this tension between an idea of reason, which attends to the sequential unfolding of thought, and an ideal of intellect (*nous*), which contemplates that which transcends temporality. In her recent study on the voice, Adriana Cavarero develops a simple and therefore useful scheme that places *logos* or the act of speech (*legein*) between the evanescence of the vocal utterance and the eternal stability of the idea. In the service of the idea, the philosopher "devocalizes" speech so that, by rendering it immaterial, thought can begin its path toward timeless verity.[13] "Ideally," Cavarero writes, "the fulfillment of the metaphysical system is a contemplative, immobile, and perpetual state that admits no discoursing—not even the silent discoursing of the soul with itself.... The voice—and this is, finally, the point—disturbs philosophy" (45). That is, the voice is located at the opposite pole of the idea, and yet both share a quality of timelessness that qualitatively distinguishes them from the linearity of *logos*. The perpetuity of the noetic truth, as well as the purely evanescent instant, admits no time. *Logos* or reason unfolds between two species of infinitude or rather between the infinite and the infinitesimal, between two realms that exceed the temporal line of human existence.

The experience of madness, as it is represented in *Le neveu de Rameau*, may be defined according to these two infinities. For the accumulating philosopher, the fulgurant instants of the nephew's behavior are clearly symptomatic of his derangement ("He noticed nothing, but went on, possessed by such a frenzy ["saisi d'une aliénation d'esprit"], an enthusiasm so near to madness [*folie*] that it was uncertain whether he would ever get over it, whether he should not be packed off in a cab straight to Bedlam ["aux Petites-Maisons"]" [*NR* 83/103]). Furthermore, from the narrator's point of view, the uncle, the composer Rameau, may also be somewhat mad ("[He] has written so many unintelligible visions and apocalyptic truths on the theory of music, not a word of which he or anyone else has ever understood" [*NR* 6/35]). Overall, Moi must admit the accuracy of the proverb that "great wits are oft to madness near allied ["il n'y a point de grands esprits sans un grain de folie"]" (*NR* 10/39). For the narrator, both the metaphysical visionary and the possessed pantomime deserve a place in the asylum. Madness is attributed to either extreme precisely because it falls below or hovers above the line of good sense.

Accordingly, in his article "Folie" in the *Encyclopédie*, Diderot describes madness in general as a deviation from the path of reason ("s'écarter de la raison"), concluding that "all excess is *folie*."[14] Extreme sensibility and extreme intellection constitute two poles equally distant from rationality ("les deux extrêmes sont également folie" [ibid.]). In *Le neveu*, in addition to the nephew's immoderately fervent behavior, there is the uncle's delusional belief in his own excessively systematic theories. Although Jean-Philippe Rameau's explications of the fundamental bass and the *corps sonore* were generally accepted by the philosophes as great advancements in the field of music theory, Moi's comment above alludes to a rejection of the composer's increasingly metaphysical tendencies, betrayed especially by his *Nouvelles réflexions sur le principe sonore* (1760). Like d'Alembert, Diderot applauded and depended on Rameau's innovations—for example, in the early essay on acoustics, included in his *Mémoires sur différents sujets de mathématiques* (1748)—while harboring both skepticism toward the composer's ambitious demonstrations and downright revulsion for his perversely mystical, quasi-Rosicrucian hallucinations.[15] Much later, in the *Leçons de clavecin* (1771), Diderot has Rameau pegged as a "systematizer" ("un systématique") who, unlike "a sensible physicist" ("un bon physicien"), "bends the facts, so that willy-nilly, he can adjust them to his ideas."[16] Rameau the composer is arguably as mad as his nephew, if not for his civic disturbances, then for his ability to invert and pervert matters of sense into an abstract, transcendent form.

The uncle's belief in system and his fondness for deductive demonstration are said to be grounded in a will to abstraction. In the nephew's opinion, the composer is "made of stone" (*NR* 79/99). He lives in a self-enclosed space, indifferent to the world and to those living around him— "He thinks of nothing but himself, and the rest of the universe is not worth a pin to him ["comme d'un clou à soufflet"]. His wife and daughter can just die when they like, and so long as the parish bells tolling their knell go on sounding overtones of a twelfth and a seventeenth everything will be all right ["cela est heureux pour lui"]" (*NR* 8–9/37). In short, he is a kind of philosopher ("C'est un philosophe dans son espèce"), the kind that we have already witnessed in the opening lines of the dialogue, where Moi presented himself in egocentric self-sufficiency. By allowing his mind to wander, by admitting that his thoughts are his *catins*, the narrator saves himself from the *folie* that deludes the composer. One might have assumed that this lapse is a mark of his inconstancy, when in fact it is the crucial element that returns him to the discursive line that is reason. Pursuing the temporal unfolding of his thinking as well as deigning to listen to the bizarre nephew are symptomatic of Moi's rationality, which rejects both the contemplative perpetuity of a *systématique* and the evanescent instant of the madman. Thought must be discursive for the Enlightened, insofar as it permits ideas to be further interrogated, qualified, and even debunked. To borrow the terms from d'Alembert's "Discours préliminaire" to the *Encyclopédie*, the man of reason must constantly negotiate between the dual lures of the transcendent map and the immanent labyrinth.

EXCURSUS: THE HOWL OF MARSYAS

> And I would humbly suggest the old fable of Apollo and Marysas. It seems to me very timely. Or more properly, it is probably always timely in any well-composed literature.
>
> —CONCLUDING LINES TO FRIEDRICH SCHLEGEL,
> *GESPRÄCH ÜBER DIE POESIE* (1800)

From the viewpoint of discursive reason, the two timeless extremes of the idea and the instant, of the infinite and the infinitesimal, are sites of madness. It should be noted, that in *Le neveu*, both poles are represented by musicians, by the systematic composer and the deranged performer, respectively. The myth of Apollo and Marsyas—a story of central importance for the history of music aesthetics—serves as a useful illustration of the dynamic tension between these two poles, which courses through Diderot's dialogue.[17] The myth not only illustrates the basic tension that organizes the work but also accounts for many points of narrative detail. A digression therefore is in order.

Apollo, the god of music, is known to have driven people mad. In this general sense, he was no different from the other Olympians, who all possessed the power to punish mortals by striking them down with insanity. Zeus stole the mind of Bellerophon, Hera goaded poor Io and compelled Heracles to murderous fury, Athena darkened Ajax with terrible delusions, and Dionysus—the explicitly mad god (*mainomenos*)—deranged all those who encountered him, whether they came in worship or denial. Apollo's inflictions, however, tended to be of a different, more ambivalent nature. As the god of healing, he was often called upon to cure the mad, as in the case of Heracles or Orestes. In the *Phaedrus*, Socrates aligns Apollo's version of madness with the art of prophecy (*mantikê*), emphasizing the word's relation to *mania* in general (244c). This gift was ambivalent indeed, something either beneficial or malevolent, detrimental or salutary. Thus, to punish Cassandra, he stole her mind and turned her into a vehicle for true predictions no one would believe.

In demonstrating the usefulness of divine madness, Socrates refers to Apollo's cult instituted at Delphi, where the young Pythia became possessed (*entheos*), transmitting divine messages in a glossolalia that would be converted into legible hexameters by the *prophêtês* on duty. The internalization conveyed by the *en-* of *entheos* or *enthousiasmos*, announcing that there is a "god within," is typical of Apolline madness and distinguishes it from the other species of Olympian-sent sufferings, which on the whole are characterized as an attack from without.[18] The way Apollo invades the core of one's psyche, establishing an uncanny, external space within one's very inwardness, confirms the musicality attributed to this god. For music takes place *inside* the listener and is therefore a perceptual experience quite unlike vision, which tends to be understood as setting up a distance between the observer and the observed. Apollo explicitly strikes from within. He *in-spires*, hence he is closely related to the Muses and poetic creation.

Whereas Io was tormented by a pricking gadfly or Orestes by frightful hallucinations, the Apolline madness of Cassandra or the Sibyl, as long as it was still considered mad—that is, before it was worked into a system of interpretation or comprehension—consisted primarily in the voice. The voice, one of the most distinguishing marks of individual existence, identity, and presence, had become alienated. The words Cassandra spoke, her self-expression, were not her own. Her voice had yielded to the god's. In the *Agamemnon* of Aeschylus, it is specifically the *daimon* that "makes her sing" (1175–76). Cicero notes that it is the god within who speaks, not Cassandra ("Deus inclusus corpore humano iam, non Cassandra, loquitur" [*De divinatione* 1.67]). This fact partially accounts for the seduction and fear of music expressed in Plato's *Republic*, where it is said to "penetrate the innermost part of the soul [εἰς τὸ ἐντὸς τῆς ψυχῆς]" (3.401d). *Mousikê*—the threefold art of word, tone, and movement—threatened to derange, to turn you into something other than what you are. Yet it is precisely this alienation that produces sense. It is only after being struck down by Apollo, only after losing *her* voice, that Cassandra became a vehicle of the true.

The story of Apollo and Marsyas, although not explicitly concerned with madness, is nevertheless structured by two opposing conceptions of musical experience that rehearse the scheme outlined above, which pits reason between the idea and the instant. In brief, the myth contrasts immediate, evanescent expression with the invasive nature of Apolline mediation, which works according to a transcendent vision or form. The encounter is presented as especially gruesome. According to Apollodorus, the half-bestial satyr Marsyas retrieved the pipes, or *aulos*, which Athena had invented and then threw away in disgust. She discarded the instrument because playing it disfigured her face, that is, "it made her face unbeautiful or deformed [*amorphon*]."[19] Exceedingly proud of his competence on the newfound instrument, Marsyas challenged Apollo himself to a musical contest. After the competition resulted in a stalemate, Apollo fatally trapped Marsyas in a second round by "turning" (*strepsas*) his lyre upside down and demanding that the pipes be inverted as well.[20] Failing to produce any sound in this fashion, Marsyas lost the contest and was condemned to suffer whatever punishment the god chose. Apollo forthwith nailed him to a tree and flayed him alive. In other words, the god deformed him in a way that recalls and radicalizes Athena's deformation. The outcome can be imagined to have been particularly garish. Ovid, for example, in his version of the proceedings, devotes excessive space to describing the details, vividly relating how the victim's sinews (*nervi*) were cruelly exposed (*Metamorphoses* 6.382–400).

The myth is generally read as a warning against hubris: one should not be so haughty as to challenge a god. I, however, would like to press the interpretation of the myth, even if exaggeratedly, because I think it speaks to a central concern of this book. Apollo wins by means of a ruse—or an inversion. The lyre can be played upside down; the *aulos* cannot. As I see it, Apollo defeats Marsyas by means of poetry itself. The participle for "turning (upside down)" (*strepsas*), from the verb "*strephô*," yields the noun "*strophê*," designating not only a "dirty trick" but also the "turn" a chorus makes in the public performance of a lyric poem, hence the poetic "strophe." Marsyas's arrogance stems from his belief that he could express himself so powerfully, so immediately, that he could even surpass a god. That is to say, he thinks he can communicate the contents of his soul without the mediation—or, better, the inversion—of poetic form. He dreams of direct expression, uncontaminated and therefore somehow "formless"— *amorphon*. Yet the god of poetry has his tricks, Marsyas is fatally incapable of the strophe, and formlessness is exposed in all its ugliness.

From one perspective, one could say that Marsyas denies language. The lyre (or *kithara*) is an instrument designed to accompany a song's words, to uphold a text with harmonic support. The *aulos*, in contrast, does not allow the voice to articulate linguistically. It pushes words away, utilizing the breath to emit nothing but pure sound. In the version given by Diodorus Siculus, Apollo is victorious not by inverting his instrument but rather by opting to sing along for the second round (*Library* 3.59.1–6). Marsyas exerts himself, pouring out his life's breath, his spirit, or *pneuma*, while the Olympian sings, his fingers plucking at the strings with relative calm. The god's dactylic and logical (verbal) control over the music contrasts with the satyr's pneumatic expenditure. Apollo blends music to word, while Marsyas almost faints from hyperventilation.

This literally alogical nature of the *aulos* no doubt contributed to its degradation in fifth- and fourth-century Athens as an instrument commonly associated with slaves and prostitutes, with drunken excess and irrational behavior. Its purportedly non-Greek, Phrygian provenance fueled the antipathy. Its use was forbidden in the education of Athenian children, and it was banished from Plato's ideal city (*Republic* 3.399c–e). Aristotle, who also refers to the *aulos* as preventing human speech, explains that Athena rejected the instrument not simply because it was "disfiguring" but because it offered nothing to the "intelligence [*dianoian*]." Thus, Aristotle concludes, the *aulos* could be of no service to "the goddess of knowledge and art"—of *epistêmê* and *technê* (*Politics* 8.1341b).

What the *aulos* is incapable of performing is the lyre's forte. The stringed instrument is the perfect artistic tool for the investigation of scientific inquiry and the determination of eternal truths. The Pythagorean advancement of knowledge of the physical and cosmological spheres, based on the numerical tetractys—that is, on the first four integers (1, 2, 3, and 4), whose addition yields the 10 of perfection—found its sonorous correspondence in the lyre's original four strings, which produced the consonant intervals of a perfect fourth, fifth, and octave. These intervals beautifully reflected the proportional relationships among the basic numbers of the universe (4:3, 3:2, and 2:1).[21] The length of the strings and the constancy of the tone provided a concrete model of the abstract order underlying all reality, a model that was simultaneously visible, tangible, and audible. Although originally constructed with four holes corresponding to the same basic pitches, the double reed of the *aulos* required an excess of breath, causing the cheeks to puff out—hence Athena's disfigurement. It yielded a comparatively uneven tone, which was generally interpreted as an ethical failing, if not an attack on universal order itself.[22]

From another perspective, one may pause at the lyre's efficacy and question its capacity to bring the voice in line with harmonic proportion.

In considering more carefully the opposition between the lyre and the *aulos*, it becomes evident that the wind instrument is much closer to the human voice, despite the fact that it does not allow the performer to articulate words while playing. Like the human voice, the *aulos* is monodic, nonchordal. The synchronic ordering of the lyre's strings, sounding out a harmony that reflects the eternal proportions of the cosmos, is as distant from an individual's singular voice as one's body is from the heaven's constellations. The flute's strain, like a sung melody, is given over to time—imprecise and variable, evanescent, mortal. The *aulos* may be illogical (preventing the *logos* from being heard), but it may also offer a self-expression that moves beyond the verbally formatted. Marsyas seems to question the voice's reduction to linguistic meaning. In light of his performance, the Apolline coordination of word and harmony seems to be purchased at the price of a strange sublimation or, again, an alienation from within.

To continue: the beautiful Apollo could not abide an instrument that obstructed knowledge. He refused to condone something that deformed both physically and morally. For this reason he gave Marsyas not merely a form but a particularly apt one. By nailing his body to a tree and exposing the viscera, he turned him into a kind of lyre—an instrument composed of wood and gut strings. The Greek term "*neuron*," like Ovid's "*nervus*," denotes "sinew" (or "tendon") as well as "lyre string." Stretched on the bark, the life that once pulsed wildly and illogically now serves to illustrate the numerical relationships that underlie a law-abiding cosmos. Apollo literally instrumentalizes the satyr. He subjugates his intemperance.

Titian's well-known depiction of the scene seems to appreciate these implications of the myth, insofar as it is Marsyas himself whom Apollo has inverted. To reinforce the interpretation, Titian's portrayal of the victim's body, with curved arms resting on the ground, replicates the shape and color of the god's viol. The symmetrical cavities at Marsyas's chest, the arc of his mouth, and even the anatomist's thin blade, are all repeated in the f-holes, bridge, and bow of Apollo. The *aulos* player believed he could be victorious with the expression of pure sound, exceeding the definitions of articulate words, but the Apolline approach to music—the god's capacity to invert and convert, to perform a strophe—teaches him that his inwardness, like Cassandra's, is subject to a gross alienation. Marsyas has his insides torn out. The mythic punishment reveals the truth of anatomy, namely, that to understand how life works, to form life into an object of knowledge, of *epistêmê*, is to bring life to an end. As technologies of comprehension, science and art give life a definition by finishing life off. *Technê* betrays its complicity with death.

To be sure, Apollo's tempering does little to conceal its violence, but it also reflects a kind of madness on the god's part, the obsession to uncover what lies within or behind the voice, the desire to learn by vivisection the mechanics of this material, so as to render it more efficient. Perhaps Apollo wants to decorporealize the voice, which would prepare it for its sublimation, like the song that issued from the decapitated Orpheus.

Apollo inverts the lyre and therefore wins the right to invert Marsyas. The lyre, it should be noted, had always been an instrument of inversion. According to the *Homeric Hymn to Hermes*, it was the infant trickster god who first created one from a tortoise shell. As the hymn relates, Hermes is strikingly adept at causing inversions, for example, when he reverses the tracks of the cattle he stole from Apollo (76–78). Happening on a tortoise by his cave, he conceives the idea of killing the animal and using the shell to form a resonating body. He persuasively mentions the "harm" that will surely occur should the animal go on living, adding: "but if you die, then you shall sing most beautifully"—ἢν δὲ θάνῃς, τότε κεν μάλα καλὸν ἀείδοις (38). He tears the living body from its carapace, in a manner that recalls the flaying of Marsyas and thereby converts the tortoise's mortal life into the immortal life of music.

Hermes' accomplishment therefore is truly a work, an *ergon*, that produces a new life by means of a death. Indeed, on hearing the sweet melodies, Apollo, who is repeatedly addressed in the *Hymn* as the "one *working* from afar or at will" (*Ekaergos*), is overwhelmed by the instrument, which he exclaims to be "wondrous work" (*thaumata erga* [440]). Whereas he has never taken pleasure "in the provocative [*himeroeis*] roar of the *aulos*," he now finds himself utterly enchanted by the lyre's strains. In the end, Apollo receives the instrument from Hermes, in compensation for the theft of the cattle. It is but one more exchange, one more inversion.

The Marsyan position rejects the lyrical program as it is here portrayed. A life purchased by death is no life. The stance has everything to do with language, hence Marsyas's reticence. The only words that Ovid allows Marsyas to express is a protest: "Quid me mihi detrahis? . . . A! Piget! A! non est . . . tibia tanti"—"Why are you stripping me?"—literally, "Why are you drawing me away from myself?"— "Ah! I repent! Ah! A flute is not worth so great a price" (*Metamorphoses* 6.385–86). Marsyas cannot bear seeing himself pulled away from himself. No music, the flute included, is worth the price of his life.

Marsyas's pain, his shock and incomprehension, confirms his suspicions of beautiful form. As a satyr, he is a figure of excess with an insatiably sexual appetite, eager to break through all limitations, all definitions. To be sure, it was the formlessness of the *aulos* that first made the instrument so appealing to him. The ugly Marsyas was attracted to that which made Athena's face *amorphon*. It offered him the possibility of remaining in the singularity of a life that is irreducible to linguistic expression, irreducible to form. It led him to think that there might be something that could stay outside the work of language and therefore defeat Apollo's wondrous *ergon*. Yet Marsyas is no match. *Ah ...Ah ...* In the satyr's final cries, we hear how the preverbal pain, by way of repetition, is already being worked into poetry. This nonsemantic though passionate scream is the last sound to be heard, as Marsyas disappears into dactylic form, as he is converted into verse. Apollo teaches the futility of the satyr's desires by revealing that anything posing to be outside the work is already comprehended by that work. As for nonverbal expression, he demonstrates that, no matter how singular, it is always subject to inversion. All expression is liable to public exposure; all life, if it is to manifest itself as life, must be ex-pressed, pressed out and eviscerated. Marsyas begins as a wordless *aulos* player and ends as a dead lyre, becoming an instrument for a language that ruthlessly works.

SOCRATIC ENERGY

> MOI: And you with a paunch like Silenus ...
>
> —*LE NEVEU DE RAMEAU*

The various motifs of the Marsyas myth, culled from different sources, bring to light a conception of language as something formative. With shifting emphases, the form-bestowing nature of verbal language becomes a cause for suspicion throughout the tradition of mad, musical representations. The Marsyan position, as I would like to present it, is a protest against certain aspects of language that it considers perverse. This protest is twofold: in the first place, it takes issue with language's exclusive claim to the production of meaning; second, it questions the way language works as an instrument of objectification, as a discursive tool for transforming the instant into the idea—something that the Marsyan invariably regards as an expropriation.

In the model of instrumental language, words accomplish the task of making sense by means of designation and subjective intention. These two functions are grounded in the classical theory of the symbol. In Aristotle's famous definition, whose influence extends across the European tradition, spoken words (τὰ ἐν τῇ φωνῇ) are symbols of the soul's affects

(*De interpretatione* 16a). That is to say, the verbalization consists of a double articulation, already manifest in the metaphor of the *symbola*, which are two pieces of a single object, held by contracting parties, that one could literally "throw together" (*symballein*). In linguistic terms, a word is a symbol insofar as it constitutes a substantial sign that must be rearticulated on a second level, which alone grants meaning. Again, it is the user of language—through the "affectations of his soul"—who guarantees the correct passage from signifying substance to significance. For this reason, the human voice (*phônê*), as the bearer or container of an utterance (Aristotle clearly describes the words as being "in the voice"—ἐν τῇ φωνῇ), is already understood as being meaningful. Here the voice is distinguished from all other sounds that occur in nature, which lack the intentionality to speak in themselves. We can certainly attach (or assign) significance to them, but this interpretive intention necessarily remains external to the sound. For Aristotle, the human production of sound as voice stands in contrast to animal sounds on the basis of the former's internal intention.

That said, however, the double articulation of symbolization complicates this definition. As already mentioned above, if the voice is the material substance that conveys meaning, then it could be regarded as having merely a mediating function that itself does not contribute to the meaning borne. Indeed, in Aristotle's model, the "soul's affects" are the ideal goal before which the material means of communication disappear. The voice must evaporate into sense. Here the material is dispensable, because it is in itself meaningless. Language seems to work by using the voice and using it up.[23]

Less ambiguously, at least in the conventional sense, designation and intentionality are present in the Greek conception of *mousikê* only by virtue of the rational *logos* that governs the harmonic and rhythmic dimensions. Without *logos*, as in the case of the solo *aulos*, designation and intentionality can be said to be missing. The pipes emit mere sound—a single articulation on the level of material alone. It is a sign that cannot be joined (or "thrown") together with sense. Marsyas, however, denies that the symbolic is the sole mode of making sense. His performance obstructs the labor involved. He questions the instrumental model of language and views the double articulation as a cruel inversion. "Quid me mihi detrahis?" From a more positive point of view, Marsyas seems to suggest that beyond communicating content, language also communicates itself. Language is not merely an instrument; it is also a voice. If language works, it is the Marsyan project to see to its unworking. Marsyan music is irrational or mad because it remains on the single level of sound, unable to convert it into a symbol or sign of (nonaudible) significance. This level of material substance is often associated with life itself—mere life—where the "ah" is heard in all its particularity: nonrepeatable and evanescent.

From the point of view of the classical tradition, such an insistence on the intransitive nature of sound is strange, insofar as it runs counter to more conventional models of song sponsored by the Muses and based on inspiration and transmission. The Muses redeem singular instances by extracting them from the *hic et nunc* and integrating them into an order that is not fleeting but lasting. As the daughters of memory (Mnemosyne), they create song by gathering pieces of immediate experience and combining them with what is no longer here. Memory is the storehouse of what is no longer. Its offspring is the Muses' work, which removes moments from present existence and arranges them into a beginning, middle, and end, into a *logos* that leads to the establishment of a form. Marsyas is a simpleton or a fool because he perceives only the present without being able to coordinate it with the no-longer-present. He cannot ascend to knowledge, which is grounded in repetition, in connecting perception with what has been perceived.

Marsyas is an idiot because he is incapable of rising beyond the "particular" (*idion*). Yet his idiocy—like Erasmus's moronic Folly—speaks some truth. The Marsyan emphasis on evanescent, nonrepeatable life shows that what is no longer here is in fact dead. Memory is less a storehouse and more a graveyard. To sing with the Muses is to mourn. Marsyas would rather forget—an impossible task!—so as to live in the pure present. We should recall that the one requirement, in the doctrine of metempsychosis, for dead souls to return to life is that they drink from the waters of Lethe, that they imbibe oblivion. Mere life seems to be the renunciation of memory itself and with it the Muses' seductive offer of immortality. Marsyas cries against being pulled out of the lived moment. Little does the idiot know that he is already lost as soon as he speaks, as soon as he formulates words that must be converted into sense. His gory ex-pression is but a consequence of his expression.

Although harboring a deep suspicion of words, the Marsyan position is not simply without language. On the contrary, it promulgates a linguistic activity that boldly reevaluates the conventional means of symbolic signification. Plato, for example, often portrays Socrates as a Marsyan type, ready to unwork the objective truths established by language. To borrow an opposition made by Wilhelm von Humboldt, Socrates questions the status of a language as an accomplished piece of work (*ergon*) and prefers to investigate precisely how language is put to work—"eine *wirkende* Kraft" (*energeia*).[24] Socrates' method of cross-examination, which is consistently allied with the quest to know himself, is to interrogate what language says by analyzing how language works. His irony shows little respect for all truths formed by language.

Accordingly, Socrates' suspicion of writing, famously outlined in the *Phaedrus*, is linked to his indifference to facts. At the head of this dialogue, Socrates responds to Phaedrus's inquisitiveness concerning mythic lore by mentioning the myriad rational explanations available. For example, Boreas's rape of Oreithyia could be reconstructed as a story of how a gust of the North Wind (*pneuma Boreou*) pushed her off the rocks to her death. "Now, Phaedrus, such explanations are amusing enough, but they are a job for a man I cannot envy at all. He'd have to be far too ingenious and work too hard [*epiponou*].... But I have no time for such things; and the reason, my friend, is this: I am still unable, as the Delphic inscription orders, to know myself." (229d–e). As Seth Benardete comments on this passage, "The universality of knowledge and the individuality of self-knowledge seem not to consist with one another."[25] Socrates' obsession with his own selfhood leaves no room for the consideration of what lies outside.

For this reason, Socrates is shocked, in the *Apology*, at his accusers' portrayal, in which he cannot recognize himself. They have him pegged as a kind of "wise man" who ponders what is above and below the earth and then misleads others with his nonsense (19b–c). To correct the situation, Socrates wants to relate something true, something authentic, but decidedly not in "beautifully refined words" (κεκαλλιεπημένους γε λόγους [17b]). He distrusts beautiful speeches, like those of his accusers, insofar as they conceal something beneath their form. Socrates is concerned more with semiotics than semantics: not what is meant by words but rather how words construct meaning. For this reason, his entire mode of cross-examining the citizens of Athens constitutes a challenge to Apollo himself, the god of beautiful forms. He explains how his friend Chaerophon once brought him to Delphi to ask the Pythia, possessed by Apollo, whether there existed a wiser man than Socrates. When Socrates heard the reply that there was no one wiser, he set out on his path of dialectical confrontations with others in order to disprove the Apolline dictum, explicitly to "prove the utterance wrong" (ἐλέγξων τὸ μαντεῖον [21c]). He unworks each interlocutor's beautiful words, which perversely allow the unwise to be perceived as wise, both to others and to themselves.

In the *Symposium*, it is Phaedrus again, now the host of the evening's festivities, who turns the party into a round of speeches devoted to Eros. Upon banishing the *aulos*-playing girls, this "father of the *Logos*" heads off the sober discussion. After each participant has had his turn, however, an intoxicated Alcibiades crashes the party and leaves the door open for the flute girls' return. With harsh words, he assaults Socrates, comparing him to Marsyas:

> Isn't he just like a statue of Silenus? You know the kind of statue I mean; those, I mean, that our craftsmen work out [*ergazontai*] with pipes or *auloi* in their hands: when their two halves are pulled open, they are found to contain images of the gods. Now look at him again! Isn't he also just like the satyr Marsyas? . . . Are you not an *aulos* player? In fact, you're much more marvelous than Marsyas, who needed instruments to cast his spells on the souls of man by the powers of his breath, and so the players of his music do still. . . . The only difference between you and Marsyas is that you need no instruments; you do exactly what he does, but with mere words [*psilois logois*]. . . . Whenever I listen, my heart leaps within me more than that of any Corybantian reveler, and my eyes rain tears when I hear them.
>
> (*SYMPOSIUM* 215A–E).

Alcibiades, the beautiful young man whose words are explicitly compared to "arrows" (219b), clearly takes an Apolline position. He thereby re-creates the god's contest against the satyr. In his biography, Plutarch reports that Alcibiades recalled the Marsyas myth when he proclaimed his distaste for the "ignoble and illiberal" *aulos*, which "robs the master of voice and speech" (*Alcibiades*, 2.5–6). Now, in the *Symposium*, he wants to pull his teacher apart, to eviscerate him, literally to strip him of his "hide" (*doran* [216d]), in order to reveal the beautiful, divine forms he believes are concealed within. The contest is staged, but Alcibiades is already handicapped, playing the dubious role of a drunken Apollo. Moreover, as Alcibiades admits, Socrates does not need the *aulos*. The power of his Marsyan words is enough to frustrate the beautiful man's will to form. Thus Plato inverts the mythic inversion—here, Apollo is defeated, and Marsyas remains intact.

One could say that Socrates' work is to unwork linguistic forms by way of a musical performance, as opposed to a precomposed set of speeches. In a famous passage from the *Phaedo*, which fascinated the young Nietzsche, Socrates confesses the dream that recurred throughout his life and that visited him on the eve of his execution: "Socrates, make music and work at it" (μουσικὴν ποίει καὶ ἐργάζου, [*Phaedo* 60e]). As he explains, he had always interpreted the Muses' command as an encouragement to do what he always did, philosophize, "because philosophy was the greatest kind of music and I was doing it [ἐμοῦ δὲ τοῦτο πράττοντος]" (61a). Socrates appears to be following the Muses' (Apolline) injunction, but in "doing" (*prattontos*) his philosophical music, he has already deviated from the letter of the command, which specifically demands "work" (*ergazou*). Regardless, Socrates has recourse to a musical metaphor to describe a method that alludes to his Marsyan character: a dialectical exchange grounded in the presence of the speakers and the immediacy of the situation. One should recall that the primary intention is an immediate self-knowledge (or *gnôsis*) that is opposed to a mediated form of knowledge of what is outside the self (*epistêmê*). The musical metaphor is important not only because it further adumbrates the nature of Socrates' speaking but also because it discloses possible aspects of language use that differ from the more common work of mediation. I would only note in passing that on more than one occasion, for example, in the *Phaedrus* and the *Apology*, Socrates refers to this musical method explicitly as "manic."

Many of the writers preoccupied with musical mad experience resist the formative impulse associated with the Apolline. In this sense, they distinguish themselves from a more conventional poetics desirous of formal arrangement. Indeed, most poets tend to reject the Marsyan desire for formlessness. Dante, for example, betrays his will to form in his invocation to Apollo at the beginning of the *Paradiso*:

> Entra nel petto mio, e spira tue
>   sì come quando Marsia traesti
>   de la vagina de le membra sue
>
> (Enter into my breast, and within me breathe
>   the very power you made manifest
>   when you drew Marsyas out from his limbs' sheath.)

(1.19–21)

Dante welcomes the inspiration that may lead to a new birth ("de la vagina"). He willingly accepts the terms of Apollo's work contract, negotiated by Hermes, whereby poetic immortality may be received. But at what price? The Marsyan writer resists this kind of redemption. There is a suspicion about shaping the immediacy and power of inward feeling into the eminently logical ordering of the lyre, which matches sound to words that are shared by all. The writers who turn to music and madness are Marsyan, insofar as they seek out ways of unworking the very language they are required to use. They recognize that the radical particularity of feeling can only be compromised by a language whose generality, required for communication, inevitably homogenizes and flattens individual emotion—hence their obsession with a writing that offers an alternative to standard signification. In brief, every Marsyan regards symbolic expression—the evaporation of the sensible sign into an ideal, nonsensible system of meaning—as a cruel perversion, an expropriation, or a kind of death.

Diderot's nephew is explicitly associated with the Marsyan position when he is described by the narrator as Silenus (NR 8/37). Moreover, the nephew's subsequent emphasis on radical singularity, his evanescent performances, and his suspicion of verbal conventions, all speak to his satiric and satyric character. (Although the genre of satire [*satura*], which refers to a random or even confused mixture of styles, is not etymologically related to the satyr [*satyrus*], which derives from Greek mythology and refers to a comic performance, the congruence of randomness and impudent comedy, not to mention the sheer homonymity, had contributed to a general conflation of the two terms. The fact that Diderot subtitled *Le neveu de Rameau* a "Satyre"—choosing to use the Greek "Y" rather than employing the more standard and etymologically clearer "satire"—suggests that the author wanted to promulgate the confusion of the two terms. I shall return to this conflation.) Besides the explicit allusion to Silenus and the melding of the satiric with the satyric, Diderot's portrayal of the nephew underscores the family resemblance. Tellingly, the very first words that the nephew addresses to the narrator lightly recall the outburst of Ovid's *aulos* player ("A . . . A . . .")—"Ah, ah, vous voilà, M. le philosophe" (NR 7/36).

The repeated description of the nephew's "lung power" ("Dieux, quels terribles poumons!" [NR 4/34]) further reminds us of Marsyas's pneumatic expenditure, as does the following account of one of his more impassioned moments: "With cheeks puffed out and a hoarse, dark tone he did the horns and bassoons, a bright nasal tone for the oboes, quickening his voice with incredible agility for the stringed instruments to which he tried to get the closest approximation; he whistled the records and cooed the flutes, shouting, singing and throwing himself about like a mad thing ["comme un forcené"]" (NR 84/103). Other details forcefully align the nephew's portrait with the image of Socrates that Alcibiades conjured in the *Symposium*: like the nephew, Socrates always catches one off guard—"All of sudden you'll turn up out of nowhere where I least expect you!" (213c); his strangeness subverts attempts at rationalization (which here Alcibiades simply blames on his drinking)—"It is no easy task for one in my condition to give a smooth and orderly account of your bizarreness [*atopian*]" (215a); he unmasks conventional beliefs, especially those bound to societal values—"He makes me admit that my political career is a waste of time" (216a); in short, he is absolutely unique—"He is like no one else in the past and no one in the present, this is by far the most amazing thing about him" (221c). "Rien ne dissemble plus de lui que lui-même."

Faced with the bewitching peculiarity of Socrates, Alcibiades' only option is to shut his ears—"I refuse to listen to him; I stop my ears and tear myself away from him, for, like the Sirens, he could make me stay by his side till I die" (216b). Here, however, Diderot's narrator parts from his classical model. Whereas Alcibiades plugs his ears, the narrator leaves them open. He is initially confident that he can find a *topos* for the nephew's oddities, for his *atopia*. As the dialogue proceeds, however, he begins to recognize that he remains vulnerable to the threat of losing himself to the sirenic voices. Still, this risk also belongs to the program. The man of reason must situate himself between two species of madness, between the transcendence of Apolline inversion and the hyperimmanence of the Marsyan instant. Here alone, in this balancing act, will the *moi* be able to establish subjectivity, that is, by directing his *logos* to the alterity of two possible deaths: the death of being a form (an *ouvrage*) and the death of being a voice lost upon emission.

2

Unequal Song

In view of the way in which the earliest societies united, was it surprising that
the first stories were set in verse and that the first laws were sung?

—ROUSSEAU, *ESSAI SUR L'ORIGINE DES LANGUES*

F OR MORAL philosophers of the eighteenth century, self-identity is
tightly bound up with the issue of self-representation. There is
concern for the capacity to give one's subjective position a form
that may be communicated to others and therefore to oneself. The rational use of language, understood as intentional and referential, works
precisely to this end. Thus the first-person narrator of Diderot's *Neveu de
Rameau* is all too eager at the head of the dialogue to present himself as
someone in control of his verbal utterances. The need to be in command
of his statements, including his self-representations, is aimed toward establishing a set identity, toward the formation of a figure—by means of
mimesis—that would adequately (completely) correspond to the subject
of language.

This process has decisively moral implications, in relation to both self
and the other. Moi presents himself as an exemplum of constancy (he is
always at the *same* café), as a rationalist capable of gathering and recon-
ciling the most disparate of elements (his thoughts are his *catins*). That is
to say, he proceeds from the belief in personal identity, which further
orients his approach to the nephew. Thus the latter's madness must be
systematized (for example, as a means for intellectual fermentation—"he
is the speck of yeast that leavens the whole" [*NR* 5/35]). Likewise, musicality must conform to a mimetic program, that is, it must become *musica
ficta*, sound absorbed into discourse, ready and able to represent or
express. To this end, Moi—who has a decided knack for splitting experience into perfect oppositions ("Qu'il fasse beau, qu'il fasse laid"), who
likes to spend his afternoons watching games of chess that neatly divide
all encounters into black and white—works to inscribe Lui's alterity into
an operative difference, so as to reinforce the logic of totality.[1]

The nephew, however, is the nonconformist, radically other, equal to nothing, a force of impropriety or even nonidentity. His madness therefore does not simply indicate his failure to represent himself rationally but rather demonstrates—perhaps like every monster—the failure of representation *tout court*. His flaunting of mimetic processes—the bizarre gestural language, the ridiculous imitation of orchestral instruments, the role-playing, and so forth—dismantles the entire mechanism. His gift for unmasking barely conceals his iconoclasm, which is not content to demolish merely images but language as well. And yet the volatility of his musical madness cannot be limited to a purely destructive function. Indeed, his unworking of language hints that there is more to selfhood than can be expressed rationally, more to life than can be molded into an identifiable figure or a representative discourse. The narrator's allusion to Alcibiades' speech—"And you, with a paunch like Silenus . . ."—in granting the nephew a Marsyan-Socratic nature, marks the noncoincidence between the madman's appearance and his interiority. His impropriety may, on the one hand, invite Apolline formation and rational reenlistment, while, on the other hand, it may suggest that there are already gods within, chthonic powers below or beyond any system of figuration, able to break any form, brazenly able to resist the draft into sense.

The fact that the nephew is a mad musician is crucial. It indicates that there may be other dimensions to language that are not included in the rationalist model. Rhetoricians, beginning with Aristotle, had long distinguished the expressive force of what is being said from its lexical meaning. In the eighteenth century, the opposition between expression and semantics, or between force and meaning, was often based on the distinction between speech and song. In verbal communication, a statement's musical properties, that is, its voice, was constituted by intonation, rhythm, accent, pitch, and so forth. The consequence of all this was that it could account for the totality of human experience without reducing it to the lexicon. Rousseau's pentecostal dream of reversing Babel, of reuniting speech and song, is directed to this quest of keeping force and meaning together. With his nephew, Diderot upsets the plan. By insistently questioning the notion of self-representation, *Le neveu de Rameau* turns representability itself into a problem. In other words, force is detached from expression. The voice is no longer understood as a medium expressive in itself but rather comes forward simply as the material substrate of language, necessary for the transmission of sense but not in fact contributing or belonging to semantics. The intensity of the eighteenth century's work to bring the alterity of madness and music back into the fold testifies to an extraordinary difficulty.

MUSIC AND THE IRRATIONAL

Toward the conclusion of the dialogue, the madman's question occasions the philosopher's confession:

> LUI: What is a song [*chant*]?
>
> MOI: I confess the question is beyond me. That's what we are all like [*Voilà comme nous sommes tous*]. In our memories we have nothing but words, and we think we understand them through the frequent use and even correct application we make of them, but in our minds we have only vague notions.
>
> (NR 77/98)

In setting a musical fool as the antagonist to the first-person narrator, the dialogue challenges conventional concepts not only of general terms but also of individual identity and autobiography, representation, and self-representation. "What we are all like" may in fact be concealing a delusion of habit, a "vague notion" that generalizes and glosses over the singularity of objective and subjective experience for the sake of communicative ease.

As an embodiment of the twin themes of music and madness, the nephew introduces a meaninglessness that turns all ontological questions into semantic ones. Exasperated by the madman's musical displays, the represented self—Moi—must rephrase his line of inquiry: rather than explore the possible meanings of "song," he turns to the meaning of words, for example, the words "*je*" and "*moi*." Certainty is abandoned. Accordingly, the dialogue as a whole is replete with confessions of the philosophe's frustration: "I was listening to him ... my soul stirred by two opposite impulses ... I felt embarrassed ["Je souffrois"] ... I was dumbfounded ["J'étois confondu"]" (NR 24/51). Hegel, who accorded Diderot's satire the crucial role of marking the end of the Enlightenment subject, explains that it was specifically "the derangement [*Verrücktheit*] of the musician" that revealed the breakdown of linguistic norms and modern man's subsequent self-alienation, his "tornness," his *Zerrissenheit*. But why this? How do music and madness work together? And what precisely is their threat to subjective knowledge and individual identity? Is all music mad and all madness musical? Or is it not rather the case that music is mad only insofar as it exposes the madness of language, which would sublimate all singularity, all uniqueness?

The questions all turn on the issue of mimesis, variously understood. Generally speaking, the charge of madness is based on a failure to represent, which includes the failure to represent oneself as a cognitive subject. Here, in the crudest terms, "madness" means "nonmimetic." Moreover, it can be applied to opposing parties. Neoclassicists disparage music as mad insofar as it is nonrepresentational, while those who distrust words complain of language's madness, that is, its incapacity to represent the soul, to be emotionally specific, to be—in Rousseau's sense—musical. A close reading of *Le neveu de Rameau*, however, shows that these seemingly straightforward positions are far more complex. If Diderot argues elsewhere for the mimetic—and therefore sane—character of music, in this text he allows his views to be seriously challenged. He exposes himself—as a thinker, as a philosopher, as a writing subject—to an intense self-interrogation.

To appreciate the challenge presented by Diderot's mad musician, one should contextualize it within the broader trends of eighteenth-century aesthetics. An especially illustrative example is the work of Johann Christian Gottsched. It may seem odd to turn to a German theoretician as a way into Diderot's text, but Gottsched's capacity to formulate injunctions of French neoclassical practice and to do so in an eminently systematic fashion warrants this approach. It is not gratuitous that he earned among his Lutheran contemporaries the dubious title of the "pope of poetry." Gottsched would have strongly disapproved of Diderot's dialogue. He was highly suspicious of music and had no patience for the madman. In his theater reviews, published weekly in the *Beyträgen zur critischen Historie der deutschen Sprache, Poesie, und Beredsamkeit* (1732–44), he rallied against the figure of the *Hanswurst*, which in his opinion should be banished from the German stage. The fool's improvised jokes and disruptive antics bore no relation to the plot at hand; they offered nothing save the muddled contents of a warped mind, "eine unordentliche Phantasie" that loudly distracted the audience from the true purpose of theatrical performance, namely, the imitation of nature.[2] The satirical (and satyrical) violence of such figures, including Harlequins, Kasperls, and Pickelherings, transgressed conventions and disrespected all Aristotelian prescriptions. Where Descartes had seen mad behavior as an example of the possible deceptiveness of sensory knowledge, Gottsched regarded the indecorous behavior of jesters as a useless display of mere *sensibilia* that hindered the mind from arriving to the meaningful and truthful realm of the intelligible. The problem finally was also national, since Gottsched viewed the Hanswurst not as a leftover from the earlier German *Possentheater* but rather as a dangerous import from the south, an invasion by the irreverent fools of the commedia dell'arte.

Significantly, Gottsched's concern with the mad player is echoed in his distaste for opera, which he also attributed to Italian origins. "[The opera is] merely a work for the senses ["ein bloßes Sinnenwerk"]: the understanding and the heart get nothing out of it. Only the eyes are dazzled [*geblendet*]; only the ear [*das Gehör*] is tickled and stunned: reason, however, must be left at home, when one goes to the opera."[3] Opera is irrational because its music, together with its spectacular visual effects, subordinates the rule of poetry. It neglects to honor the correct function of music, which according to Gottsched should be entirely subservient. The description here is perfectly classical, modeled both on the Horatian dictum of instruction and pleasure (*aut prodesse aut delectare*) and on the tripartite division of the Platonic soul. When properly imitative, art pleases and instructs, affecting both the heart (*thymos*) and the understanding (*nous*), respectively. The sensual shock of opera, however, works on desire alone—Plato's *epithymia*— which usurps the position of the heart and mind. The condition is analogous to the case of the tyrant, whose soul is described in the *Republic* as steered solely by appetitive desire at the expense of understanding and heart and who therefore is explicitly characterized as a madman (9.571a–573c). To escape connotations of madness, music must be satisfied with being the handmaiden of verbal sense and emotional veracity.

According to Gottsched's genealogy of poetic forms, music's true role had always been supportive and compliant. To this end, music had to be fundamentally repeatable. He understands the regularity of epic representation in dactylic hexameter as a repetitive pattern of return that lends coherence to the linear unfolding of narrative. Gottsched emphasizes the sense of turning ("Umkehren") in the terms "*strophe*" and "*verse*" (from "*vertere*"), taking each line as a melody that returns to the beginning.[4] Correct imitation is grounded in word's power over tone—a mastery that is carried out by reiteration, by turning melody around and converting it to mimetic purpose. Operatic song is dazzling, stunning, and finally mad because here the force of music is all too eventful, not permitting the repetition decisive to Gottsched's program. Like the intrusion of the Hanswurst, operatic effects derail the discursive sense of the story.

Gottsched associates music with the problem of madness, because both are based on spontaneous sensuality with no regard for intelligible or well-grounded emotional experience. The transalpine heat no doubt contributed to the infectious threat perceived by the northern man of cool, clear-headed reason. The peril, however, not only consisted in figures of the commedia dell'arte or in spectacles by settecento impresarios: Italian instrumental music, boldly divorced from words, was incomparably dangerous.

Nonvocal music was the maddest of all, since it denied art of any mimetic function. Without textual supervision, musicians were deemed incapable of being imitative. That is to say, mere music could not represent the particular in a communicable form that could be cognitively grasped.

However differing in their rationale, many eighteenth-century theorists remarked on music's struggle with representation, be it physical or psychological.[5] On the one hand, the vague semantics of purely musical pieces was taken as a frightening incapacity to represent nature. On the other hand, in regard to interior experience, the unexpected and frequent changes in emotions could be considered as a kind of frenzy, imitating the passions of someone without rational consistency. For example, in the opinion of Noël Antoine Pluche, sonatas are like the expressions of madmen, who pass from laughter to tears and from joy to anger without any comprehensible motivation.[6]

It is Jean-Jacques Rousseau who most avidly attempted to reverse these pejorative opinions. While sharing Gottsched's view of language as having its origin in song, while insisting as well that music is most effective as a melody committed to the representation of human passion, he disagreed that music constituted a threat to mimesis. On the contrary, the menace came from verbal language, whose articulations severed expression from its original efficacy. For this reason, Rousseau praised the superiority of the Italian language, which he felt retained more of the natural accents of original speech, as opposed to the unmelodious, overarticulated patterns of the French. If music was considered mad, it was only because societal conventions alienated the individual. For Rousseau, language was indeed a matter of *turning* music—of Gottsched's *vertere*—however, not as a positive conversion of the sensible into the intelligible but rather as a negative perversion that cheated words of their original, musical power. Where Gottsched believed that the imitation of nature required word's mastery over tone, Rousseau argued that only music could revitalize the cold abstractions of verbal language.

Although Rousseau's theoretical positions undo Gottsched's disapproving assessment of music as an art allied to the irrational, his writing nowhere addresses the theme of music and madness in an explicit and extended fashion. That fell to Diderot, whose disruptive, unstable, and musical nephew occasions a reexamination and complication of all the terms involved. *Le neveu de Rameau* not only deals with the problem of representing external reality or internal states but more radically scrutinizes the idea of mimesis itself.

"*Vertumnis, quotquot sunt, natus iniquis.*" With this epigraph from Horace's *Satires*, Diderot places the nephew beneath the sign of "the adverse or unequal [*iniquis*] Vertumni," that is, under the protection of the gods in charge of alternating the seasons. Their name—also derived from the verb "*vertere*"—posits the nephew as an allegory of change itself, with all its connotations of conversion, perversion, and inversion. As a Marsyas, however, the nephew does not invoke an inversion of the formless into the formed but rather a perversion of the formed into the formless. Better, he effects an inversion of inversion. Thus, in Diderot's text, doctrines of mimesis are unworked, exposed to the difficult tensions between semblance and deviation, difference and repetition, propriety and impropriety. With its portrayal of a mad musician who acts and is described as someone "differing from himself," the dialogue draws out the semantic, moral, and ontological implications of every mimetic operation. The nephew punctures the philosopher's masterful control, by means of a series of bizarre impersonations that demonstrate the madness implicit in every imitation. Theories of semblance—from Rousseau's dream of social transparency and communal equality to notions of self-sameness that ground individual identity—are disrupted by this insane lover of Italian opera and a kind of Hanswurst in his own right, who is nonetheless unequal to everyone, including himself.

MIMESIS: CRATYLUS AND THE ORIGIN OF LANGUAGE

Despite Gottsched's and Rousseau's rather straightforward positions, imitation has never been a simple affair. The classical tradition that coursed through eighteenth-century aesthetics reveals instead a fundamental ambiguity. As will be shown, Diderot's contribution to this tradition is highly significant insofar as it aggravates many of the tensions that others would ignore.

One may begin with the reduplicative form of the Greek word "*mi-mê-sis*" itself, which could be taken as an iconic depiction of the term's duplicity. Someone like Plato's Cratylus would hear the term "*mimesis*" itself as an imitation of imitation, for Cratylus believes that names work in the same way as music, that each name puts forward in its phonetic makeup a description of the very thing it names. He regards the words of language as established by nature (*physei*), and that is the main point of contention against his antagonist, Hermogenes, who understands words as set by convention. Hermogenes takes language as working according to posited law or *nomos*, not natural but arbitrary. Cratylus, on the contrary, hears words as mimetically motivated. For him, language is not an arbitrary system of signs at all but, rather, naturally true.

In Hermogenes' view, Cratylus is mad. His refusal to "speak clearly" likens his speech to prophecy (*manteia* [384a]), which Socrates, in the

Phaedrus, defines as one of four types of divine madness. But it is not merely Cratylus's tendency to obfuscate that marks him off as a madman. After Socrates defends Cratylus by establishing that a word is indeed an "imitation" (*mimêma*), he chides him for implying that mimesis is simply a matter of perfect similarity, unadulterated by difference: "Now then, Cratylus, those things that are named by names would suffer ridiculously [γελοῖα . . . πάθοι] if they should be entirely similar in every respect, for everything would be doubled, and no one would be able to say in any case which is the thing itself and which the name [τὸ μὲν αὐτό, τὸ δὲ ὄνομα]" (432d). The ridiculousness of Cratylus's position consists in the desire to override the gap inherent in every repetition. Despite his generous disposition toward Cratylus's idea of mimesis, Socrates cannot abide the suppression of difference: "Do you not perceive how far images [*eikones*] are from possessing the same qualities as those things they represent?" (ibid.)

To illustrate, Socrates turns to the idea of personal representation: "The image must not by any means reproduce all the qualities of that which it imitates, if it is to be an image. . . . Would there be two things, Cratylus and the image, if some god should not merely imitate your color and form . . . but should also make all the inner parts like yours . . . should place beside you a duplicate of all your qualities? Would there be in such an event Cratylus and an image of Cratylus, or two Cratyluses?" (432b–c). Socrates realizes that, no matter how one understands imitation's truth, its *vraisemblance*, mimesis is always problematic. As a re-presentation (a reenactment or a repetition) of what is naturally given, imitation works according to a duplicitous logic. Its energy derives from the irresolvable tension between the same and the different. The split between the first phoneme (*mi*) and the second (*mê*) marks a difference held together by semblance. Cratylus is laughable because he confuses repetition with equivalence. He fails to recognize that positing equivalence entails a degree of inequality.

In a passage from the *Physics*, Aristotle respects the double, alternating logic of imitation in a comprehensive definition of art: "In general, on the one hand, art [*technê*] accomplishes those things that nature is incapable of working out [*apergasasthai*], while on the other hand it imitates those things" (199a 15–17). In the first place, art takes and finishes what nature leaves unworked, while, in the second place, it produces something entirely new that belongs and does not belong to the natural— something connected to the natural by way of similarity yet unbound from it by way of difference. The distinction between completion and invention complicates the terms of the debate between Hermogenes and

Cratylus. On the one hand, *technê* proceeds with what nature itself has given, albeit unfinished, while, on the other hand, the technical consists in the conventions that determine a representation to be true. In either case, *technê* is both motivated and arbitrary. Consequently, it allows two conceptions of the natural to emerge that depart from the Cratylist belief in nature as plenitude: in regard to imitative invention, nature is deficient (there is now something in the world that is not entirely natural), and, in regard to artistic completion, nature is simply idle—incapable of work—*désœuvrée*.

Throughout *Le neveu de Rameau*, Diderot respects the complexities of the mimetic enterprise. For example, when pressed into giving a definition of his own art, the crazed nephew makes a declaration full of qualifications: "Song is an imitation, by means of sounds of a scale, invented by art or inspired by nature, as you please, either by the voice or by an instrument, of the physical sounds ["des bruits physiques"] or accents of passion" (NR 78/98). Following the clear announcement that "song is an imitation," the nephew's remark immediately falls into a number of duplicities, reminiscent of Aristotle's alternative between the naturally given and pure invention. The statement is in fact an exercise in alternation, almost to the point of parody, whereby imitation is grounded in a series of possibilities: art or nature, voice or instrument, sounds or accents. In this way, mimesis turns out to be the principal object of the satire: a presumably identifiable topic that eludes identification.

Elsewhere, however, in other writings on music, Diderot shows himself to be allied with a less complicated understanding of the mimetic function of music, one that is clearly in line with the philosophical program associated with Rousseau. A great impetus behind this program came from Jean-Baptiste Dubos, who deployed the Cratylist distinction between natural and arbitrary signs by distinguishing the musical language of the passions, which was "instituted by nature," from articulated speech, which is merely conventional.[7]

Rousseau famously employed this distinction in his essay on the origin of language, which posits an original identity of word and tone founded in a life of passion and strong emotion. The subsequent rationalization of speech was literally a disenchantment, whereby language lost its naturally given accent in increasingly conventional articulations. One may still hear the passionate tone in modern French—for example, in the vowels and the internalized nasal sounds—but this natural accent is all but lost in the articulations of the tongue and teeth. For Rousseau, the dental and fricative modifications of sound—hallmarks of northern languages—express a neediness that drives men to possession and therefore to isolation. Arguing against Condillac, who attributed language's origin to need, Rousseau sees the primary motivation in desire and pleasure, that is, in those passions that bring men together.[8] Here Rousseau betrays his Cratylism by referring to the impassioned "m" of *"aimer,"* whose expression of love is replaced by the dental articulation of need in *"aider."*[9] A single letter, then, is sufficient to remove mankind from a life of immediacy in nature to a world of cold reflection, where nature is to be articulated, utilized, and used up. As he remarked earlier, concerning the inarticulate languages of nature: "You will find that Plato's *Cratylus* is not as ridiculous as it may seem" (ROC 5.383). Nonetheless, Rousseau can hardly escape the double bind that mimesis imposes. In revealing language's proximity to its source, accent also establishes its distance. As Derrida tirelessly points out, the origin is already divided by a necessary articulation.[10] The replacement of "m" with "d" is but a mimetic symptom of mimetic duplicity.

In the *Phaedrus*, Socrates has recourse to the very same Cratylist-Rousseauist argument, concerning genealogical features of language. The explicit subject of Socrates' remarks is not the love that joins men together but rather the madness that brings men close to the gods: "It is worthwhile to bear witness that the men of old who invented names did not consider madness to be shameful or disgraceful, for they would not have connected it [the word *"mania"*] with the noblest of arts, that which judges what is to come, which they called the manic art [*manikên*]. . . . But the men of today tastelessly insert a *tau* and call it the mantic art [*mantikên*]" (244b–c). The word *"mania"*—consisting of only nasals and vowels and therefore softly evocative of Rousseau's *"aimer"*—undergoes the same dental articulation that distinguishes original speech from the speech of today. The "t" introduces the idea of art or *technê*, the rational, calculated procedure that is necessarily subsequent to the irrational, incalculable moment of divine inspiration. The structure of the *Phaedrus* suggests that the event of manic immediacy enjoys a nearness to the source (the gods or the Muses) that is afterward articulated in the reflective work of philosophy. In the same way, Socrates' "mad" speeches (*manikôs* [265a]) are followed by the labor of explanation. Madness, be it prophetic, ritualistic, poetic, or erotic, is understood by the work it accomplishes after the fact. Rousseau, whose "pure language" would be described by Hölderlin as divinely inspired by the mad god Dionysos, is indeed insane, if he believes it can occupy the site of origin, uncontaminated by the conventions—the *nomoi*—that mediate that event through the articulations of language.[11]

Rousseau's political program is also based on a story of discontinuity and decadence: the inequality that pervades modern society is a direct result of the articulations that split human communities, for example,

into subordinate and dominating groups, into possessors and the disen-
franchised. To correct the injustices caused by inequality, it would be necessary to re-enchant language itself, to dissolve its articulations and
restore its natural accent.[12] The reaccentuation of language would return
humanity to an original, transparently communal state founded on
compassion—on *la pitié*—that first allowed one man to recognize and
identify with the vocal utterances of another as a representation of his
passion, joy, fear, or pain. In Rousseau's view, it was this experience of dis-
covering semblance in another that first established not only community
but also the feeling of being an individual, whose existence was inex-
tricably bound to the fact that one belonged to a community.

Rousseau's statements on music correspond well with this scenario. The
Querelle des Bouffons, which broke out in 1752 with the Paris performance
of Pergolesi's *La serva padrona*, compelled Rousseau to specify his position. His emphasis on melody or song (*chant*) as a language of the heart
argued against the mathematical practice of harmonic systems like the
one proposed by the composer Jean-Philippe Rameau, who essentially
treated music as lifeless acoustic material to be manipulated, controlled,
and tempered. From Rousseau's point of view, Rameau perpetuated the inequality inherent in Cartesianism by removing music from its source in
lived experience.

For the most part, throughout his career, Diderot shared Rousseau's position by referring to music as an expression of the passions, grounded in
sensibility. In the *Leçons de clavecin* (1771), Diderot explains that a succession of musical sounds should "know how to speak to the soul and to
the ear and know the origins of song and of melody, whose true model is
in the depths of the heart ["au fond du coeur"]."[13] Earlier, Diderot had developed a theory of gesture and pantomime, for example, in his *Lettre sur
les sourds et muets* (1751) and the *Entretiens sur le fils naturel* (1757),
whereby preverbal or extraverbal affective movements of the body could
introduce a more natural, less conventional language into theater. "Inarticulate words" (as in impassioned cries or sudden exclamations), "violent
emotions," inflections of "voice and tone," corporeal gesticulations—all
could reenergize the performance and return to it the "accent of truth."[14]
Despite his distaste for the theater, Rousseau's partial contribution to the
Querelle des Bouffons, his opera *Le devin du village*, fondly acknowledges
his friend's work by incorporating a pantomime scene onstage.

Rousseau's opera, written as an intermezzo, makes a formal allusion to
the opera buffa, which developed from the comic intermezzi performed
between acts of an opera seria. In this regard, the opera buffa performed a
structural role analogous to ancient comedy, to the Satyr plays that disrupted

the graveness of tragic performances. Entirely untrained in the art of composition, Diderot offered his own intermezzo in the wake of the *Querelle*— not an opera buffa but rather a dialogue, *Le neveu de Rameau*, which bears, in the orthography of the manuscript, the subtitle "Satyre." Like the actors in the Italian intermezzo, who exploited improvisatory elements of the commedia dell'arte, Rameau's nephew performs the satirical functions of overturning social norms and conventions of language. His wild pantomimes, his irreverent behavior, and his virtuoso display of accent are all reminiscent of the opera buffa. They would at first appear to execute the Rousseauist agenda of igniting the cold conventions that rob human expression of its heart. A master at impersonating accents, the nephew could recharge language by way of mimesis, which for Rousseau would demonstrate man's similarity to his neighbor. The nephew's musicality, however, fails to unite men into an ideal community of shared compassion. On the contrary, his bizarre performances are more pitiful than pitied. As a madman and outsider, he neither exists in nor belongs to a community. As a social parasite, he is more needy than loving. Rather than solving the problem of inequality, the musical language of this depraved man's heart seems to perpetuate it. Here, contrary to Rousseau, the nonsemantic force of song becomes a cause for breaking all identification. It is important to stress that this function runs counter not only to Rousseau's theory but also more remarkably to the majority of Diderot's own aesthetic positions. The autobiographical self—*le Moi*—has indeed found its antagonist.

IDENTITY AND DIFFERENCE

Let us return to the dialogue's epigraph, taken from Horace, *Satires* 2.7: "Vertumnis quotquot sunt natus iniquis." Ernst R. Curtius, in the concluding excursus to his *European Literature and the Latin Middle Ages*, recommended that the motto should be taken as an invitation to read Diderot's text together with the entirety of Horace's satire.[15] Indeed, the correspondences are great. In Horace's poem, the slave Davus takes advantage of December's Saturnalia ("libertate Decembri" [4]), impersonating a free man to berate his master. The figure of the slave-cum-master literally evokes the opera that instigated the *Querelle des Bouffons*, Pergolesi's *La serva padrona* (*The Servant Mistress*), in which the outspoken housemaid Serpina cunningly tricks her master into marriage. The festival of the Saturnalia— which, incidentally, resonates with the term *"satura"* by paronomasia—takes place during the days that fall outside the calendar. A time outside of time, it is the appropriate place—just once a year—for the inversion of all hierarchical ordering. Analogously, Diderot's narrator remarks how he makes the exception of conversing with madmen like the nephew but "once a year" ("Ils m'arrêtent une fois l'an" [*NR* 5/35]). Like the nephew, Davus takes his master's claims of constancy to task. He argues that most men are fickle, like one Priscus, who lived a life of capriciousness ("vixit inqaequalis" [10]). One day a "rake" (*moechus*) the other a "sage" (*doctus*), you could say Priscus was "born beneath the unequal Vertumni, however many there are" (14). When Davus directs his diatribe against his master, accusing him of the same moral variability, the latter loses all patience. He shouts, looking for a weapon, for a stone or arrows. Davus counters: "aut insanit homo aut versus facit" (117)—"The man's either insane or making verse"—linking the poet's act to madness, while reiterating the perversity of versification. As deities in charge of alternating the seasons, the Vertumni are perfectly musical, insofar as music is the art of time par excellence, an art of process, change, and alternation. The Vertumni confer a capacity for turning things into something else, for effecting conversions and inversions. In Horace, they are predicated with adversity or inequity (*iniquis*), although it is difficult to ascertain in what fashion. As regulators of seasonal change, they may be contrary to Priscus, who follows no order whatsoever. Yet it is also arguable that the Vertumni are the agents of change itself, imposing inequality on those born under their influence. Are they constant and therefore "unequal" to those inconstant? Or are they inconstant, "unequal" to everything and everyone? These questions complicate the function of Diderot's epigraph. Furthermore, although the majority of readers assign it to the nephew's character, it is perfectly possible that it reflects the narrator's as well.[16] Certainly, the nephew enjoys neither communal identification nor self-sameness—"Rien ne dissemble plus de lui que lui-même." Yet, as I have shown, Moi is no more an exemplum of perfect constancy. Indeed, Horace's satire suggests that it is the one who fancies himself so that is most open to accusation. Hence fixed concepts of identity become shaken, be it the subjective identity that grounds vocal utterances or the productive identity that establishes something as a work of art.

It is the nephew's lack of subjective stability that prepares him for satirical disruption, which he carries out by way of musical performances, and this musicality in turn pokes holes in the narrator's sense of selfhood.[17] As Plato observed, madness, especially the madness provoked by music, is terribly infectious.

In assuming a wide range of masks, the nephew is capable of exposing society itself as populated by masked personalities. In this sense, his unmasking is congruent with the Rousseauist scheme. A master of accent, he reminds us all of our natural origins, breaking down all conventions and cultural articulations. In this way, he resembles the master actor of Diderot's *Paradoxe sur le comédien*, who is able to appropriate a vast variety of identities, precisely because he himself lacks one. The great actor, paradoxically, must be empty. He must have "no sensibility," if he is to be able to "imitate everything."[18] Like the nephew, he must be—to borrow a phrase from Lacoue-Labarthe—a "subjectless subject."[19] One might presume that the actor's vacuity is closely akin to the nephew's derangement. As I shall show, however, the similarities between the nephew and the actor can hardly be maintained.

The series of performances by which the nephew interrupts the dialogue clearly demonstrates his mimetic, musical talent: "He wept, he cried out, he sighed; his gaze was either tender or soft or furious: he was a woman swooning with grief ["une femme qui se pâme de douleur"], a poor wretch ["un malheureux"] abandoned in the depth of despair, a temple rising up, birds falling silent at sundown, waters either murmuring in a place solitary and cool, or tumbling in torrents down the mountain side. . . . It was night with its shadows, it was darkness and silence, for silence itself can be depicted in sound. He had completely lost his head ["Sa tête était tout à fait perdue"]. Exhausted with fatigue, like a man coming out of a deep sleep or a long distraction, he stood there motionless, dazed, astonished" (NR 84–85/104).

Here is no insensitive, calculating actor but rather a hypersensitive victim of overwhelming passion. The madman's enthusiasm is opposed to the actor's detachment. Instead of exhibiting the empty subjectivity of the great mimetic actor, the nephew seems to undergo a loss of subjectivity altogether.[20] Like Cassandra, he acts as though there is a god working inside of him ("avec l'air d'un energumène"). The trancelike state does not suggest cool distance but rather complete ecstasy. The nephew may start out as an actor, appropriating an array of masks to be used according to calculated intent, but he ends up deranged, identifying himself with the masquerade. His ecstasy reveals that the distance that kept the disinterested actor safe has been flooded over. This sublime experience, this loss of self, implies that the nephew, contrary to the actor, does have a subjective identity, for a loss of self depends on the fact of having a self to begin with.

Whereas the mimetician puts nature to work, the nephew is idle or *désœuvré*. Rousseau defines genius as the capacity to render emotion by means of accents; he even declares, like Diderot's narrator, that genius can "make silence itself speak."[21] The nephew, too, can make silence speak, not out of some genial prowess but rather out of the passive experience of losing himself. When asked why he never produced a work of art of his own, the nephew confesses: "I had persuaded myself that I was a genius, and at the end of the first line I can read that I'm a fool [un sot], a fool, a fool" (NR 98/115). The comédien, who actively practices his work of appropriation onstage, finds his shadow in the madman, who unmasks society by passively losing himself behind an endless array of masks. The nephew, then, is restless, in constant motion without being active in the subjective sense, that is, he is active without doing anything. His inexhaustibly frantic behavior barely conceals his idleness. He is unable to produce anything of lasting worth.

In aesthetic terms, the nephew's entirely ephemeral improvisations betray a conception of music that rests more on temporal performance and audition than on composition. The compositional paradigm in music stresses the authority of the composer's subjective identity, which is thus preserved from any possibility of error, misinterpretation, or corruption. The potentially disfiguring aspects of a public performance are thereby relegated to accidents, which in no way detract from the transcendent essence of the work. A musical opus thereby enjoys a privileged status, distinct from and uncontaminated by all performance histories. In other words, the accomplished work of art is situated outside time, undisturbed by the immanent, material conditions of musical production. Music historians have defined this idea as the "work-concept," which in fact is an innovation of the modern period.[22] The performative paradigm in music challenges this view by asserting the horizontal, existential conditions of production and audition. From this standpoint, taken to the extreme, an unplayed piece of music is no music at all, just as language does not exist apart from individual utterances.[23] The immanent circumstances of the musical instruments and the individual performers, the intent of the conductor and the preoccupations of the soloists, the concert hall's acoustics, the seating plan, the attire, the weather—all these contribute to the piece's actualization and severely undermine any belief in the fixed identity of a composition. In this regard, the performative paradigm underscores music's fundamental temporality, its transitoriness and ungraspability.

While the composer's accomplishments may secure his legacy for posterity, the nephew's performances simply pass away with the time needed to carry them out. The evanescent quality of these displays calls attention to an experience of music that is presubjective—before identity, before a reflective sense of personhood. The nephew—possessed by lyrics not his own—disrupts models of authentic expression or original composition. Along these lines, Roland Barthes speaks of the voice's "grain," where the voice itself is emphatically something "not personal": "It expresses nothing of the cantor, of his soul; it is not original . . . and at the same time it is individual: it has us hear a body which has no civil identity, no 'personality,' but which is nevertheless a separate body." Thus, he concludes, "the 'grain' is the body in the voice as it sings," which is "in no way 'subjective.'"[24]

Bent on securing a transcendent, subjective position, Diderot's narrator enters into portraits and descriptions of the nephew that belie his indebtedness to a specific hermeneutics, namely, a will to circumscribe this musical dementia by some kind of theory. He is eager to convert the nephew's mad pantomime into an imitative, expressive art form so as to make it comprehensible, a conversion that could reinforce the narrator's own position as a subject of language. The narrator, in other words, clings to a Rousseauist position, which strives to reveal the mimetic quality of music, even to show that music is a kind of heightened, naturally motivated language. But mimesis is not so simply steered. This fact is precisely what shakes the narrator when he unplugs his ears and begins to listen to the mad musician.

Earlier, in his *Lettre sur les sourds et muets* (*Letter on the Deaf and Mute*), Diderot shared Rousseau's hope that mimesis could reinstate societal equality. Ironically, he did so by keeping his ears plugged. The *Lettre* relates how, during a theatrical performance, Diderot stuffed his ears, to the astonishment of his companions, asserting that in this way he could better observe the mimetic content of bodily movements.[25] He goes on to report a meeting with an anonymous deaf-mute during a chess match at the Café de la Régence. To this point, the anecdote perfectly foreshadows the philosopher's encounter with the nephew, who also appears over chess at the selfsame café. As in *Le neveu*, the chance meeting leads to the topic of music. The *Lettre* describes how the deaf man was taken to the apartment of Père Castel in order to learn his reaction to the famous "color harpsichord."[26] After a brief performance on Castel's *clavecin oculaire*, which involved a succession of colors appearing alternatively on a screen, Diderot's deaf examinee concludes that music is "a particular way of communicating," that instruments are analogous to "speaking organs" that produce expressive signs. He therefore confirms Rousseau's assertion that "melody not only imitates, it speaks." For Diderot, the deaf-mute's experience demonstrates that there is "sense [*sens*] in sounds [*sons*]." In other words, it substantiates Castel's theory and the philosophes' presupposition, namely, that music functions linguistically, generating a kind of text. Diderot's inference begs additional credibility by way of paronomasia: a mimetically charged rhetorical device, based on the visual appearance of the written word, which here emphasizes the underlying association of "*sens*" and "*sons*." Music is thereby redeemed, but only on the basis of vision, only for the deaf or for philosophers with ears plugged.

The initial topic of the *Lettre sur les sourds* is grammatical inversions, for example, the postpositioning of the adjective in French. As Diderot argues, this kind of articulation obscures the historical development of language based in sensory experience, where qualities precede the recognition of substantives. In direct contradiction to Condillac, Diderot asserts that the articulateness of the French language essentially reverses natural perception by placing adjectival modifiers after the common noun.[27] To introduce the topic of inversion, Diderot offers an epigraph from Vergil:

> Versisque viarum
> Indiciis raptos; pedibus vestigia rectis
> Ne qua forent.

The words, which thematize the act of turning (*versis*), are taken from the *Aeneid*, book 8, where Cacus—driven by madness or furor ("furiis Caci mens effera" [line 205])—steals cattle from Hercules and to conceal his crime reverses their tracks by dragging them backward into his cave. Beyond the manifest theme of inversion, however, Diderot's citation masks a deeper comment on epistemological presuppositions. A turn to Vergil's text immediately shows that Diderot himself has inverted this description of inversion:

> atque hos, ne qua forent pedibus vestigia rectis,
> cauda in speluncam tractos versisque viarum
> indiciis raptos saxo occultabat opaco.
>
> (and these [bulls and heifers], lest their tracks show the right way,
> were dragged by the tail into the cave, and reversing their paths'
> traces, he hid the stolen herd behind a dark rock.)
>
> (*AENEID*, BOOK 8, LINES 209–11)

Although Diderot does not explain his use of the citation, his intention in reordering the words is perfectly clear. Where Vergil's lines proceed from reflection to action, Diderot's manipulation demonstrates how the act precedes the thought. In Vergil's text, Cacus ponders possible consequences ("ne qua forent") and then acts accordingly ("versisque viarum indiciis raptos"). Diderot's rewriting, on the contrary, places the fear clause after the deed is done. This order is congruent with the *Lettre*'s larger claims. What language hides most of all, the *Lettre* eventually concludes, is its own tracing to an origin in gestures, in bodily action. Diderot's consideration of the deaf and mute therefore wants to invert linguistic inversion. It targets the poetic art that glosses over human movement, for example, Vergil's spondaic smoothness, which converts into art the sweaty toil of dragging livestock by the tail.

$$— \quad — \mid — \quad — \mid — \quad — \mid — \quad — \mid — \quad \cup \quad \cup \mid — \quad —$$

cau-d(a)—in-spe-lun—cam-trac-tos—ver-sis-que-vi—a-rum

But there is more. Implicit in this epigraph is an allusion to the *Homeric Hymn to Hermes*, where the infant god steals Apollo's cattle and, by cunning art (*technê*), reverses their tracks to conceal the crime.

δολίης δ' οὐ λήθετο τέχνης
ἀντία ποιήσας ὁπλάς, τὰς πρόσθεν ὄπισθεν,
τὰς δ' ὄπιθεν πρόσθεν.

(And he did not forget cunning art [*doliês . . . technês*],
reversing [*antia poiêsas*] the hooves, making the front behind,
and the hind before.)

(HYMN TO HERMES, LINES 76–78)

When Apollo discovers the transgression, when he recognizes the crafty, poetic deed [*poiêsas*], Hermes offers in compensation his newly invented lyre—an instrument, we recall, made from a live or mortal tortoise, whose shell was converted into a deathless, resonant body.

If Diderot's *Lettre* proceeds, with ears plugged, to understand verbal inversion and the inequality it breeds, *Le neveu de Rameau* marks an even greater complication by keeping philosophy's ears open to the implications of this hermetic music and to sounds otherwise suppressed. In the name of the Vertumni, the text signals how philosophical retroverts may themselves suffer inversion. As I have already noted, at the dialogue's opening, the narrator begins by presenting himself as a man of theory, shutting his ears to the bustle ("écoutant le moins que je pouvois"), happily engaged in speculative conversations with himself alone. When the nephew arrives, however, he explicitly unplugs his ears. Shocked and confused, he gropes for comprehension. He attempts to render the madness into conceptual schemes. His only option is to muster textual forms, which invariably come up short. Like Apollo, he tries to transform the Marsyan nephew into an instrument of sense, but, like Socrates, the nephew is always ready to break apart whatever form is imposed.

CRISIS AT THE CAFÉ DE LA RÉGENCE

The intellectual climate of the *Encyclopédie* fostered great optimism, thanks in large measure to the conviction that language, when used properly, was perfectly efficacious. In converting every aspect of human knowledge into discursive shape, the project's contributors intended to promote the free circulation of ideas, which would thereupon provide the basis for an egalitarian community. As the article "Language" by the Chevalier de Jaucourt asserts, language use presupposes a degree of equality: "Ever since man felt driven by taste, need, and pleasure to join together with his companions [*semblables*], it was necessary for him to develop his soul in relation to another, and to communicate its situations."[28]

Diderot's musically mad nephew upsets this scenario, insofar as he is presented as someone fundamentally improper and dissimilar. As a text fraught with division, the dialogue as a whole appears to be a grand experiment in testing the efficacy of language as well as problematizing the notions of personal identity that it grounds. Division is so evident in *Le neveu* that it may be said to constitute its very theme. A dialogue in the truest sense, it derives its narrative energy from the clash of antagonistic forces. The process of opposition is already initiated with the title itself, which blatantly names two distinct personages. The differences between the celebrated composer Jean-Philippe Rameau and his idle nephew, Jean-François, are encapsulated in the title's contrast between proper name and common noun (*le* neveu *de* Rameau) as well as between what is original and what is subsequent, between creator and epigone, composer and performer (*le neveu* de *Rameau*). On the level of both form and content, these basic oppositions go on to organize many of the discussions in the body of the dialogue, articulated more specifically between fame and obscurity, success and failure, productivity and sloth. Thus a guiding division is established between the interlocutors as they consider and debate issues in morality, ethics, politics, and aesthetics.

Prima facie, philosophy thus confronts its other; the subject of language confronts the subjectless subject. The divisions, however, not only separate the enlightened freethinker from the cynical madman but also split the author himself in two. The psychomachia, which divides his soul into two opponents (Moi and Lui) leads to the exposure of the multiple distinctions endemic to language use: between the author and narrator, between Diderot and Moi, between the writing subject and his uncanny double, the represented subject.

Such mimetic divisiveness questions the efficacy of language and thereby weakens the viability of the *Encyclopédie*. Diderot suffered this skepticism, especially in the years following the project's public condemnation in 1759. Would the work withstand the violence of time? Could its validity persist in the hands of posterity? In his article on the term "*encyclopédie*," that is, in the project's highest mode of self-reflection, Diderot never refers to posterity as a timeless realm of truth; instead, tellingly, no less than four times, he characterizes future readers as "our nephews." "The goal of an *Encyclopedia* is to assemble the knowledge scattered across the earth's surface; to set forth [*exposer*] its general system among those with whom we live and to transmit it to those who will come after us; in order that the works [*travaux*] of centuries past might not be useless for the centuries to come; that our *nephews* [*nos neveux*], becoming better instructed, may become at the same time more virtuous and happier and that we may not die without having been worthy of the human race [*genre humain*] (s.v. "Encyclopédie," 5.635; my emphasis).[29] As an elaboration of one of these nephews, Lui reminds the encyclopedist that the hope of posterity—of continued progress toward a more learned, more virtuous, and happier future—must entertain the risk of perversion.

Still, despite his perversity, Diderot's mad musician does communicate. That is, he speaks and sings, even though the significance of his utterances is persistently questioned. With this characterization, Diderot seems to present the possibility of expressing pure difference in spite of but also by way of the conventional system of signs called language. One episode serves as an especially good illustration: the story of the Renegade of Avignon.

Just past the dialogue's midpoint, the tale of the Renegade brings both the philosopher and his companion to the point of exasperation. Eager to demonstrate his "excellence in degradation," the nephew introduces the vile man, who won the confidence and protection of a kind, wealthy Jew, only to betray him to the Holy Inquisition and escape with his fortune (*NR* 74–76/94–96). Of all the anecdotes related by Diderot's fool, this one stands alone in bringing both interlocutors to the point of having nothing left to say, to a limit beyond which there may be no further communication. Moi is at a loss: "I didn't know whether to stay or run away" (*NR* 76/96). The nephew's vicious celebration of betrayed trust, anti-Semitism, murderous greed, and travestied justice, however, is not merely repulsive for the man of the Enlightenment. On the contrary, the storyteller himself, whether overcome by mad delight or embarrassing shame, also seems compelled to give up on language. For both men, language has run its course. The nephew reverts to one of his discomforting routines, performing a confused "fugue," while the narrator retreats into contemplation, entirely unsure as to what to do. Diderot frames the story of the

Renegade as if it reached a degree of immorality so deep, so thorough, that the promise of verbal communication, grounded as it were in the selfsame structures and beliefs that underwrite moral behavior and judgment, were no longer possible.

The dialogue, however, does not end here but instead turns to a full discussion of music. The topic was already broached by Moi, whose only comment on the Renegade's crime concerns the "tone" of the nephew's voice in telling it. "I don't know which strikes me as more horrible, the villainy [*scélératesse*] of your renegade or the tone in which you talk about it" (*NR* 76/96). The nephew's use of language demonstrates that depravity has permeated both content and form. The criminality of what is said corresponds to the wickedness of how it is recounted. Thus the details of the story readily conflate the protagonist with the storyteller. The Renegade's plot, which deployed language as a tool for deception and manipulation, perfectly parallels the narrative act of Lui—a veritable nihilist bent on dismantling language's relation to truth. Both the nephew and the con man come across as thorough liars, as grand abusers of communicative trust. The possibility of a set correspondence between words and things or even between utterance and intention has been exposed as something altogether fragile and exploitable.

There are many hints that a kind of semantic disintegration has taken place: the Renegade's utterly deceitful use of speech; the vulgar stereotype of the Jew unable to read past the literal; and even the resonance of the name Avignon, a place that marks the schismatic history of the church, possibly serving as an allegory of how the transcendent ground of meaning may be contested. On the level of narration, there is the dubious boasting of a madman whose capacity for dissimulation and self-contradiction is frightening. The crime of the Renegade, who betrayed the trust confided to him and sent a man to a cruel death, matches the talk of a fool, who reneged his commitment to true speech and thereby consigned language itself to an auto-da-fé.

It is out of this crisis that music comes to the fore, both as a topic for debate and as a performative evasion. Lui withdraws into his bizarre routines, while Moi presses for definitions of what music is, what it does, and to what end. The philosopher's cross-examinations are answered by crazed pantomimes of orchestral fanfares and operatic displays. Altogether, following upon the Renegade story, the twin theme of music and madness emerges precisely where language breaks down as a vehicle of truth. The musicality of language, the tone of what is being said, fascinates the philosophe insofar as it reveals an embodied—malicious—voice beyond denotative meaning. Semantics is no longer sufficient for understanding language as a means of communication. Rather, it comes forward as a medium through which one can dissimulate. The nephew's conglomeration of operatic snippets exploits this dissimulating capacity.

Nonetheless, phoenixlike, the semantic project is resurrected so as to attend to its own limitations vis-à-vis musical experience. In addition to extended discussions on the essence of music, the reader is offered further mad performances by the nephew, spectacles whose frenzied appearance occupy a space of nonmeaning that challenges the philosopher's desire for comprehension. Questions on the possible meaning of music parallel concerns over the nonmeaning of mad behavior. If madness constitutes a nonsignifying relation to some metaphysical regime of meaning, then this text suggests that music stands in an analogous relation, a relation of non-signification as conventionally understood. The crucial point, however, is that despite this failure of signifying logic, thanks to music and madness, language does carry on. Even after speech has been evacuated of meaning, there emphatically is more to say.

SATIRE, INEQUALITY, AND THE INDIVIDUAL

Subtitled "Second Satyre," *Le neveu* should be read in connection with two other pieces, with which it bears many similarities: *Satire I, sur les caractères et les mots de caractère, de profession, etc*, first published in Grimm's *Correspondance littéraire* (October 1778), and a very brief, un-published dialogue simply entitled *Lui et Moi*.[30]

Lui et Moi, clearly a predecessor to *Le neveu*, relates another encounter between a philosophe and a villainous interlocutor. An opening paragraph sets the scene. Despite the many occasions on which Moi had been duped, he continued to lend money to this rascal (*coquin*), who recently had the audacity to use the funds to finance a satire against his very own bene-factor. Now, after some months, Moi chances upon Lui, who appears haggard and malnourished. This time Moi refuses to succumb to pity; this "leech" (*sangsue*) is beyond reform, and Moi is beyond compassion. The dialogue reaches the same level of horror that followed the nephew's an-ecdote of the Jew and the Renegade—"I was seized by horror" (715). Here, however, the moral shock is not overcome by music; the conversation does not continue. Instead, the text ends abruptly, leaving the philosopher's ab-horrence to resonate in silence. Diderot stops writing when his characters stop talking. Here, at least, nihilism has the last word.

Satire I deals with the diversity of human character. Yet, unlike La Bru-yère's earlier project, Diderot's investigations are in search of infinite dif-ference, irreducible to rationalization or typology. Like *Le neveu*, this text is also governed by epigraphs from Horace's *Satires*, from the first poem of the second book:

Sunt quibus in satura videar nimis acer, et ultra
legem tendere opus

(There are those to whom I may seem too harsh in my satire, and that I seem to stretch the work beyond the law)

(*SATIRES* 2.1.1)

Quot capitum vivunt, totidem studiorum
milia

(A thousand living persons, as many thousand desires)

(2.1.27)

Thus Diderot adopts Horace's satiric program, namely, to investigate language's capacity to register the fine nuances of individual emotion and passion—a particularly harsh or impassioned project that would move beyond conventions ("ultra legem"). Like Diderot, Horace places himself in the text as a represented subject, an uncanny double, a figure explicitly to be seen ("videar"). Here the satirical voice does not yet fall to a deranged nephew but rather to the first-person narrator, whose sharpness would cut through all representations, including his own.

Specifically, in seeking out the detailed differences of individual expression, *Satire I* contributes to Diderot's refutation of the mechanistic arguments put forward by Helvétius, whose *De l'esprit* (1758) claimed that all men are born exactly the same, that human diversity is merely a result of education and general environment. Helvétius writes, for example: "It is therefore certain that intellectual inequality ["l'inégalité d'esprit"] . . . does not at all owe its excellence to being innately better or worse organized but rather to the different education that they receive in diverse circumstances."[31] To correct this view, Diderot insists on human *in*equality. He stresses the influence of natural, innate aptitude in shaping each human character as a unique being. As Diderot argues, this condition has obvious consequences for the understanding of language: "Is it possible that, human organization being different, the sensation may be the same? Its diversity is such that, if each individual were able to create a language analogous to what he is, there would be as many languages as there are individuals. One man would say neither hello nor good-bye like another."[32] Although indispensable for intersubjective communication, language's generalizations all but efface the particularity of human sentiment. The faint hints of an individual's speech can only be heard in the person's tone: not in what's been said but how it's been said. As in Cratylus's laughable aspiration, musicality should present language before or beyond conventional agreement, beyond *nomos*—*ultra legem*, so to speak, like Horace's acrid satire.

As already suggested, *Le neveu de Rameau* is the story of how the philosopher chose to listen to this mimetic cry not as a dissolution of socially unjust articulations but rather as the siren song of inequality. There is a resolve here to get behind a legality that would establish equality or a rectification of natural differences. The ethical problems are obvious. Is there a way to respect individuality without allowing for gross injustices? Is the effacement of singularity—its equalization—not a worthwhile price to pay for societal justice? To what extent does the divisive nature of the individual—of the genius, for example, or the madman—belong to the collective? And can one even speak of an individual apart from this collective?

The singular, unequal music of the madman's language seduces the moralist to flirt with injustice. To be sure, as a madman the nephew matches the horrific lechery of the *coquin* in *Lui et Moi*, but as a musician he emits a tone that entices the philosopher to stay rather than flee. The highly individual, unequal music of his language draws the philosopher in. The anecdote of the Renegade and the Jew—two figures of alterity—fills the philosopher with such horror that he would have fled, had it not been for the nephew's masterful tone. The pessimism of *Lui et Moi*, which rests on the decidedly nonmusical, noisome qualities of the parasitic leech, is healed by the hope of hearing something beyond language.

Le neveu de Rameau, whose conclusion leaves us uncertain as to who will have the "last laugh," could also be read as an honest consideration of human inequality in response to Helvétius's biological egalitarianism. Certainly, the nephew is nothing if not unequal. Unlike *Satire I*, however, this radical inequality suggests that perhaps the search for an individual voice—including the authorial voice—is from the start faulty. The concept of identity—which is grounded in some idea of equality, in self-sameness over time, in the potential for repetition—is unable to cover the nephew's baffling individuality. *Le neveu* pursues the unique, but does so by relaxing ideas of identity in order to consider the possibility of an individual who is split among many voices, always different and never equal to himself.

The word *"inégalité"* in fact occurs only once in the entire dialogue (that is, without repetition), tellingly during the course of the story of the Renegade and in explicit relation to tone. Lost in reflection, the narrator excuses himself: "I am thinking how variable your tone is ["je rêve à l'inégalité de votre ton"], sometimes high, sometimes low" (NR 74/94).

Throughout the dialogue it is tone that produces the split between morality and art. Tone is the way one's speech manifests itself as unequal to intention. As the nephew confesses, he reads Molière in order to disguise his true aims, in order to be avaricious without sounding avaricious, to be a hypocrite without sounding hypocritical (NR 60/82). He is like and unlike the actor—imitating but really imitating imitation.

The shift to questions of tone reinforces the hypothesis that the entire issue of inequality is associated with music and the problem of meaning. Whereas conventional discourse is presumably based on the transparent circulation of selfsame identities, musical discourse introduces a different kind of conversation. After attempting to define music, the narrator must confess that "the question is beyond" him. For him, the vagueness of the term "chant" opens on to the issue of vagueness in general. As in *Satire I*, in good empiricist fashion, words are regarded as being too general, too conceptual, to register the subtleties of individual experience. The nephew would agree, were it not for the possibilities offered by musical expression. For him, language may still represent the particular fine points of personal emotion as long as it is wedded to music. Individuality is saved, but only if speech becomes a tune, only if articulation yields to accent.

To this end, the nephew pronounces: "*Musices seminarium accentus*: accent is the nursery bed of melody" (NR 79). The statement rehearses the general position of Rousseau's *Origin of Language* essay, namely, that the loss of accent in modern language is concomitant with its rationalization. Where Rousseau insists on the function of similarity in mimesis, however, Diderot recognizes that all semblance is grounded in difference. Unequal to everyone, including himself, the nephew's ecstatic performances work at cross purposes to his subjective statements: music (tone, accent, rhythm, the cry) cannot express personal identity because the very principle of identity is already a result of a demusicalization—a disenchantment. Music can indeed restore song to speech, it can effectuate the desired reenchantment, but it cannot abide identity, which is simply a construct of convention, repetition, and personal memory. By performing madly in strictly irreversible time, the nephew demonstrates that the notion of identity is already at a far remove from its origin in song. The "I" only emerges with the establishment of the community, with the articulations that halt the evanescence of ephemeral accents and convert acoustic experience into a lasting work to be identified and memorialized. The nephew's improvisations resist the assignation of an opus number. His music unworks the drive to pull existence out of time.

In this regard, *Le neveu* illustrates the materialist epiphany expressed by d'Alembert in the dream recorded by Diderot. Deep in a fevered trance, d'Alembert shouts prophetically in staggered prose, as his caretakers, the physician Bordeu and Mademoiselle de l'Espinasse, listen on: "And you talk of individuals, you poor philosophers! Stop thinking about your individuals ["Laissez là vos individus"] and answer me this: Is there in nature any one atom exactly similar [*semblable*] to another? . . . No . . . Don't you agree that in nature everything is bound up with everything else, and that it is impossible for there to be a gap in the chain? Then what do you mean with your individuals? There is no such thing; no, no such thing."[33] As d'Alembert's guests go on to discuss, not only identity but the entire notion of individuality (as an essence identifiable across time) is grounded in a fragile belief in self-sameness. It is all but a result of the capacity for memory, which each nerve fiber possesses to varying degrees. Music, the most Vertumnal of arts, has, according to Diderot, the most powerful effect on our nervous system. It is therefore best equipped to qualify the idea of personal identity as a purely physiological symptom. As in d'Alembert's delirious ravings, the nephew's rhapsodies reveal the fragility of this convention and the reality of atomic, musical inequality. The nephew's madness reveals our existence as ever-changing, unrepeatable, and irreversible. It shows us that our self-sameness is grounded in self-difference. It exposes our individual sense of self as a metaphysical, mimetic delusion.

The nephew's identity consists in the constant loss of identity; impropriety is all that is proper to him. He is in fact a figure of pure alterity: "Nothing is less like him than himself." In short, he is what he performs. In connecting music and madness, Diderot's text elaborates the fundamental—mimetic—tension between the singular and the general, repetition and difference, between poles that are at once distant and near, shared and isolated: from a place somehow the same but always unequal.

Gottsched, Rousseau, and Diderot's philosopher (Moi) all share the conviction that art should be mimetic; they differ, however, not only on what mimesis is but also on what is and is not capable of accomplishing it. Gottsched privileges the semantic weight of words and therefore reserves a merely ancillary role to music, which in itself, as pure sound, is nonsemantic. For him, mimesis is strictly imitation—that is, the re-presentation or depiction of something anterior. The *representandum* is the original element that renders every imitation as secondary, whose only substance is derivative. Mimesis as such may be related to either external or internal experience. In both cases, be it the imitation of *la belle Nature* or of personal emotion, mimesis is best achieved when language imposes its rational, narrative energy on the musical material, when it turns music into patterns that are repeatable and therefore knowable. When music, however, is not bound to the semantic clarity of words, it becomes threatening as an irrational or mad force; its mere sensuality overtakes the guidance of either the heart or the mind; art becomes neither pleasurable nor instructive.

The mimetic imperative is no less great in Rousseau, but with an emphasis on the originality of the expression, which promotes it above the status of being a secondary, derivative copy. For him, the expression has substance in itself. While granting the signifying capability of words, Rousseau nevertheless recognizes verbal language as somewhat deficient. Its tendency to abstract, to present mere concepts sundered from the singular power of life, is the cause for the inferior mimetic capabilities of words. Thus human expression is better served by music in general and by melody in particular, for melodic inflections alone may dissolve the articulations of rational language and reintroduce an original accent. It is language's suppression of this accent that renders society's individuals mad, insofar as they are deprived of a more authentic relation to themselves and to others. The restoration of music within language therefore promises the reestablishment of human equality: a society grounded in justice and full transparency. It is important to note that Rousseau's mimeticism is here bound to a Cratylist idea of motivation and has little to do with "representation" in the neoclassical sense. The mimetic force of accent in fact imitates or "re-presents" nothing. That is to say, it is recognized as the true expression of one's inner experience. Ultimately, the only way to ensure equality is to have everyone imitate nothing (*The Social Contract* is clear on this point in relation to "sovereignty" and the "general will").[34] A musicalized community—a community in accord—consists of individuals who participate in an authentic expression of their inner self, equally and therefore justly.

In the majority of his writings on music, Diderot seems to agree with Rousseau's position on the mimetic potential of personal expression. His theories of gesture and pantomime all work together to create an art of accent that unworks the cold conventions and abstractions of verbal designation. His satires, however, reveal that the utopian dream of social equality is not served by the restitution of accent. On the contrary, the mimetic power of music is a kind of violence that reveals infinite difference and radical inequality—*Quot capitum vivunt, totidem studiorum milia* (A thousand living persons, as many thousand desires). Hence the nephew's performances confirm the rationalist's fears: music is mad, not simply because it upsets one's communicative relationship to others but also because, as an art of nonrepeatable time, it unhinges one's relationship to oneself. The terrifying lesson of the nephew's musicality is precisely this: nothing differs more from ourselves than ourselves; nothing is more evanescent. Despite major differences, then, Diderot's text at least shares with Gottsched's neoclassicism the suggestion that the musicality of language may be mad. Together, in varying ways, they respond on either side of history to Rousseau's valuation of nature and the natural, including the natural motivation of language in song. Hegel, who, as I shall discuss, had recourse to *Le neveu* in order to formulate his own anti-Rousseauist position, introduces the terms of this debate into a philosophical discourse that will play a significant role in the development of the link between music and madness, particularly in Kleist and Hoffmann. The mad musicians who inhabit the fiction of German romanticism are, in a certain sense, but modulations or variations of the themes introduced by Diderot's deranged performer.

3

Resounding Sense

SOMETHING HAPPENED. Whether or not one allows for disconti-
nuities in the history of ideas, one could agree that something
took place, something that would have to wait for posterity before
its significance could begin to be sorted out, discussed, and assessed, and
then only after it had been granted a form. The marvelous publication
story of Diderot's *Neveu* is pertinent: the author's stubborn suppression,
Goethe's translation from a subsequently lost manuscript, the retrotrans-
lation of the German for the first French edition in 1821, and so forth, until
finally in 1890, more than a century after the author's death, the discovery
of the text, in Diderot's own hand, by one Georges Monval, librarian of the
Comédie Française, who purchased the manuscript from a bookstall
along the Seine, long after the work's effects had been felt.[1]

To speak of the initial reception of *Le neveu de Rameau* is to speak of an
echo, of a text removed from its origin and recorded across the Rhine by
no less an engineer than Goethe, whose yielding prose enchanted generations of German readers and writers from Hegel to Freud.

In 1805 Diderot's text came before the public as a work whose place in
the burgeoning German literary canon had already been prepared. More a
welcome expatriate than a humble migrant worker, *Rameaus Neffe* arrived
in brilliant local dress. The fact that the original French was nowhere to be
found simply added to the effect. For Foucault, regardless of the unusual
publication history, it was only now, at the height of German romanticism,
that Diderot's dialogue and the event it registers could address a com-
petent audience. Thus, posthumously disseminated from a nonlocalizable
source, the text's illustrious career began. "The eighteenth century was
unable to understand [*entendre*] the full meaning of *Le neveu de Rameau*.
And yet something happened, at the very time when the text was written,

promising a decisive change."[2] In Foucault's view, the book could only work after the fact—*nachträglich*.

A BREAK IN THE GRAND CONFINEMENT

What, then, did happen, and why the essential untimeliness? Why did this event have to wait for the future to become manifest in a comprehensible form? Foucault's reasoning seems clear. His *History of Madness*, which attempts to trace a broad reevaluation of insanity, makes a historical argument first by proposing an epoch of "the grand confinement," where madness as unreason (*déraison*) had to be forcefully sequestered from rational society, and subsequently by announcing the "birth of the asylum," where the mentally ill were reintroduced into society, albeit under the moral watch of the psychiatric doctor. The shift from a discourse of isolation to one of medical treatment—both of which are viewed by Foucault as mechanisms of oppression and subjugation—is marked by two crucial signposts: 1656, which witnessed the establishment of the first *hôpital général* to house about 1 percent of Paris's population, and 1793, when Philippe Pinel, the mythic "liberator of the insane," assumed the directorship of Bicêtre. What happened with *Le neveu de Rameau*, therefore, is that "for the first time since the Grand Confinement," decades before the Revolution, that is, decades before unreason could reenter society as mental illness, "a madman once again became a social personage."[3] And yet, as Foucault asserts, the eighteenth century failed to understand or hear—*entendre*. Ears were not yet ripe. Instead a "great fear" of contagion was sparked, which threatened to attack the moral and cognitive security of the bourgeoisie. An adequate hearing would have to wait for another day, when madness would no longer be perceived as fatal but rather as a vital component of human experience, say in the fantastic visions of the German romantics or in the supple dialectic of German idealism.

Despite Foucault's cautious disavowals, the teleology implicit in his *History* is evident. It is not fortuitous that one of the first and most influential appropriations of *Le neveu* is found in Hegel's *Phenomenology of the Spirit* (1807), which assigns the mad musician an absolutely central role in the analysis of Enlightenment culture. Moi's incomprehension and uncertainty ("I didn't know whether to stay or run away" [*NR* 76/96]) is replaced by the idealist's recognition of Spirit's manifestation in the form of a "higher consciousness" (*PG* 389/319). The Foucauldian threshold has been crossed. The dialogue cedes to the dialectic, in Jena rather than Paris, in the nineteenth rather than the eighteenth century.

Before looking further at the way Hegel responded to Diderot, it is prudent to pause a moment and reflect on the general nature of such philosophical appropriation. The tradition of rendering madness discursive—intelligent, informative—is long and prestigious. At least since Plato, the evanescent voice of madness has been made to yield to philosophy's sustained eloquence. In the *Phaedrus*, the voice falls to Socrates, specifically in his second speech, his "palinode," which he spouts forth "madly" (*manikôs* [265a]), sparked by the fulguration of his *daimonion* (242c). The myth of the charioteer therefore motivates the remainder of the dialogue. What is proclaimed in mad inspiration requires interrogation and careful unfolding: the birth of philosophy. Similarly, the four species of divine madness (*theia mania*) that Socrates lists in his enthusiasm are all defined by and confined to a teleology. Each is revealed to have a purpose (*telos*) that constitutes its realization: prophetic madness results in benefits for the state; ritual madness cures disease; poetic madness glorifies; and erotic madness leads directly to the philosophical project itself (244c–245b). Upon "listening" (*êkousamen*) to the divinely inspired words, Socrates sets out on the philosophical pursuit of truth (278c). This subsequent appraisal of the mad moment therefore cannot itself be mad. Accordingly, in reference to the role of madness in the *Phaedrus*, Silke-Maria Weineck writes: "The accountable nature of madly engendered meaning generates the necessity of a critical paraphrase that must not be mad itself. . . . The very privilege of mad speech disinherits the mad speaker of his product. The speaker can never claim mad speech as his own *while he is mad*."[4]

In many respects, this structural motif rehearses the oracular practices at Delphi, where the entranced Pythia Melissa spewed forth in obscure glossolalia what was subsequently deciphered by the officiating priests in relatively lucid hexametric form. But Socrates had his doubts about the poetic industry. As for Foucault, he repeatedly suggests that a process of integration takes place in the case of Rameau's nephew, whose "existence" indicated rationalism's "reversal, which could only be understood or heard [*entendu*] in the age of Hölderlin and Hegel."[5] The implication is that to give Diderot's mad musician a hearing, one must deal with the great echo chamber of Hegel's *Phenomenology of the Spirit*, whose pages resound with nephew's voice.

THE EMERGENCE OF THE MAD MUSICIAN

A survey of French literature from the late seventeenth and early eighteenth centuries seems to corroborate Foucault's assertion on the eventlike quality of *Le neveu de Rameau*. It demonstrates that Diderot's portrayal of a musically gifted madman is quite unique for the period. Foucault, who does not entertain the possible links between the nephew's insanity and his musicality, would have done well, then, to secure a place for music as well within his "grand confinement." Although music certainly did not suffer from the same kind of societal isolation, and although theoreticians and philosophers of the time regularly treated musical topics, there is nonetheless remarkably little representation of musicians or musical experience in works of literature. It is as if literary artists had plugged their ears to music. The preponderance of Orphic themes in the poetry of the Pléiade failed to find resonance in the later period. In fact, one can now detect a decided antagonism on the part of literature against the musical arts. Writers of the Golden Age and beyond regularly protested against their treatment by composers. Boileau, whose libretto had been insultingly rejected by Lully, famously retorted: "Music does not know how to tell a story" ("La musique ne saurait narrer").[6] Voltaire, who equally suffered from the impossible demands of Jean-Philippe Rameau, complained to Charles Hénault that the renowned composer was simply "mad" (*fou*).[7]

The anger heard in these assessments is connected to the conventional belief espoused by men of letters, namely, that music should be subservient to words, for words alone could make *tragédie lyrique* meaningful. In the opinion of the rationally minded, music should remain the handmaiden of poetry. As a consequence, purely instrumental music troubled writers all the more for its apparently complete abandonment of sense. In his *Spectacle de la Nature* (1746), the abbé Pluche regards music without words as merely pleasurable. In a judgment that recalls Athena's suspicions concerning the *aulos*, Pluche finds that instrumental music "amuses the ear without presenting any thought to the mind." Its sounds are entirely "devoid of meaning" ("destitués de sens") and thereby neglect to fulfill art's primary function, which is to convey moral principles in an intellectually comprehensible fashion.[8] To introduce this potentially meaningless, idle, immoral art in a work of literature and moreover to treat it somewhat positively with a protagonist no less insane, no less unproductive or immoral, would be for the majority of eighteenth-century authors unthinkable in every sense of the word.

Diderot's figure of the mad musician does appear to address this unthought, providing a place for this banished, doubly fearful topos. And certainly the later age to which Foucault refers was in a far more favorable position to entertain the nephew's madness as something worthy of thought, if not wholly commendatory.

The ground for Hegel's reception of the text was prepared not only by Goethe's translation but also by the earlier flourishing of *Empfindsamkeit*, the Sturm und Drang and early romanticism in German literature. Here madmen thrive, for example, in Christian Spiess's *Biographien der Wahnsinnigen* (1795–96), Tieck's *Der blonde Eckbert* (1797), or Jean Paul's *Titan* (1803). Nor is there a lack of musically inclined outsiders. In Adolf Knigge's *Die Reise nach Braunschweig* (1792), we meet an itinerant flute virtuoso, a Vertumnal type who travels under various pseudonyms and in diverse dress. Like Diderot's nephew, his nearly demonic power poses a serious threat to moral society, enchanting music lovers and seducing man-crazed (*manntollen*) women, whom he proceeds to rob and abandon.[9] Concerned less with the moral sphere and more with the dark recesses of melancholy, the *Nachtwachten des Bonaventura*, published anonymously in 1803, features a horn-wielding, mildly deranged protagonist, who begins his rounds when the world of reason goes to sleep. The watchman is obsessed with music, which he sees explicitly as an antidote to poetic aspirations: an "antipoeticum." He consigns the night to troubled souls and mad auditory hallucinations, for example, the mysterious song that only those about to die can hear: "the first sweet sound from the distant beyond."[10]

Literature of course was not the only home for mental disturbances. The year 1805—the very year in which Goethe's *Neveu* translation appeared— saw the opening of the Psychische Heilanstalt für Geisteskranke in Bayreuth, the first asylum to be established in the German states—a liberal-minded institution, clearly designed according to the standards set by Pinel. Outside the medical profession, philosophy, too, now appeared ready to converse with insanity. Kant had already recognized the necessity of including an analysis of mental derangement in order to fill out his study of mankind: "Anthropology requires at least an attempt at a general outline of this most profound degradation of humanity which seems to originate from Nature."[11] Madness ("amentia"), insanity ("dementia"), and delirium ("insania") may substitute common standards of meaning—a "sensus communis" for a "sensus privatus"—but this peculiarity was nevertheless still meaningful; it still made sense.[12] Kant, however, still agreed with earlier opinions that deemed madness incurable. For him, any cure would require the use of subjective understanding, which is precisely what the madman lacks. By Hegel's day, this estimation was beginning to be reevaluated. Most significantly, madness came to be perceived as something emphatically curable.[13] The popularity of visiting the mentally ill—the fashionable *Irrenhausbesuch*—signaled the general willingness within society to accept the once-banished other back into its domain.[14] Again, this freshly welcome neighbor often betrayed a musical disposition. "Der Besuch im Irrenhause" (1804), by Friedrich Rochlitz, editor of the *Allgemeine Musikalische Zeitung*, not only reflects the trend

properties of words, theorists pointed to the opacity of individual sentiment, whose communication relied on something beyond semantics and syntax, on something more mysterious, like the dark processes of intersubjective sympathy.

As early as 1715, in his *Traité du beau*, Jean-Pierre Crousaz claimed: "One's ideas are easily expressed, but it is very difficult to describe one's sentiments; it is impossible, even, through language, to give an exact understanding of them to those who have not had similar experiences."[18] The antiverbalism of Crousaz's statement, which was subsequently rehearsed in the work of Charles Batteux and the abbé Dubos, would be exploited later in the century by German theoreticians claiming the preeminence of music for expressing the subtle distinctions of human feeling. British empiricism also made significant contributions. In *Das forschende Orchestre* (1721), Johann Mattheson anticipated the full blossoming of *Empfindsamkeit* by elaborating on the work of John Locke and others, basing his musicology on the dictum that "sentiment [*Empfindung*] is the source of all ideas."[19] By the middle of the century, the prominent Berlin journals of Friedrich Wilhelm Marpurg—*Der critische Musicus an der Spree* (1749–50) and the *Historisch-kritische Beyträge zur Aufnahme der Musik* (1754–78)—worked further to transmit French aesthetic and British empiricist thought to German intellectuals concerned specifically with musical topics. For example, an associate of Marpurg, Johann Adam Hiller, in his weekly *Nachricthen* (1770), persistently argued against neoclassical concerns over music's presumed cognitive muddle: "Without being restricted by words, [the composer] can choose feelings [*Empfindungen*] which could be classified under one or the other passions, or even which seem to belong to more than one. And even assuming that one did not know how to classify this or that feeling of a composer, these feelings nevertheless originate in the human soul and its feelings. . . . Often many things can be expressed, which we do not know how to label with names."[20]

Descartes's fear that the excessive onslaught of conflicting passions can "eradicate or pervert the use of reason" had been transformed into something desirable and commendable.[21] The shift, it should be noted, was far from a clean break. Most aestheticians regarded *Empfindsamkeit* as a moderating force that balanced the excesses of rationality and brute sensuality. Thus Johann Georg Sulzer advocates sentimentality's place in the arts, while warning against its immoderate use, which would make feeling something "shameful . . . effeminate, weak, and unmanly."[22] At any rate, Diderot's nephew, who demands "exclamations, interjections, suspensions, interruptions, affirmations, [and] negations" (*NR* 87/105), could now find a response not only in German aesthetic theory but also in the sentimental, impassioned style of C. P. E. Bach's volatile fantasias.

Empfindsamkeit was based on a reworked understanding of the body that had far-reaching epistemological implications. In the earlier paradigm, the *res cogitans* of Cartesianism had been essentially incorporeal, a being transcendent to the body, which itself was relegated to the objective (that is, nonsubjective) sphere of *res extensae*. Now, by rendering the body biological or organic, as opposed to a lifeless, soulless thing in extension, the vital materialists of the eighteenth century, Diderot among them, collapsed the rationalist dualism that grounded meaning in the mind over and against the physical and the physiological. They thereby introduced a way to conceive of music not in deficient terms—say, as an art that could not think for itself or that needed the guiding intelligence of words—but rather in terms of corporeal, physical expression.[23] As a language of feeling, dependent more on sympathetic resonance than on cognitive understanding, music had already bypassed the confining dictates of reason.

The theoretical statements of Johann Gottfried Herder concerning music, however brief, played a pivotal role in the development of musical *Empfindsamkeit*. In one sense, he rehearsed the general ideas inherited from the French and English traditions, while, in another, he pointed toward a conception of musical experience that moved beyond the by-now-popular notion of music as a language of feeling.[24] In *Kalligone* (1800), his "metacritique" of Kant's critical philosophy, he takes issue with Kant's judgment that music is but a "beautiful play" ("schönes Spiel") of feelings and instead posits its source in "our inmost being." Musical experience has little to do with rational agency; rather, our very nerve fibers constitute a clavichord of sorts, which vibrate in "involuntary reaction," allowing the body itself to express itself spontaneously, automatically, without recourse to the dualistic structures of rationalism.[25] Diderot had already suggested as much in the letter to Mademoiselle de la Chaux that he appended to the *Lettre sur les sourds*: "In music, the pleasure of the senses depends on its particular effect [*disposition*], not only on the ear, but on the entire nervous system. If there are heads that resound ["têtes sonnantes"], there are also bodies, which I would like to call harmonic."[26]

Similarly, for Herder, all musical sound is the result of striking the exterior of bodies, which makes their interior perceivable. Music is simply a reverberation, a resounding from within, an echo responding to impulses from without.[27] As the next chapter discusses, Herder argues strongly against Kant, who had asserted that musical pleasure lies merely in the enjoyment of mathematical proportions. Instead, Herder's empiricism ascribes musical pleasure to basic corporeal responses, which are essentially involuntary and noncognitive. Music is therefore meaningless in the strict sense, eluding human understanding, yet still significant inasmuch as it affects mankind's relation to the world. What is expressed here belongs to the German fascination with nonrational dimensions of human experience, of which madness was but an extreme case. Notably, this enthrallment was greatly nourished by the nonrational workings of musical production.

Goethe's early work—so marked by Herder's influence—provides many signs of changing attitudes to irrationality. Moreover, it reflects an appreciation for new theoretical views of music's meaning and effects. Already in his first novella, *Die Leiden des jungen Werthers* (1774), there are even hints of madness's proximity to musical experience, especially in the protagonist's fervid, if not delirious passion for folk song and Ossianic abandon. In the novella's first part, in the description of the famous dance scene, music is explicitly said to have "opened" the guests' "senses to feelings," to have made them "more susceptible to impressions."[28] It is this particularly vulnerable, musically induced state that will continue to mark the sentimental hero's mad, impossible love, which eventually drives him to take his own life.

The novella, however, also links music to madness as a possible cure. Exactly one month after the dance, the sentimental Werther describes the salutary effects that music has on his soul:

[Lotte] is sacred to me. All passion [*Begier*] is silenced in her presence. I never know how I feel when I am near her; it is as if my soul turns about in every nerve.—She has a melody that she plays on the piano with the force of an angel, so simple and so spiritual [*geistvoll*]! It is her favorite song; she only has to strike the first note and all pain, confusion and caprice ["Pein, Verwirrung und Grillen"] are cast from me. I believe every word about the ancient magical power ["der alten Zauberkraft"] of music. How her simple song affects me! And she knows how to apply it, often when I would like to shoot a bullet to my head! Then, the confusion and gloominess ["Irrung und Finsternis"] of my soul disperses, and I breathe freely again.[29]

The scene is reminiscent of the legendary powers of David's harp, which alone could rid King Saul of the evil spirit of melancholy that tormented him (1 Samuel 16:14–22). Goethe would continue to employ the motif of the curative force of music throughout his career, from the "Heavenly tones" of Faust's "Night" to the late *Novelle* (1828), where it is the child's flute playing and song that calm the ferocious lion.[30] For the author who studied piano and then cello as a young man and whose mother and father both excelled on musical instruments, the beneficial properties of music were always colored by a certain nostalgia, by a longing for a simpler, more natural existence.[31] It is precisely music's blissfulness, however, that can render the contrast with the present world all the harsher. In *Werther*, toward the year's end, Lotte's piano playing brings the doomed young man to uncontrollable tears and inconsolable despair. He shouts for her to stop and is asked to leave (December 4). A possible cure for madness, music can always become its possible cause.

I do not consider it fortuitous, therefore, that the principal representatives of mental disturbance and irrationality in *Wilhelm Meisters Lehrjahre* (1795–96)—the harpist and the child Mignon—both display a peculiarly strong relation to music, be it a source of natural, excessive feeling, a remedy for psychic torment, or an expression of a solitary, incomprehensible life. The "mournful strains" of the harpist, sung directly after the disastrous fire in book 5, strike Wilhelm as "the consolations of someone who feels he is near to madness ["der sich dem Wahnsinne ganz nahe fühlt"]." The final stanza, the only one that Wilhelm is able to recall, is paradigmatic of a new consideration of derangement:

> An die Türen will ich schleichen,
> Still und sittsam will ich stehn,
> Fromme Hand wird Nahrung reichen,
> Und ich werde weiter gehn.
> Jeder wird sich glücklich scheinen,
> Wenn mein Bild vor ihm erscheint,
> Eine Träne wird er weinen,
> Und ich weiß nicht was er weint.
> (Let me linger by the gate
> Unobtrusive, silently,
> Pious hand will give me food,
> I move on to other doors.
> Every one will show delight
> Just to see my face out there,
> Down their cheeks a tear will fall,
> Why they weep, I do not know.)[32]

The verses exhibit the solitude, sympathy, and self-opacity haunting romantic perceptions of madness straight through the later tradition, which would be powerfully drawn to these lines, from Schubert and Schumann to Hugo Wolf.[33] It is important to note that the first edition of *Wilhelm*

Meister included printed melodies for the lyrics, prepared by the Kapell-meister Johann Friedrich Reichardt, Goethe's close friend. This composer would play host to a new generation of poets and philosophers at Giebi-chenstein, his luxuriant estate outside Halle. Here Goethe and Schiller, the Schlegel brothers, Novalis, Tieck, Jean Paul, and others were treated to musical soirées featuring Reichardt's latest *Vertonungen* of the most recent poetry.[34]

Among the ranks of frequent visitors was the celebrated Johann Christian Reil, who since 1789 worked as Halle's chief physician (and had the opportunity to treat Goethe himself on more than one occasion). Reil specialized in a field that would eventually be called "Psychiatrie," a term he himself coined in 1808.[35] Reil's *Rhapsodieen über die Anwendung der psychischen Curmethode auf Geisteszerrüttungen* (Rhapsodies on the ap-plication of psychiatric cure methods for the mentally disturbed, 1803) exerted an immediate influence not only in the medical community but also in literary circles, thanks both to its richly evocative, metaphorical style and to Reil's association with Reichardt's romantic haven at Giebi-chenstein. Aside from the blatant aspirations to high poetic style, Reil's book is noteworthy in pleading for the humane treatment of the insane. A man of feeling in every sense, Reil did more to eradicate the demonization of the mad than any other before him. With Rousseau, but without his ve-hemence, he faulted the progress of civilization for the increasing numbers filling the asylums.[36] Indeed, Reil reformulated most species of insanity as symptoms of societal alienation. Above all, it was the pronounced musi-cality of this rhapsodic psychiatrist that directed, throughout roman-ticism, a synthesis of philosophy and poetry, a blending of physiology and aesthetics, that strove to reveal the continuum between normalcy and mental abnormality.

HEGEL'S READING OF *LE NEVEU*

The new receptiveness to psychological disturbances, instigated by notions of sentimentality and corroborated by institutional, philosophical, and scientific reforms, prepared Hegel to recognize in *Rameaus Neffe* that the "derangement [*Verrücktheit*] of the musician" is a sign of modern man's necessary self-alienation (PG 387/317). In the *Phenomenology of the Spirit*, the nephew provides the best illustration that culture (*Bildung*) is a realm of self-estrangement. For Hegel, Diderot's fool is a figure that stands both within and outside the Enlightenment, someone who exhibits its inherent contradictions while being able to recognize them as such. The problems that the nephew's characterization therefore exposes become crucial moments in the *Phenomenology*'s grand narrative, devoted to Spirit's relentless striving toward self-consciousness.

Zerrissenheit

From a broader perspective, one might surmise that Diderot's text merely constitutes but another literary instance of a philosophical analysis, just as Sophocles' *Antigone* belongs to "The Ethical Life" (*Sittlichkeit*) of Antiquity and the narration of the "Beautiful Soul" in Goethe's *Wilhelm Meisters Lehrjahre* to the world of "Morality" in the sections preceding and following. Diderot's *Neveu*, however, should not be regarded simply as one of a series of literary exempla. Presented as an embodiment of "tornness" (*Zerrissenheit*), Diderot's *persona inæqualis* serves a more fundamental function, representing the deep divisions that foretell every move to higher forms of consciousness.

In the second section of *Phenomenology*'s sixth chapter, Hegel leaves the harmonious, natural realm of ancient Greek civilization and moves to the modern world of culture, where consciousness is regarded as essentially disharmonious. The happy balance that the polis enjoyed—between divine and human law, the family and the state, the feminine and the masculine—is now disrupted by a Spirit (*Geist*) that tears apart and breaks down everything that is stable in society. This Spirit of Culture is the "tornness" itself, the *Zerrissenheit*, that reveals the life of culture as one of perversion and inversion. The basic cause for this general breakdown is the contradiction between what could be called a natural state and an actual one, between the naturally given and its nonnatural actualization. Hence the word for culture—"Bildung"—seems to lose all connotations of natural development, common among most romantic writers. Instead, it functions in stark opposition to everything that may be taken as nature. Culture is the realm wherein nature—be it brute sensory data or the immediate feelings (*Empfindungen*) ascribed to a personal subject—is worked on and altered. The implication is that the natural is always deficient and requires a cultural transformation. In brief, understood specifically as an actualization, *Bildung* enacts a double articulation, converting the evanescence of the natural and offering it to the universality and constancy of the actual.

Above all, it is the subjective self that undergoes the greatest metamorphosis. Hegel writes: "It is . . . through culture that the individual acquires standing and actuality [*Wirklichkeit*]. His true *original nature* and substance is the alienation [*Entfremdung*] of himself as Spirit from his *natural* being. This externalization is, therefore, both the purpose and the existence of the individual" (PG 364/298; emphasis in original). The "actuality," or *Wirklichkeit*, that marks this process of alienation shows the "work" (*Werk*) involved. The operation of *Bildung* is therefore a process of self-formation: "This individuality forms itself [*bildet sich*] into what it intrinsically is, and only by so doing *is* it an *intrinsic being* [*an sich*] that has an actual existence [*wirkliches Dasein*]" (ibid.; emphasis in original). Just as the happy world of the Greek polis had to yield to the dissonant unhappiness of modernity, so the self in some natural state must cede to the cultural processes by which it becomes actual. Hence Hegel's decisive conclusion: "Although here the self knows itself as *this* self, yet its actuality consists solely in the setting-aside of its natural self" (ibid.; emphasis in original). Culture, then, is the realm of *Zerrissenheit*, insofar as it hosts a shape of consciousness that is what it is only by way of self-alienation. In the world of *Bildung*, "nothing has a spirit that is grounded within itself and indwells it, but each has its being in something outside of and alien to it" (PG 361/295). Modern consciousness is what it actually is by not being what it naturally is. Consequently, where the realm of nature was happy, the world of culture is basically one of despair.

But what precisely was this happiness, and why the need for discontent? Already in the introduction to the *Phenomenology*, in a light allusion to Plato's allegory of the cave, Hegel warned that the path of philosophy is an arduous one: "Whatever is confined within the limits of a natural life ["Was auf ein natürliches Leben beschränkt ist"] cannot by its own efforts go beyond its immediate existence; but is driven beyond it by something else, and this uprooting [*Hinausgerissenwerden*] entails its death. Consciousness, however, is explicitly the Notion [*Begriff*] itself. Hence it is immediately something that goes beyond limits ["das Hinausgehen über das Beschränkte"], and since these limits are its own, it is something that goes beyond itself. ... Thus consciousness suffers the violence [*Gewalt*] at its own hands" (PG 74/51). In Hegel's grand dialectical scheme, the violent power, or *Gewalt*, of consciousness is the force that will allow Spirit to break from its prereflective state in nature. It loosens the bonds to contingent and evanescent existence and lets Spirit continue on its path toward the Idea, which relinquishes particularity for universality. In this sense, the second part of the *Phenomenology* rehearses the opening of the first, which refutes empiricist claims that posit what is perceptually given as the proper basis for knowledge. The brief experiments that Hegel conducts in his chapter "Sense-Certainty" serve as grounding examples for this argument. The realm of *Bildung* is the hard, historical lesson that permits philosophy to ground truth truthfully. For this reason, Hegel describes the world of culture by employing a historical narrative that passes from the European absolutist state, through the Enlightenment, to the French Revolution. Rather than retrace the complicated steps and reversals that make up Hegel's account of culture, it is sufficient to recognize that, throughout, the epoch is defined as a period where the self's "actuality" (*Wirklichkeit*) is achieved at the expense of its "natural self." The opacity of the soul's particularity—like every phenomenon of the "Now"—is due to its evanescence: its immediacy "immediately passes away" into a phenomenon for others. It is transformed into something knowable, which by definition stands opposed to that which is already gone. In other words, the self's reality can only be had through the externalization that establishes subjectivity as split. Diderot's nephew emerges as a philosophical hero insofar as his musical madness—"the derangement of the musician"—announces this fundamental split, which the narrating man of Enlightenment (Moi) failed to grasp and which the idealist of Jena could now enlist in Spirit's service.

Hegel characterizes the nephew and the philosophe as representatives of an "ignoble" and a "noble" consciousness, respectively. In the simplest terms, the noble consciousness regards its individual will as congruent with the will of the state, while the ignoble considers state power as an oppressive, antagonistic force. Where the ignoble consciousness is always on "the point of revolt," the honest man of the Enlightenment remains complacent. Ultimately, however, this noble consciousness is compelled to realize that the state power that he had thought to be "good" is in fact "bad," especially as the monarch devolves into a self-serving despot. One by one, all the fixed values that stabilized the life of the noble consciousness fall apart in contradiction. The "good" becomes the "bad," the "bad" becomes the "good"—every evaluation suffers an inversion. "It is this absolute and universal inversion [*Verkehrung*] and alienation of the actual world [*Wirklichkeit*] and of thought: it is *pure culture* [*reine Bildung*]. What is learnt in this world is that neither the *actuality* of power and wealth ["die *wirklichen Wesen* der Macht und des Reichtums"], nor their specific *Notions*, 'good' and 'bad,' or the consciousness of 'good' and 'bad' (the noble and ignoble consciousness), possess truth; on the contrary, all these moments become inverted, one changing into the other, and each is the opposite of itself" (PG 385/315; emphasis in original). The universal inversion is of course a necessary consequence in the world of culture, where, as I have already mentioned, the self is itself only by being what it is not. Of the two types of consciousness, however, it is the "disrupted" mind of the ignoble and mad musician that is able to cope with culture's inherent contradictions. As for the noble consciousness, it finds it more and more difficult to deal with the perpetual breakdown of its rigid distinctions between the "good" and the "bad." In the end, the philosophe has nothing left to say. For this reason, Hegel grants victory to the nephew, because he (Lui) recognizes the truth that Moi ignores.

The *Zerrissenheit* that the base consciousness reveals not only portrays everything in culture as a source of unhappiness but also frustrates the simplicity of writing in the first person:

> The "I" is this particular "I"—but equally the *universal* "I"; its manifesting [*Er-scheinen*] is also at once the externalization and vanishing of *this* particular "I", and as a result the "I" remains in its universality. The "I" that utters itself is *heard* or *perceived* [*vernommen*]; it is an infection [*Ansteckung*] in which it has immediately passed into unity with those for whom it is a real existence, and is a universal self-consciousness. That it is *perceived* or *heard* means that its *real existence dies away* [*verhallt*]; that its otherness has been taken back into itself; and its real existence is just this: that as a self-conscious Now, as a real existence, it is *not* a real existence, and through this vanishing it is a real existence. This vanishing is thus itself at once its abiding; it is its own knowing of itself, and its knowing itself as a self that has passed over into another self that has been perceived and is universal.
>
> (PG 376/308–9; EMPHASIS IN ORIGINAL)

Even though they are ignorant of the fact, Diderot's narrator (Moi), no less than the monarchy ("L'état c'est moi"), enjoys "real existence" only insofar as his "real existence" has vanished. His externalization through language—his textualization—permits existence to be realized, but only as something "perceived" or "heard" [*vernommen*], that is, as something whose ground is "outside of it."[37] In writing "I," I must suffer a self-disavowal. The autobiographical gesture, writing the word "I," is a move into self-exile or even self-extinction. The pure feeling self cannot be represented, cannot be perceived or heard without losing itself. Under different circumstances and facing different revolutions, Rimbaud will formulate the same notion by unworking grammar itself: "JE est un autre" ("I is an other").

In a larger sense, the Vertumnal nephew embodies the dialectic itself, a figuration of the awareness of the mutual implication and contamination of all opposing pairs. The perverting force of the madman's behavior overrides and blurs all rational distinctions. Therefore, for Hegel, the nephew "has the last laugh" on the narrating Moi, whose "noble," "honest consciousness" consists precisely in establishing strict but fragile borders between opposites, for example, between the good and the bad, the self and the nonself. The nephew's concreteness corrects the abstractness of the moral perspective; his maddening aesthetic dismantles the clear but lifeless distinctions posited by the moralist.[38] These distinctions are unworked by the idle nephew, whose remarkably vigorous *désœuvrement* exposes the vacuity of everything, both abstract representations and singular expressions. The "Sense-Certainty" chapter already demonstrated that language—which is "self-consciousness existing for others"—is more truthful than subjective intention: "In language, we ourselves directly refute what we *mean* to say" (PG 91/60). Private "meaning" (*meinen*) is to be distinguished from public "saying" (*sagen*). The "work [*Werk*] of thought," reveals that personal intention (meine *Absicht*) or opinion (Mein*ung*) fails to rise to the universality of truth, to the *Allge*meine. Faced with the truth of Lui, the meaning of Moi's words truly has nothing to say. This is the crucial point. Hegel's nephew is not the spontaneous, frenzied, "subjectless" voice of immediacy but rather the very incarnation of mediation and tornness that is culture. In the *Phenomenology* he is not a Marsyas awaiting inversion and vivisection but rather the inverter himself, somewhat akin to Socrates, who always drove the noble Alcibiades mad.

Nature and Culture

Hegel's overall program may indeed find its primary illustration in Diderot's *Neveu*, but not without some degree of interpretive violence. Altogether, the *Phenomenology*'s sixth chapter features three separate quotations from the dialogue. Each is highly decontextualized, given without attribution and tightly rewoven into the fabric of Hegel's argument.

The first citation is summoned to clarify the deficiency of "natural individuality," defined as a merely "assumed existence" ("ein *gemeintes* Dasein"), which must be posited back to an origin that literally never took place (PG 364/298). "Natural being" is a "*kind* of existence" (emphasis in original), an "espèce," whose confirmation rests on false pretenses. To explain, Hegel utilizes the nephew's own definition of the term "espèce" as "the most horrid of nicknames; for it denotes mediocrity and expresses the highest degree of contempt" (ibid.). Here Hegel betrays his strong, eminently philosophical method of reading. In returning to the context of the remark in Diderot's text, we find that the nephew is not discussing "natural being" as an "espèce." On the contrary, he applies the term to what Hegel would call mediated, "actual existence." The nephew is explaining the futility of trying to educate his son. How can one form a child into something that contradicts his innate tendencies? "Education being continually at cross purposes with the natural bent of the molecule, he would be torn between two opposing forces and walk all crooked down life's road like a lot of them who are equally inept at good or evil and whom we call 'types' [*espèces*], the most frightening of all epithets because it indicates mediocrity and the last stages of the contemptible" (*NR* 90/108). In this passage, the nephew portrays the feeling soul not as an "assumed existence" but rather as an original nature that must be defended from the pull into Hegel's substantial self. The nephew is arguing that any attempt to correct one's natural disposition is useless at best and breeds dullness at worst.

In direct contradiction to the nephew's exegesis, then, Hegel claims that education or *Bildung* does not produce a mediocre "kind of existence" but rather allows the individual to become substantial or actual or real. For the philosopher, it is the "assumed existence" of something called "natural individuality" that is the mediocre type, a "kind of existence" to be disparaged. Although the nephew clearly calls the acculturated person a "type," Hegel's own philosophical program compels him to understand the nephew's words as describing the natural, that is, uncultured sort. That is because for Hegel the nephew represents a higher consciousness, which must recognize the natural self as something inferior. This first citation is programmatic, insofar as it reveals the strategy that the philosopher will use throughout, employing Diderot's words in a way that transcends, and even may contradict, the character's intention.[39]

The second quotation is more readily attributed to Diderot's text, even though the author's name is nowhere cited. This is where Hegel explains that the Spirit of Culture, manifested in the ignoble consciousness, is alone capable of recognizing the inversions and perversions of every notion maintained by the noble or simple consciousness of the Enlightenment. For the latter, the garrulity of the former is simply "the derangement of the musician." In a direct quotation from Goethe's translation, Hegel presents the unequal rambler as the one "who heaped up and mixed together thirty arias, Italian, French, tragic, comic, of every sort; now with a deep bass he descended into hell, then, contracting his throat, he rent the vaults of heaven with a falsetto tone, frantic and soothed, imperious and mocking, by turns" (*PG* 387/318; cf. *NR* 83/102). This is Moi's description of Lui's most memorable performance, whose ecstatic quality appears to illustrate the nephew's argument that music should be based on natural expression as opposed to academically procured rules (*NR* 82–83/101–2). Again Hegel ignores the context. Specifically, he neglects to point out the nephew's naturalism and instead utilizes the description to present a mode of human expression that eludes the "noble consciousness." Hegel's deployment further violates Diderot's narrative by claiming that Moi finds

Lui's mad performance entirely strange and incomprehensible, when actually the narrator notes his own "admiration" and "pity." In any case, at this point Hegel interjects a comment, before continuing with a further citation:

> To the tranquil [i.e., noble] consciousness which, in its honest way, takes the melody of the Good and the True to consist in the evenness of the notes, i.e., in unison, this talk appears as a . . . "rigmarole [*Faselei*] of wisdom and folly, as a medley of as much skill as baseness, of as many correct as false ideas, a mixture compounded of a complete perversion of sentiment ["völligen Verkehrtheit der Empfindung"], of perfect shamefulness, and of complete frankness and truth. . . . It will be unable to refrain from entering into all these tones and running up and down the entire scale of feelings from the profoundest contempt and dejection to the highest pitch of admiration and emotion; but blended with the latter will be a tinge of ridicule which spoils them."
>
> (*PG* 387/318)

Hegel's brief explanation appears to interrupt a continuous citation; however, the second quote is taken from an entirely different section of Diderot's text, from Lui's earlier imitation of a "pimp" (*proxénète*) attempting to seduce a young girl (*NR* 24/51). Then, without any punctuation, Hegel grafts yet a third passage, which is presented as a direct quotation but is in fact a paraphrase of Moi's description of the same performance reported in Hegel's first quote (*NR* 83–84/103).

Hegel's citational practice betrays the same kind of "perversion" attributed to the nephew qua Spirit of Culture. Like an echo, he cuts and splices snatches of text, which thereby transcend and rework the original. In this regard, Hegel's strategy reflects his philosophical project. As noted, "intention" (*Meinen*) is the untruth that can only arrive at truth by becoming what it is not. The truth of "saying" (*Sagen*) belongs to the side of philosophy, which can articulate what Diderot's text said, in contradistinction to what it meant. Furthermore, this montage, or cento, in addition to revealing the dialogue's truth, also illustrates how an individual's truth—for example, the truth of the *Phenomenology of the Spirit*—can only emerge in the dialectical confrontation of more than one particular text. Hegel's philosophy forms (*bildet*) Diderot's satire in the same way that latter molds the former.[40] Through intertextual violence (*Gewalt*), Hegel listens to the "derangement of the musician" and finds in his "allpowerful [*allgewaltigen*] note" the reconciliation that will "restore Spirit to itself" (*PG* 387/318). In this way, the idealist philosopher hopes to correct the insufficiencies of a purely rationalist standpoint. He reveals that the first-person narrator (Moi) or even "the self" (*le moi*), grounded in the "self-identical" ("das sich Gleiche"), is but a moment toward the truth: "what is self-identical is only an abstraction, but in its actuality [*Wirklichkeit*] is in its own self a perversion" (ibid.). Philosophy therefore *works*.

SENTIMENT DE L'EXISTENCE

Philosophy works insofar as it brings about "actuality" (*Wirklichkeit*) by giving form to the natural, which is otherwise something insubstantial, a mere assumption, "ein gemeintes Dasein." Hegel's appropriation or misappropriation of Diderot's text strives to reveal what the nephew says as opposed to what he meant, just as the nephew's performance can bring Hegel's own words out of the sphere of mere opinion (*Meinung*) and into the realm of truth. He cites the nephew's naturalism to argue against naturalism and to actualize his own idealism. In other words, Hegel turns the nephew's perversion and derangement against both him and himself. This dialectical work could be said to temper the nephew's nature in a way that recalls the tempering of the naturally given overtone series.

This analogy is especially pertinent when we think of Rousseau's arguments against the uncle Rameau, against a mathematization that destroys the naturally endowed voice. In the introductory notes to his translation, Goethe already advised that any understanding of *Rameaus Neffe* must take into account the historical *querelle* between French and Italian music, between Rousseau's beloved Mediterranean melodists and Rameau's harmonic system, which was "mannered in a way that is . . . divorced from all authentic artistic truth and simplicity."[41] Hegel assumes the role of Rameau, who worked to reconcile the inconsistencies of naturally produced tones by way of a system based on temperament.

This musical historical process, like Hegel's own dialectic, is rich in theological implications. It begins with Andreas Werckmeister (*sic!*), whose *Musicalische Paradoxal-Discourse* (1707) provided one of the first theoretical justifications for temperament. For Werckmeister, the so-called Pythagorean komma should be regarded as a *felix culpa*: a symptom of mankind's fall that rendered the natural overtones of our mundane reality imperfect or impure and therefore in need of salvation.[42] What Rameau (and later Hegel) would view as a response to God's command to perfect the given, Rousseau would simply see as a sad removal from our origins in nature.

Hence Hegel's implicitly anti-Rousseauist position, with which he concludes the passage dealing with *Rameau's Nephew*: Reason should not give up "the spiritually developed consciousness it has acquired, [it] should not submerge the widespread wealth of its moments again in the simplicity of the natural heart, and relapse into the wilderness of the nearly animal consciousness, which is also called Nature or innocence" (PG 389/318).[43] Rousseau's nostalgic dream of a natural, musical language is thereby dispelled.

For Rousseau, music was the art most capable of expressing human feelings (*sentiments*) irreducible to words. A momentous episode in his late *Rêveries du promeneur solitaire* (1776–78) provides a key description of the state that Rousseau longed for and Hegel disparaged. It is found in the *Fifth Promenade*, where the author relates "the happiest days of his life," spent on the small island of St. Pierre in the middle of the Lac de Bienne. It is a place of refuge and solitude, a site unspoiled by cultivation, seldom visited, and therefore an asylum from all of society's ills. Centeredness and containment are emphasized throughout, so the sketch of the island at the lake's "center," "naturally circumscribed and separated from the rest of the world" (ROC 1.1048), may be regarded as mirroring the text of the *Fifth Promenade*, situated at the very midpoint of the collection's ten "walks."[44] Here, moreover, the writer can "circumscribe himself" ("se circonscrire" [1040]), untroubled by desires and passions, devoting himself to "idleness" (*oisiveté*), if not "worklessness" ("*far niente*" [1042]).

It should come as no surprise that his time on the island is "cradled" by natural sounds, by the original music of Nature: "the cry of eagles, the songs [*ramage*] of some birds, and the pulsing rushing of the torrent that falls from the mountain" (1040). This natural music overwhelms the articulations of a subjective position over and against the objective. In auditory experience, the perceiver cannot distinguish himself from the perceived. Subjectivity, reflection, and thinking are replaced by a simple "feeling of existence," entirely turned in on itself, self-sufficient (like the island of St. Pierre), with nothing external to it: "Le sentiment de l'existence depouillé de toute autre affection" (1047)—"stripped" (*depouillé*) of all other sensations and passions, indeed of all otherness, which grounds the possibility of reflection. Thus, at night, the continuous noise of the tide ceaselessly strikes his ears, "making him feel his existence with pleasure, without taking the effort to *think*" (1045; my emphasis). At times Jean-Jacques sets off on a little boat, all alone, letting the water take him where it will, lost for hours in reverie, with no determined objective or goal. Again, subjectivity is displaced; the "je" appears only to be negated: "There the sound of the waves and the agitation of the water, fixing my senses, chasing all other agitation from my mind, would plunge it into a delightful reverie in which night often came upon me *without my having noticed it* ["sans que je m'en fusse apperceu"] (1045; my emphasis).

For Hegel, this simple, nonreflective feeling is but a nonconscious emptiness, awaiting the alienation that would allow the reflective turn back to oneself, which alone is the birth of self-consciousness. Rousseau calls for no externalization. Prereflective and in the immediacy of the moment, one may still enjoy the pleasure of feeling "one's own existence" ("sa propre existence"), "which suffers no emptiness in the soul that would need to be filled" (1046–47). Reflection would introduce an inequality, a difference out of which would emerge the distinction between subject and object. This manifestation of the "I" would disrupt the gentle pulsation of nature's music and put an end to the song of equality: "If the movement is uneven [*inégal*] or too strong it awakens; in reminding us of the objects around us, it destroys the charm of the reverie" (1047). The "charm," from the Latin word for "song" (*carmen*), would succumb to a rude disenchantment.

Hegel's dialectic could have no patience for this existential feeling "stripped" (*depouillé*) of all exteriority. He would not allow the possibility of self-consciousness without reflection. For him, such a state is altogether unconscious and such a subject is necessarily a "corpse" (*depouille*). Whereas Rousseau asserts this immediate feeling of self and in fact takes it as an achievement, Hegel understands it solely as a prelude to philosophy, which alone may articulate what this "sentiment" actually says. For Hegel, Rousseau's musical loss of subjectivity—his musical madness—is wrong in believing it can express something philosophy cannot. In Hegel's hands, the madness of the musician ceases to be a source of fascination, admiration, desire, or fear but rather becomes a fundamental moment in the process of actualization. For this reason, the nephew, according to Hegel, is not really mad at all: "fully aware of its confused state" ("dieser sich selbst klaren Verwirrung" [PG 387/318]), the torn consciousness exhibits a higher stage of development over the simple mind. In unworking the language of simple abstractions and the natural standpoint, the nephew's *Zerrissenheit* permits language to perform its true work of introducing the concrete universals that ground self-consciousness.

Rousseau wants auditory experience to give access to a feeling of self-existence that is immediate, preconceptual, and prereflexive. Hegel's dialectical project, however, demonstrates that any sense of self, any self-consciousness, is necessarily dependent on a self-objectification, on a self-expression mediated by language. Self-consciousness is "being for others"; it is only by being reflected in the other that I can become myself. But Hegel need not have the "last laugh." The *Naturphilosophie* of Friedrich

Schelling, Hegel's other Tübingen schoolmate, may be understood as continuing a more Rousseauist strain and developing it along the lines of a transcendental idealism far different from Hegel's. Concerning Hegel's requirement for alienation and subsequent reflection, Schelling reverts to Rousseau's lexicon: "In Hegel's philosophy the beginning relates to what follows as a simple nothing, as a lack, an emptiness, which is filled and is admittedly felt as emptiness, but there is in this as little to overcome as there is in filling an empty vessel."[45] Where Hegel sees only an "assumed existence" ("ein gemeintes Dasein"), Schelling sees Nature.

Rousseau touches precisely on this feeling—prereflective yet still belonging to oneself—in his *Fifth Promenade*, tellingly by way of natural sounds and rhythms, in bird songs and rushing water. This moment—of greatest significance for Hölderlin and his generation—would seem at last to remedy Rousseau's fears of self-loss and expropriation. For the nature of auditory experience, as adumbrated here, discloses dimensions of human life irreducible to reflective understanding. This track will be pursued by the German romantics, from Wackenroder on, who all owe a great debt to Rousseau. Hegel, however, remained skeptical. He seemed to accept as true the rumors and allegations that the Genevan philosopher was insane. To be sure, Hegel valued music much higher and more respectfully than did someone like Kant. Consequently, his thoughts on musical composition and reception, with particular emphasis on the art's temporality, had an enormous influence on later aesthetic theories. For Kant, who generally ignored music's temporal nature, the art of sound was merely a pleasurable play of sensations, offering nothing to the understanding and therefore hardly an art at all. For Hegel, however, as the later lectures in *Aesthetics* reveal, music held a privileged position in his philosophical system. Nonetheless, his discussion of music seems to be haunted by a Rousseauist naturalism, which he consistently fought to denigrate. The way Hegel enlists music to perform dialectically appears like an attempt to rescue the art form from Rousseau's mad program, just as the *Phenomenology* strove to put the derangement of Diderot's musician to work. Work is the only cure for madness, Hegel asserts in the *Philosophy of Mind*, but what if music were stronger than Hegel's philosophical will? What if it were able to unwork the system? What if music was inherently, incurably mad?

Dispersed across the writings and lecture notes outside of the *Phenomenology*, Hegel provides separate definitions of music and madness, which appear strikingly correlative. In his *Lectures on Aesthetics*, music is consistently regarded as an art of "pure interiority," which may be taken as analogous to his brief but important statements in the "Anthropology" of

his *Philosophy of Mind,* where insanity is primarily understood as a re-
version or withdrawal to interiority, as a "sinking into inwardness" with
no relation to external reality.[46] Parallel passages can be readily accumulated. These separate definitions seem to reveal not only music's af-
finity to madness but also the "moment" music and madness share with
the "natural self" discussed above. Hegel understands all species of madness
as a regression to an archaic state of simple feeling (*das Gefühlsleben*).[47]
The madman withdraws into his interiority, cuts himself off from the
outside world, indeed "circumscribes himself" in a manner reminiscent of
Rousseau on the island of St. Pierre.[48] To be sure, music for Hegel, is an art
form—a "sensible manifestation of Spirit"—and therefore qualitatively
different from a psychological disorder. Nonetheless, the fact that Hegel
defines music as "the obliteration . . . of the whole of space" and a "complete
withdrawal" signals at least some points of contact between the aesthetic
experience and the mental state.[49]

The connection becomes particularly clear in Hegel's discussion of the
"violent power of music"—"die Gewalt der Musik"—which bears striking
similarities to Rousseau's account from the *Fifth Promenade.* To begin, he
defines music in terms of inwardness, that is, as a nonrelation to space and
spatial figures that, together with the "purely evanescent" quality of sound,
permits it to "penetrate the arcanum of all the movements of the soul" and
therefore to cause consciousness to be carried away "by the ever-flowing
stream of sounds."[50] Concerned exclusively with interiority, music annuls
the representational distance that distinguishes the observer from the observed. Since subjectivity is grounded in its relation to the outside (its existence for others), music's obliteration of external space, its iconoclastic
removal of anything that may be represented "out there," potentially leads
to a loss of subjectivity altogether. Musical performance offers no concrete,
externalized object for the listener and therefore fails to maintain the
distance between the subjective and objective poles of aesthetic experience. It consists of "purely abstract sound in a temporal movement,"
which allows it to be a vehicle for purely interior content (*Aesthetics,*
157/908). For Hegel, it is this capability, and not something inherent in
music itself, that has caused tradition to speak about music's violence, its
"all-powerfulness" (*Allgewalt*). Music is not mad in essence, but potentially maddening.

For this reason, music must be put to work: "Music is spirit, or the soul
which resounds directly on its own account and feels satisfaction in its
perception of itself. But as a fine art it at once acquires, from the spirit's
point of view, a summons to bridle the emotions themselves as well as
their expression, so that there is no being carried away into a bacchanalian

rage or whirling tumult of passions, or a resting in the distraction of despair, but on the contrary an abiding peace and freedom in the out-pouring of emotion whether in jubilant delight or the deepest grief" (*Aesthetics*, 197–98/939). From the point of view of Spirit, music may be said to work like a concept, resolving the dissonance of particularity into the concord of the universal. Its maddening potential must be bridled so as to keep Spirit on its true path. The simplicity of life feeling (*Gefühlsleben*) must be brought face to face with difference, so as to generate a dialectically charged, concrete sense of individuality, self-consciousness in relation to the world. Analogously, lunatics, according to Hegel, should be made "to think about other things . . . to occupy themselves mentally and especially physically; by working, they are forced out of their diseased subjectivity and impelled towards the real world."[51] As early as the *Phenomenology*, Hegel had implemented his technique, latching on to the "derangement of the musician" only to reveal its task for philosophy. The nephew's bacchanalian rage was bridled, violence was averted, and the *persona inaequalis* could expose how difference may be held together in sameness, just like a concept. Something happened. The age had become ready to hear the madman and assign him his task. And yet the madness—especially in its musical form—would continue to defy the workhouse. Its violence had hardly been exhausted.

4 🌿

The Most Violent of the Arts

LUI: Our art, the most violent of all.
—*LE NEVEU DE RAMEAU*

B Y THE late eighteenth century, the idea that music could have violent effects on the listener had become a commonplace. As a language of the passions, music was said to enjoy immediate access to the volatile life of the emotions and was therefore considered inordinately powerful, dangerously sensuous, and morally problematic. The pleasure that musical experience unquestionably afforded could readily—unforeseeably—turn into the greatest displeasure. Joy could at any point yield to pain. Whatever enabled music to lighten the spirits, wipe away despair, or embolden the faint-hearted also made it capable of befuddling the clear thinker, driving the resolute into perplexity, or even sinking those already unstable further into madness. The listener was viewed as having little choice but to undergo the experience of submitting his or her subjective will to music's intoxicating power. To listen was to put one's autonomy at risk.

This experience of engulfment and imposing heteronomy caused music to be regarded as an exemplary case of the sublime, that is, as something that eluded definition, comprehension, or representation. From a historical perspective, the discourse on music's sublimity—instigated by the ancient treatise *Peri hypsous*, which was attributed to Longinus—flourished in close association with the development of the symphony. Majestic, forceful, and, perhaps most important, without the determination of text, the symphony could readily—sublimely—resonate with something prereflexive or presubjective, having disallowed any representational ground in which an individual subject might find itself reflected. The sublime therefore should, at this basically experiential level, be taken as antimimetic in the strong sense, as that which renders figuration nearly or even entirely impossible.

The first wave of theory that attempted to make sense of the musical sublime could do little but register this effect. For example, Johann Peter Schulz's article "Symphonie" in Sulzer's *Allgemeine Theorie der schönen Künste* (General theory of the fine arts, 1771–74) stands simply as a repository of eighteenth-century characterizations of a music considered "vast," "unpredictable," and "altogether overwhelming": "The symphony is especially skillful [*geschickt*] in expressing grandeur, solemnity, and the sublime."[1] Edmund Burke, Immanuel Kant, and Johann Gottfried Herder treated the topic of the sublime somewhat differently, with less emphasis on the qualities inherent in the work of art and more on the subjective processes involved in the aesthetic experience.[2] Here theory is aimed toward some kind of recuperation. The views and conclusions, however, vary considerably and only receive partial reconciliation in later work, for example, by Christian Friedrich Michaelis, whose essays on the musical sublime began to appear five years after Kant published his third *Critique* in 1790.[3] Overall, one could say that the new focus adopts as its first premise the passivity of hearing, which should be opposed to the activity of sight. Vision was assigned more to the realm of beautiful objects, which could be measured, compared, and appreciated by the eye. The ear, on the contrary, was thought to be a vulnerable organ, unable to maintain the safe distance required for rationalization. Throughout the tradition, music had been recognized as that which overwhelms distance—it "plunges down into the innermost recesses of the soul" (καταδύεται εἰς τὸ ἐντὸς τῆς ψυχῆς), as Socrates remarked in the *Republic* (3.401d). For that reason, as recommended for Plato's ideal city, music should be rigorously constrained, legislated, or justified. For the eighteenth century as well, music could be perceived as dangerously violent, insofar as an individual's identity was at stake. Now, by aligning audible experience more specifically with notions of sublimity, the problem became even more acute, turning explicitly on the issue of representability. The identity of the individual subject, including the identity of a collectivity (community, *Volk*, nation, and so forth)—grounded like all identities in a system of representation—was severely challenged by notions of the sublime, understood, as it was, as the very failure or impossibility of representation. If recuperation were to be had, music's function in representational (mimetic) procedures would need to be clarified.

Thus theories of the sublime (qua loss) strove to define modes of compensation or gain. Burke, for example, offers a notion of "delight," derived from the popular Alpine descriptions of John Dennis, whereby the fear before terrible grandeur is complemented by a safe fascination from a distance. Kant further analyzes this feeling, in the third *Critique*, not on the basis of self-preservation but rather on the subject's desire to know, on the drive to enlarge one's cognitive faculties. For Kant, the loss suffered in the experience of the sublime strictly affects the uncomprehending imagination, whose disability acts as an occasion for reason to demonstrate its superiority. The case of Herder, as we shall see, is more difficult to ascertain. His discussion of the sublime, primarily in the *Viertes Wäldchen* and the *Kalligone*, when taken together with his account of church music in *Cäcilia*, leads to a new conception of community, but one that departs significantly from conventional ideas of identity. Wackenroder's *Berglinger* novella, treated at this chapter's end, may be read in relation to Herder's portrayal of fusion and singularity, particularly in its treatment of sacred music. The hypersensitivity of Wackenroder's doomed composer, manifested throughout by a proneness to sublime ecstasies, reveals how the violence of music holds important ramifications for the association of music and madness.

THE MUSICAL SUBLIME IN LONGINUS AND BURKE

Music's acknowledged violence was indeed a pressing concern among eighteenth-century aestheticians. The assiduous demand that music be subordinated to a text is symptomatic of their disquiet. Verbal language or at least some species of linguisticity (for example, music as a language of passions) was deemed necessary to maintain art's mimetic principle, which would militate against irrational, confusing, or ambiguous emotionalism. Semiotic structures or actual text should provide the extramusical, ideational content that would safely escort the listener through the vague labyrinths of sound and thereby prevent total submersion. The long-standing tradition of polyphony, with its melismatic meanderings and dense harmonic texture, had always constituted a threat against representational clarity. Now, with the development and growing popularity of instrumental forms like the sonata and symphony, general anxieties were greatly precipitated.

This anxiety is already discernible in Rousseau's insistence on the shared origin of language and music. His craving for individual expression motivated his vociferous championing of melody over harmony and barely concealed his concerns about purely instrumental music. Rousseau, whose devotion to the ardor of tones was inexhaustible, himself suffered from the same fatigue that he heard in Fontenelle, whom he portrayed as crying out "in a fit of impatience ["dans un transport d'impatience"]: *Sonata, what do you want of me* ["*Sonate, que me veux tu*"]?"[4] The impatience is but an expression of a deep fear. Unbridled by words, music would be free to exert its violence. Its violation of sense, as well as its violating effect on the listener, would move unchecked with indomitable potency.

In setting Fontenelle's celebrated bon mot in a state of "transport," Rousseau invokes the key issue underlying all the debates not merely about music's relation to words but also about music's sublimity. "*Transport*"—the term Boileau used for "*ekstasis*" in his 1674 translation of the Longinian treatise *On the Sublime*—signaled for the epoch the experience of being overtaken by a work of genius. Sublime was that which overpowered the subject, that which by its vastness, its irregularity, its magnitude, or its brute strength carried the listener away. Like Ganymede, the individual was said to be ripped from mundane existence and borne up to divine heights, to a supersensible realm.

The author commonly referred to as Longinus is very clear that this encounter is both excessively violent and fundamentally auditory: "For extraordinary passages do not lead listeners [τοὺς ἀκροωμένους] to persuasion, but rather transport them out of themselves [i.e., lead them into ecstasy: εἰς ἔκστασιν].... By exercising power and irresistible violence [δυναστείαν καὶ βίαν ἄμαχον], these things reign supreme over every listener." Whereas persuasion appeals to the listener's rational faculties ("our persuasions are usually under our own control [ἐφ' ἡμῖν]"), the sublime claims us as its victims. Thus, because of its essential violence (*bia*), Longinus can oppose the experience of the sublime to one that is "pleasing" (πρὸς χάριν).[5]

As a "listener" (*akroômenos*), Longinus's victim suffers specifically from the formidable power of the acoustic. It is the ear that is assaulted by sublime violence. The analogy with music therefore is never too distant and sometimes emerges quite explicitly. Concerning how the words of a speech should be arranged, Longinus refers to how tones are fitted together, namely, by the art of *harmonia*. *Harmonia* (originally a carpentry term that, when applied to music, given Greek monody, signifies the fitting together of tones in a melody) "is not only a natural instrument of persuasion and pleasure [πειθοῦς καὶ ἡδονῆς], but also a wondrous instrument of grandeur and emotion [μεγαληγορίας καὶ πάθους]" (par. 39, sec. 1, 284–85). When the pleasurable experience of being rationally persuaded cedes to an irresistible power, the effect can be devastating:

For the *aulos* induces certain emotions in those who hear it [τοῖς ἀκροωμένοις]. It seems to carry their minds away and fill them with Corybantic frenzy [ἔκφρονας καὶ κορυβαντιασμοῦ]. It sets a particular rhythmic movement and forces them to move in rhythm. The listener has to conform to the tune, though he may be utterly unmusical [κἂν ἄμουσος ᾖ παντάπασι]. Yes, by Zeus, the very tones on the *kithara*, which are simply without meaning [οὐδὲν ἁπλῶς σημαίνοντες], by the variety of their sounds and by the combination and harmonious blending [μίξει τῆς συμφωνίας], often exercise, as you know, a wondrous spell. . . . Must we not think, then, that composition, which is a kind of *harmonia* in words . . . casts a spell on us?

(IBID., PAR. 39, SECS. 2–3, 284–87)

The emphasis on emotional arousal, compulsion, and even madness (ἔκφρονας καὶ κορυβαντιασμοῦ)—all observable in musical experience— here illustrates how words might act. The asemantic qualities of the voice may overpower rational distance: "the listener has to conform." Yet, for Longinus, the exemplum of music is ultimately no more than a figure of speech with limited applicability. In the course of this very passage, Longinus adds parenthetically, "And yet these are only images and bastard counterfeits [εἴδωλα καὶ μιμήματα νόθα] of persuasion, not a genuine activity [ἐνεργήματα γνήσια] of human nature" (par. 39, sec. 3). In the end, the "simply meaningless" phenomena of tones (οὐδὲν ἁπλῶς σημαίνοντες) do not serve as a fully adequate correlative to the true work (*energêma*) of the human mind. Hypnotic rhythms and rousing musical modes trigger nothing more than an automatic reaction. In the end one is dealing more with bewitchment or psychagogy than with proper, mindful oratory.

Longinus's offhanded debasement of musicality as something derivative (εἴδωλα καὶ μιμήματα νόθα) is a reaction to a fear of music's power evident throughout the Greek literary tradition. It is noteworthy that the Homeric epics begin and end with aggressive auditory experiences. Responding to the pleas of the priest Chryses that his daughter be set free, Apollo descends on the Achaean camp, his bow and quiver "sounding out with rage" (ἔκλαγξαν . . . χωομένοιο, [*Iliad* 1.46]). He shoots his invisible arrows, punishing Agamemnon's men with pestilence and conflagration: "From his silver bow there came a terrifying sound [δεινὴ . . . κλαγγή]" (49). In this passage, Homer gives the term "*biós*" for "bow," rather than the more usual "*tóxon*." The choice, however, is particularly apt. Although etymologically unrelated, the word "*biós*," which refers to the bowstring, effectively resonates with the "violence" (*bía*) that is visited upon the Greek warriors.[6] As if from a clear blue sky, the fierce missiles, dispatched with the bow's frightening *klang*, attack and disorient the company. There is no escape from the painful suffering.

The sounds of the deathly bow will be heard again in the *Odyssey*, when the vengeful hero, disguised as a stranger, plucks the bow before the suitors, who thereupon realize that fate is near: "[Odysseus] lifted the great bow [μέγα τόξον] and scanned it on every side—even as when a man well-skilled in the lyre [φόρμιγγος ἐπιστάμενος] and in song easily stretches the string about a new peg, making fast at either end the twisted sheep-gut—so without effort did Odysseus string the great bow. And he held it in his right hand, and tried the string, which sang sweetly beneath his touch, like to a swallow in tone. But upon the suitors came great grief, and the faces of them changed color, and Zeus thundered loud, showing forth his signs [σήματα φαίνων]."[7] Odysseus's murderous rampage begins by assuming the role of a trained musician, not unlike the wrathful, bow-wielding Apollo. It is as though the epic is extrapolating what remains a simple (and therefore inexhaustibly complex) analogy in Heraclitus's fifty-first fragment, where the bow and the lyre are offered as examples of agreement in difference. Pascal Quignard, who refers to these two instances at either end of Homer's epics, points out the analogy between the god's bow, which inexplicably sends a resonating death from a distance, and the lyre's sound, which invisibly pierces the atmosphere above.[8] Similarly, thundering Zeus, whom the Romans translate as *Iuppiter tonans*, is only perceivable by the ears. The tone's import is as powerful as it is unavoidable.

Divine sound must be obeyed. Its power is violent, insofar as it overtakes the listener's rational control. Therefore, it may even violently quell violence. Again, at the head of the *Iliad*, Athena—invisible to all save the half-immortal Achilles—perceptually "appears" (*phainomenê*) primarily by way of voice (1.198ff). She bids the hero to hold off from slaying Agamemnon. Despite his fury, Achilles complies, recognizing prudence: "For the gods ever hear the prayers of him who has obeyed them"—ὅς κε θεοῖς ἐπιπείθηται μάλα τ'ἔκλυον αὐτοῦ (1.218). The later Romance and Germanic traditions will portray every listener as obedient. The English "obey," like the French "*obéir*" (from the Latin "*oboedire*," "to listen to"), succinctly makes the point. German semantics, too, often exploits an etymological connection between the words for hearing (*Hören*), belonging (*Gehören*), and obeying (*Gehorchen*).[9] If one stresses this relationship, the act of hearing becomes thoroughly passive. The implication in German is that one understands oneself as the property of another ("I belong to him"—"Ich gehöre zu ihm") or that one complies to the will of another ("I obey him"—"Ich gehorche ihm"). In hearing, one lets oneself be steered or be regarded as part of a whole. In sum, one belongs (*gehört*) to whom one hears (*hört*), and one hears whom one obeys (*gehorcht*).[10]

Edmund Burke, whose *Philosophical Enquiry into the Origin of our Ideas of the Sublime and the Beautiful* (1757) played a most significant role in shaping the European discourse on the sublime, likewise emphasizes the sense of hearing.[11] For Burke, "the ruling principle of the sublime" is "terror," which "robs the mind of all its powers of acting and reasoning."[12] It does so, overall, by exploiting the failure of vision. It is obscurity that best contributes to the arousal of terror, insofar as it prevents us from "accustom[ing] our eyes," thwarting our efforts to make "a great deal of the apprehension vanish" (54). Although Burke speaks little of the musical arts, he consistently stresses the primacy of the audible over the visual in cases of the sublime. In describing what he considers to be the cool distance with which one regards a painting, he refers to the abbé Dubos, who clearly considers vision as the superior sense in citing the following lines from Horace's *Ars poetica*:

Segnius irritant animos demissa per aures[13]
Quam quae sunt oculis subjecta fidelibus

(Things sent to the ears affect the soul more sluggishly
Than those that are laid before the faithful eyes)

(180–181)

As Burke explains, Dubos gives preference to painting because its visible presence bestows a strength exceeding the effectiveness of poetry. Hence, as Horace seems to suggest, the listener is always inactive or lazy or passive (*segnis*).[14] For Burke, however, it is precisely this idleness—this *désœuvrement*, so to speak—that, in neglecting the work of trustworthy vision, constitutes the key factor in the production of the sublime. It is indeed our ignorance of things, our incapacity to see clearly, that causes all our admiration and chiefly excites our passions. "Knowledge and acquaintance make the most striking causes affect but little" (2.2, 56–57). Therefore, regarding the sublime, the judgment of Dubos must be reversed: its power manifests itself emphatically *per aures*.

If sight is the exemplary sense of rationality—of clarity and cool, contemplative distance—then hearing is the sense that occasions the collapse of spatial relations, of the safe boundary between perceiver and perceived. In the article "Music" in his *Allgemeine Theorie der schönen Künste*, Johann Georg Sulzer reflects on the physiological basis of the distinction between musical and visual experience. By nature, argues Sulzer, the ear enjoys an "immediate connection" to the heart. Since the medium of air, through which musical tones travel to the ear canal, is "much rougher" (*viel gröber*) and "more corporeal" than the ethereal element of light, the effect of sound is all the more violent: "Thus, because of the violence [*Gewalt*] of the blows that are had [from music], the aural nerves ["die Nerven des Gehörs"] extend their effect throughout the entire nervous system, which does not happen in sight. And so it can be understood how one could exert by means of tones a violent power ["gewaltige Kraft"] on the entire body and, consequently, on the soul" (3.422). The "sense of hearing" ["das Gehör"] has the "strongest power [*Kraft*]" on the passions; therefore a tone off key, for Sulzer, is far more upsetting than a repulsive color in painting. Sulzer alludes to the many stories that speak of "music's influence on certain diseases," and, while conceding that many reports may be entirely "mythical" or "fantastic" (*fabelhaft*), he nonetheless affirms on the basis of observing music's effects on the body that there is good reason to believe in music's capacity to alleviate as well as exacerbate human illness. "It can by no means be denied that people suffering from heavy attacks of delusion ["in schweren Anfällen des Wahnwitzes"] are somewhat calmed by music, while the sane can be overcome by a passion so intense ["in so heftige Leidenschaft"] that they reach a slight degree of frenzy [*Raserey*]" (3.427). Hence Sulzer consistently speaks of music's "exceedingly violent force" ("allgewaltige Kraft" [3.422])—a sublimity that would captivate the generations to follow.

For Burke, it is the invisible quality of sound that is decisive. In vision, the distance between observer and observed allows mastery or withdrawal—options that hearing practically abolishes. Space is overcome or even eradicated, leaving no room for cognitive detachment. Further, not only as something invisible but also as something lacking solid materiality, sound permeates the most obdurate obstacles. Tones travel across distances, penetrating enclosures, transgressing all boundaries, including the barrier that separates a subject's inwardness from the environment. Music crosses the threshold (*limen*) that separates Orpheus from his lost Eurydice. Sound passes beneath the threshold—*sub limen*—subliminal and sublime.

In his studies from the 1930s on the phenomenology of listening, the psychologist Erwin Straus recognizes this sublimity in the compulsion to move one's torso when listening to music. As mentioned above, Longinus also noted how even a person with no musical inclinations feels compelled to sway before a powerful auditory experience. For Straus, this is a demonstration of how acoustic phenomena modify body experience by shifting the center of ego consciousness from the base of the nose to the navel.[15] This transposition of the site of subjectivity entails the replacement of intellectual, cognitive activity with a more immediate, and therefore less clear, experience of mere existence. Consequentially, the perception of space is altered. To illustrate, Straus emphasizes the qualitative differences between color and tone. In purely optical experience, color always adheres to its object; it is always "over there, that is, in a direction and at a distance, somewhere vis-à-vis ourselves. The colors are both bounded and boundary setting; they confine space, differentiating it into partial spaces ordered sideways and in depth" (7). For this reason, visual activity is the ground and model for "theoretical scientific knowledge" (5). A resonating tone, on the contrary, fills up space. Although we may ascertain from which direction a sound is coming, the resonance itself detaches from its source and thereby frustrates theoretical confidence; hence music's capacity to overpower.

Straus's further observations on acoustic phenomena offer a useful explanation for the distinction I made between the single and double articulations, respectively, of the Marsyan and Apolline positions. For Straus, music is more purely acoustic than noise, insofar as it can erase altogether the conscious desire to discover a referent source. In order to determine the origin and significance of an unfamiliar noise, the acoustical joins forces with the optical. As in most cases of sense perception, the "pathic" moment of immediate sensation blends with the "gnostic" moment of reflection. Musical experience, however, reveals that the pathic moment of perception need not be merely a preliminary step or stage toward the gnostic but rather an essential element of its own. In other words, some kind of meaning can be had without having recourse to the second level that all symbols demand. Essentially pathic, musical experience may hold off the gnostic altogether and thereby lead to a new appreciation of the material aspect itself as substantial.

For writers of the late eighteenth century, this pathic experience comes very close to formulations of the sublime. A thinker like Kant, as may be expected, could not abide forfeiting the subject's autonomy to this material sphere. His persistent definition of subjectivity as freedom demanded transcendence, which, to stay with Straus's terms, meant the reaffirmation of the gnostic. Musical experience, however, would prove to be an exceptionally difficult test case.

KANT'S ABDICATION

I have already commented on how, in the introduction to the *Phänomenologie des Geistes*, Hegel describes consciousness as the Notion or Concept (*Begriff*) itself. That is to say, consciousness should be capable of passing beyond the limits of "a natural life" ("ein natürliches Leben") and thus of transcending its own limitations, including the extreme limitation of death. This self-overcoming reveals the violence (*Gewalt*) that consciousness exercises against itself—"Consciousness suffers the *Gewalt* at its own hands" (PG 74/51). Alexandre Kojève, in his seminal *Introduction to the Reading of Hegel* (1947), elaborates on this idea of mortal violence by associating it with the generation of meaningful language. Paraphrasing Hegel, Kojève emphasizes the "finitude" that allows an essence to be taken away from mere (evanescent) existence: "Hegel says, if dogs were not *mortal*—that is, not essentially *finite* or limited with respect to duration— one could not *detach* its concept from it—that is, cause the Meaning (Essence) that is embodied in the real dog to pass into the *non*living word."[16] In this idealist mode, language works by committing ontological murder. In a rehearsal of the Apolline inversion, one could say that language violently nullifies beings and transforms them into entities, whose ideal (noncontingent, enduring) status is henceforth sheltered by—or entombed in—the Word.

In assigning *Gewalt* to consciousness, Hegel essentially employs an argument that could be derived from Kant's analysis of experiences of the sublime in the *Kritik der Urteilskraft* (*Critique of the Power of Judgment*, 1790). For Kant, the forces of nature that threaten our physical well-being (the "dynamic sublime") or frustrate our abilities to comprehend (the "mathematical sublime") can be met by a counterforce, namely, the power of reason (*Vernunft*). Because we are rational and not merely sensate beings, we can transcend our corporeal vulnerability and the cognitive shortcomings of our imaginative capacities (*Einbildungskraft*). The loss suffered in the experience of the sublime solicits reason to counteract by raising the mind to a higher level that exerts violence against violence—a *Gegen-Gewalt* (*KU* sec. 28, 259–60/143).[17]

While the sublime surpasses the senses' capacity for measurement, it also permits reason's power to overcome the limitations of sensory comprehension, thereby arousing in the subject a "feeling of [its] supersensible vocation" ("Gefühl [seiner] übersinnlichen Bestimmung" [*KU* sec. 27, 257/141]). In Kant's analysis, the violence of the sublime—*das Erhabene*— ultimately lies not in the object perceived but rather in the rational subject that raises itself—*erhebt sich*—above the merely sensible, above what Hegel would call "ein natürliches Leben": "Sublimity must be sought only in the mind of the one who judges, not in the object in nature" (*KU* sec. 26, 256/139). Analogous to Hegel's *Begriff*, the sublime, precisely as a rational counterviolence, introduces the universals of law and morality by negating concrete particularity. Thus, according to Kant, we are able to recognize "the superiority of the rational vocation [*Vernunftbestimmung*] of our cognitive faculty over the greatest faculty of sensibility" (*KU* sec. 27, 257/141).

In sum, Hegel and Kant, at least in this case, share a transcendental idealism that aims to correct or undo the empirical tradition of the sublime by transferring *Gewalt* from the object to the subject. As discussed, Hegel's idealism formats this process entirely in terms of language and subjectivity, by demonstrating how the contingencies of existence may be integrated into a higher order. The relation Kant establishes between failed imagination and victorious reason correlates precisely to this power of a subject's language to recuperate the particular into the universal.[18] The experience of the senses, the realm of mere life and immediate perception, is marked by an evanescence that binds us to the state of nature. As in the Marsyas myth, freedom is gained in our passage to the universal, but only by demonstrating the unfreedom of mere life. Thus idealism puts the sublime to work for the personal subject.[19]

Although Kant's analysis of the sublime requires a much fuller exposition, it is for present purposes sufficient to take note of this fundamental transference of power. Kant's idealist interpretation bears important consequences for theories and representations of music and its potentially maddening effects. This may come as a surprise, since Kant does not explicitly link his discussion of music with his analysis of the sublime. Nonetheless, in attending closely to the text, crucial analogies may be discerned, analogies that touch directly on the topic of music and madness.

Kant's appraisal of music is ambivalent at best and altogether disparaging at worst. A crucial hint for recognizing this ambivalence is Kant's incapability of deciding whether music is "beautiful" (universally valid) or "agreeable" (valid only according to private taste).[20] In section 51 of the *Critique of Judgment*, devoted to the division of the fine arts, Kant tellingly describes music, on the one hand, as "the beautiful play of sensations" and, on the other, as an art of "agreeable sensations" (*KU* 325/202). The vacillation between these two poles persists in the following sections. Upon defining the "art of tone" (*Tonkunst*) as that which "speaks through mere sensations [*Empfindungen*] without concepts," he regrets its failure to provoke reflection (*Nachdenken*), while recognizing that it "moves the mind [*Gemüth*] in more manifold and, though only temporarily, in deeper ways [than poetry]" (*KU* sec. 53, 328/205). Music's "charm" (*Reiz*) is appreciated, yet only in the area of "enjoyment" (*Genuß*) and not "culture" (*Cultur*). The listener demands frequent changes, so as to avoid "antipathy" (*Überdruß*), and may only find charm in music's communication of affects, which it does so universally by means of appealing to shared human sensations and mathematical proportions (sec. 53, 328–29/206). If one were to judge the value of an art form according to what it contributes to the enlargement of the cognitive faculties, then one would have to say that "music occupies the lowest place among the fine arts." If, however, one simply judged according to an art's "agreeableness" (*Annehmlichkeit*), than one must accord music the "highest place" (sec. 53, 329/206).

Throughout, music shares a position with the pictorial arts, which are also defined as a "beautiful play of sensations," by means of color rather than tone. Yet the fact that music provides but a "transitory" impression, as opposed to a picture's durability, means for Kant that the former cannot "promote the urbanity of the higher powers of cognition" (*KU* sec. 53, 329/206). In other words, whereas a painting leads upward from the sensorial to the ideational, music carries "determinate ideas" down to "sensations" (sec. 53, 330/206–7). Therefore, Kant famously concludes, "there is a certain lack of urbanity in music":

> Primarily because of the character of its instruments, it extends [*ausbreitet*] its influence further (into the neighborhood) than is required, and so as it were imposes itself, thus interfering with the freedom of others, outside of the musical circle, which the arts that speak to the eyes do not do, since one need only turn one's eyes away if one would not admit their impression. It is almost the same here as in the case of the delight from a widely pervasive smell ["durch einen sich weit ausbreitenden Geruch"]. Someone who pulls his perfumed handkerchief out of his pocket treats everyone in the vicinity to it against their will, and forces them, if they wish to breathe, to enjoy it at the same time; hence it has also gone out of fashion.
>
> (*KU* SEC. 53, 330/207)

Like an inescapable odor—however pleasant, however agreeable—music tracks down everyone within range, rudely and without regard.[21] Unlike the eyes, the ears have no lids. They must drink in whatever assails them. Despite talk of delightfulness, contamination is clearly suggested. The objectionable outsider crashes the city gates, transgressing the boundaries of courtesy like an unwelcome visitor, crude and unfashionable. What is worse, for an unsuspecting philosopher who moves through the day without the benefit of Circe's warning, the noise pollution pouring out of these Sirens disturbs one's own freedom to think. Kant remarks in a testy footnote: "Those who have recommended the singing of spiritual songs as part of the domestic rites of worship [*Andachtsübungen*] have not considered that by means of such a *noisy* (and precisely for that reason usually pharisaical) form of worship they have imposed a great inconvenience on the public, for they have compelled the neighborhood either to join in their singing or to give up their own train of thought ["ihr Gedankengeschäft niederzulegen nöthigen"]" (*KU* sec. 53, 330/207; emphasis in original).

These remarks on music's encroaching effect raise certain questions when related back to Kant's earlier discussion of the sublime, especially concerning the key issue of *Gewalt*. At the head of section 28, Kant distinguishes between "power" (*Macht*) and "violent power" or "dominion" (*Gewalt*), in order to clarify that sublime objects in nature cannot dominate us in our rationality: "*Macht* is a capacity that is superior to great obstacles. The same thing is called *Gewalt* if it is also superior to the resistance of something that itself possesses *Macht*. Nature considered in aesthetic judgment as a *Macht* that has no *Gewalt* over us is *dynamically sublime*" (*KU* 260/143). Music, however, apparently does have *Gewalt* over the philosopher's intellectual business (*Gedankengeschäft*), forcing him to "put down" or even "abdicate" (*niederlegen*) his thought processes. The counterforce of reason, which rescues the imagination in its failure to comprehend the sublime, apparently fails in the case of music. The subject submits "against its will." Its "freedom" is disrupted. The question, then, is whether Kant's ambivalent attitude toward music lies in its undeniable, irresistible, and perhaps unconquerable violence. Is his indecisiveness symptomatic of a basic incomprehension? To be sure, Kant alludes to, while also suppressing, the "violent power of music"—*die Gewalt der Musik*. Even Hegel, as we have seen, admits music's "Allgewalt." Would this violence threaten to dismantle the sovereign workings of reason? Is music's "lack of urbanity" but a euphemism for its indomitable sublimity?

As Kant acknowledges, his thoughts on the sublime in the third *Critique* (as in the earlier *Observations on the Feeling of the Beautiful and the Sublime*) were motivated by the work of Edmund Burke, where the sublime is an imperious, overwhelming force, predicable exclusively to the object encountered, be it natural or artistic. The fact that Kant transfers this power to the subject constitutes his greatest innovation. The move is in keeping with a new formulation of aesthetics that reassigns investigations away from the qualities of objects toward the functioning of the subject. He thereby modifies a long-standing tradition that associated the sublime effect with a domineering might that rendered the subject passive, stupefying rational control. Where Longinus and Burke saw the overpowering poignancy of rhetoric, Kant evokes reason's resistance and insistence on truth.[22]

Kant had no tolerance for oratory, which he condemned as a "deceiving" art, bent on "robbing minds of their freedom" (*KU* sec. 53, 327/204). His aversion to music's "lack of urbanity," which "interferes with the freedom of others," corresponds to this leeriness. For the same reason, he removes the experience of the sublime away from the Longinian auditorium and instead situates it in the philosopher's den. Yet Kant's empowerment of the subject barely conceals its dark side. Although he reinterprets the imagination's failure as an opportunity for reason's success, he does so by significantly raising the psychological stakes. The implementation of a rational counterforce stages an agonistic encounter between the human subject and the overwhelming object, whereby the former can in fact lose to the latter. Kant puts the subject's very status at risk.[23] He endows the subject with the capacity to stand up to the violence of the sublime but simultaneously allows the possibility of defeat.

The vulnerability of Kant's gambit may be discerned in his discussion of infinity. As in all the examples of the sublime, the loss at the level of the imagination is compensated by a gain at the level of reason. Infinity cannot be "comprehended" by our sensory apparatus but is conceivable rationally (sec. 26, 254/138). In other words, the Longinian listener receives from Kant the privilege of hearing "the voice of reason" ("die Stimme der Vernunft"): "Now the mind [Gemüth] hears in itself the voice of reason, which requires totality for all given magnitudes, even for those that can never be entirely apprehended although they are (in the sensible representation) judged as entirely given" (ibid.). Kant could hardly have chosen a more volatile metaphor. Indeed, what exactly is this "voice" and how does reason's audition escape the threat implicit in other scenes of hearing?

The "voice of reason" appears elsewhere in Kant's work, notably in the *Critique of Practical Reason*, where it functions as the universal compulsion to rationality in questions of ethics. As in the third *Critique*, the voice of reason is silent. Indeed, it is without any subjective ground, for the moral law must be purely formal, universally applicable, with no recourse to moral feelings or personal will: "Were the voice of reason with respect to the will not so distinct, so irrepressible, and so clearly audible [unüberschreibar] for the commonest man, it would drive morality to ruin."[24] Unlike Socrates' exclusively personal *daimonion* and unlike Rousseau's deistic "voice of nature," Kant's "voice of reason" is perfectly formal—and it is precisely for this reason that no one is capable of "crying out over it" (unüberschreibar).[25] This is certainly not a physical voice—evanescent, überschreibar—and yet it is still a "voice." Rather than accept that Kant is simply reverting to a conventional metaphor, it would be fruitful to press the usage, which makes moral man first and foremost a submissive listener.[26]

No thinker was perhaps more astute in exposing the hidden vulnerabilities of Kant's system than Johann Gottfried Herder. In the *Kalligone* (1800)—an extended critique of Kant's aesthetics—Herder essentially reverts to empirical premises in order to challenge what he regards as the philosopher's misguided idealism. Although Herder agrees with Kant in interpreting the experience of the sublime as an elevation, he is not ready to abandon the realm of the pathic on the basis of a priori speculation. In the simplest of terms, for Herder, Kant's method ultimately ignores man's sensate, physical existence in the world. For the sake of a particular idea of freedom, Kant has left the human subject without a body—a ghost lost in a spectral reality. The silence of the latter's "voice of reason" is therefore especially telling. For Herder, much can be learned from listening to that which is anything but silent. If music threatened to cause Kant to abdicate thinking, it would serve as Herder's very paradigm of thought—not in spite but rather precisely because of music's paradigmatic sublimity.

COMMUNITY AND HERDER'S CONCEPTION OF MUSIC

Herder's *Viertes Wäldchen*—written between 1769 and 1770 but published only posthumously—was initially conceived as a critical response to the work of Friedrich Just Riedel, professor of philosophy at Erfurt, whose compendious *Theorie der schönen Künste und Wissenschaften* appeared in 1767. What resulted, however, was Herder's earliest and most elaborate aesthetic theory to date, including a sustained reflection on the sense of hearing and the art of music.

Reminiscent of Lessing's famous analysis of the differences between word and image in the *Laokoon* (1766), Herder makes a sensualist distinction between the aesthetic experience of sight and that of hearing. Since it proceeds by comparison, measurement, and conclusion, the sense of sight is "the most artistic [*Künstlichste*], the most philosophical sense."[27] The objects perceived by the eye alone—which Herder believes to be two-dimensional, unless sight works in concert with touch—lie before us at a cold distance. The perception of sound, on the contrary, occurs "more deeply within our soul" (292); its effect is akin to "intoxication" (*Berauschung* [336]). Whereas the optical takes place spatially, the acoustic unfolds successively in time, which works "most deeply and immediately" on our soul (ibid.). That is what accounts for music's intense effect on human emotion. Herder therefore disparages music theories that attempt to explain harmony on the basis of intervallic relationships or the resonance (*Schall*) derived from the division of the monochord or from the overtone series. According to Herder, these types of explanations should be regarded as spatializations or intellectual abstractions of music. The reduction of music to space ignores the successiveness of the art and thereby fails to elucidate its powerful impact on the listener.

To come to a truer understanding of what happens in musical experience, Herder turns to physiological, materialist arguments. He refers to the ear's coils, the tympanum, and the aural nerves, which he portrays as a "stringed instrument." More specifically, our aural apparatus is capable of receiving tones either in an "adverse" (*widrig*) or "smooth" (*glatt*) manner (348). It is the latter that is perceived as "pleasant" (*angenehm*), thanks to the sound's evenness. This pleasantness furthermore can be divided into two main types: "The nerve is homogeneously strained, and at once the fibers become tenser; or it is relaxed [*erschlaffen*], and the fibers gradually overflow, as though gently dissolving ["wie in eine sanfte Auflösung"]. The former is the same kind of feeling that we name the *feeling of the sublime* in the soul; the latter is the *feeling of the beautiful*, pleasure" (348–49; emphasis in original). Here, Herder's agreement with Burke is perfectly recognizable, and he proceeds in fact to accredit the "real discoveries" made by the British writer. Although he regrets the fact that Burke did not pursue his investigations further into the realm of hearing, he clearly appreciates the empiricism that grounds the *Enquiry*. Yet, while Herder will remain true to the orientation in experience, by the time of the *Kalligone*, he cannot subscribe to Burke's (nor, for that matter, Kant's) strict distinction between the beautiful and the sublime.

Instead of drawing a firm border between the two, Herder's *Kalligone* strives to reveal the fluid passage from one to the other. He suggests we follow the ancient artists: "How varied the noble Greeks exercised their capacities, with the beautiful as well as the sublime!"[28] The *Kalligone* gives a list of examples, including the heavens and the sea, that we can certainly experience as both sublime and beautiful—"only a spoiled mind ["ein verwöhnter Sinn"] is able to separate the two" (686). The instance of the gentle and awe-inspiring heavens, the perception of the ocean alternating between stormy waves and calm surface—these blatantly polyvalent cases—are hardly the exception but rather the rule for Herder's aesthetics in general and his theory of music in particular.

For Herder, music is an art of movement, which is to say of alternation, namely, between discordance and harmony. Music is paradigmatic of Herder's aesthetics because it is constituted by a succession of tension and relaxation, dissonance and consonance. For this reason, music is ideally suited for expressing conflicting emotions like love and despair. It artistically captures the cyclothymia that falls beyond the reach of verbal language. As he argues in his essay on the origin of language (*Abhandlung über den Ursprung der Sprache*, 1772), words are too lucid (*deutlich*).[29] Herder therefore reinterprets the experience of the sublime: he uses Burke's empiricism to correct Kant's abstraction into disembodied rationality, while taking Kant's concept of elevation to disprove Burke's assertion that the feeling of the sublime consists primarily in terror (however distanced or, in Burke's terms, "delightful").[30] Herder's listener moves through successive phases of awe and comprehension, but without the forfeiture of the corporeal standpoint that Kant requires.

Moreover, the feeling of awe need not be, pace Burke, painful. For Herder, the force of the sublime that transports us into ecstasy is a divine gift: "a heavenly breeze that lifts us and strengthens us."[31] To consider this rapture as fearful is to deny the role of the divine in our lives. Rachel Zuckert summarizes the point well: "One will find such experiences painful ... according to Herder, only if one is committed to an 'arrogant' conception of oneself, or of the human self in general, as the sole source of value in the world, or only if one is 'tyrannical' enough to desire so to establish oneself."[32]

This last point correlates back to Herder's physiological argument, wherein the ear is a "stringed instrument" finely tuned to receive the sound impressions that strike the tympanum. Such a portrayal removes Herder significantly from mimetic conceptions of musical art. Music is neither the representation of emotional content nor the expression of individual passion. On the contrary, if music is said to be expressive at all, it is the expression of something transindividual, something communal, plural: "Music plays within *us* the clavichord that is *our* own most intimate nature."[33] That is to say, the violence of music lifts us beyond our individual sense of identity, beyond our cold rationality. As resonating bodies, we undergo an experience that reveals what exceeds feelings of individual subjectivity. It would be considered a loss only if subjectivity were the exclusive ground of our self-definition.

The loss of subjectivity—which for Kant would mean a maddening failure of autonomy—is for Herder the opportunity to reinterpret selfhood and community. One of the clearest expressions of this reinterpretation comes from a brief essay on church music from 1793, simply entitled *Cäcilia*. To begin, Herder employs once again the eye/ear distinction in order to define a species of the musical sublime particular to sacred music. The distinction yields an opposition between church hymns, which are nonpersonal, and what he calls "dramatic" or "characteristic" music, that is, musical pieces that depict personal traits or expressions. The difference between these two species of music evokes again the opposition between the aural and the visual. "Every syllable that a poet or an artist speaks in order to present himself ["um sich zu zeigen"] harms the effect of the whole and becomes intolerable for the pure feeling. Dramatic and church music are almost as different from each other as ear and eye."[34] Church music is "sublime" insofar as it displaces the individual, rational subject away from the center of the aesthetic experience and replaces it with the divine. Here Herder again questions the validity of judging experiences of sublimity as something necessarily painful or frustrating. From Herder's theistic point of view, the awe that is felt therein should lead to recognizing the subject's low standpoint in relation to what is higher or greater. This recognition informs the "humility" (*Demuth*) that is the physical and moral precondition for regarding the sublime as an experience of height. As such, the sublime cannot be a source of pain (challenging the sovereignty of mankind) but rather is a source of admiration (reminding the human subject of its relative position in the world). In *Cäcilia*, church music inspires admiration precisely because it reinforces the holistic picture of the world wherein the individual subject rediscovers its place before the divine. Any assertion of individuality would therefore "harm the effect of the whole."

In Herder's definition, dramatic music is that which features the voices of individuals, as in arias or duets, where the singers step forward to make themselves heard, to "show themselves" ("sich zu zeigen") in a space that is emphatically visual. It therefore contributes to the spatialization of music that Herder distrusted in the *Viertes Wäldchen*. Church music, by contrast, is nonrepresentational: "Here no person shows himself [*zeigen sich*] here nothing is represented [*repräsentiert*]. There are only pure, invisible voices that immediately speak with our spirit and hearts" (261).

Nonrepresentability, a hallmark of the sublime, is a consequence of this "internalization" (*Verinnerlichung*) that essentially dissolves the external space dominated by vision. This interior experience, however, does not give way to the expression of personal identity but rather to an attitude of devotion. Feeling is still to be had in church music: not the pathos of an individual life but rather the ecstasy that drives a person out of him- or herself beyond subjectivity. The nonrepresentable nature of the hymn or the chorale moreover implies the nonrepresentation of one's self. "Before the community [*Gemeine*], the single person loses. . . . Not only its entire appearance with all its gestures, the words of its voice also lose all effect. This word must already be taken from its mouth and have become *universal song* ["*allgemeiner Gesang*"], a word addressed to all human hearts" (265; emphasis in original) Choral singing therefore involves "the deepest humility [*Demuth*]," an "annihilation and melting away before God"— "Vernichtung und Zerschmelzung vor Gott" (262).

The obliteration of the subject before the universal characterizes the sublimity of sacred music as a specifically Catholic phenomenon. Tellingly, Herder's *Cäcilia* essay was sketched out after the author returned from an extended trip through Italy. As will become clear in the writings of Kleist, the Protestant attitude comes to be regarded precisely as the kind of self-affirmation that prevents the ecstatic dissolution of subjectivity that Herder viewed as the essential element of the sacred music experience. The exceedingly rational position of conventional Protestantism—but not, say, Pietism—was touted as a resistance to or a counterforce against the sublime, which should be approached with caution. Kant's theory of reason's counterviolence clearly belongs to this project.[35] From a musical-historical perspective, one could ascribe the Protestant introduction of the aria, the duet, and the recitative in church music to this leeriness. The Protestant paradigm was based on an ideal associated with the culture of *Empfindsamkeit*, whereby voices joined together without sacrificing a sense of selfhood. This ideal depended on the shared experience of individuality, that is, of a subjectively expressive existence that would confirm the subjectivity of the other.

The Catholic ideal adumbrated in Herder's essay rests on a particular ideal of community that is nonsubjective, nonindividualistic. Here there is no human voice that may be cognitively shared by other human consciousnesses. There is only God's voice, or the power of music. "The sacred voice speaks out from heaven; it is God's voice and not a human voice" (265). This universality—or Catholicity—reflects God's unity and is accomplished by rendering identity invisible. "This invisibility" ("diese Unsichtbarkeit") defines the essence of spiritual music, which affirms the unity of the divine. Herder therefore concludes: "The unity, for which the first church was so palpably and greatly ["so fühlbar und groß"] set up, has more or less disappeared from our Protestant churches" (261).

Yet it remains unclear how one should construe this idea of community. If the unity of which Herder speaks is figured as a kind of identity, it would by definition contradict the fundamental notion of community as the dissolution of identity and its attendant mechanics of representation. The fact that this identity would be understood from a divine rather than a human perspective does not eradicate the problem: "here nothing is represented." What idea of community are we speaking of, then, once the system of representation is surrendered? And what kind of art form is church music if it fails to produce a medium in which a community may find itself reflected?

The work of Jean-Luc Nancy may be useful here, especially if we take Herder's "unity" as "singularity." For Nancy, singularity does not contradict the idea of community. On the contrary, it proves to be constitutive of it, especially in its ecstatic mode. In discussing Rousseau and Hegel (through the lens of Georges Bataille), Nancy writes: "Singularity never has the nature or the structure of individuality." In order to draw out the implications of this idea of singularity, he borrows freely from the lexicon of the sublime: "It is linked to ecstasy: one could not properly say that the singular being is the subject of ecstasy, for ecstasy has no 'subject'—but one must say that ecstasy (community) happens *to* the singular being."[36] Singularity, then, could be thought together with the single articulation of voice—like the aulic voice of Marsyas—that does not express something else in a semantic sense but rather expresses simply itself: its physical presence, its place in the moment, its finitude. Elsewhere, Nancy focuses on the voice that is prerational, before *logos*—"There is voice before speech"—and relates it to his understanding of community: "Voice is always shared; in a sense, it is sharing itself. A voice begins with the entrenchment of a singular being."[37] The community that is ecstasy allows this singular voice to present itself without representing any subjectivity. The voice, then, is purely relational, resisting subsumption into an identifiable meaning yet still participating in a community that is nothing other than "a plurality of singular beings."[38]

Opposed to the idea of society—which is comprised of subjective, individual voices worked into an idea of some common identity—the notion of community is, for Nancy, always that which proves refractory to the work of representational meaning. In brief, the community is "inoperative" (*désœuvrée*): "Community necessarily takes place in what Blanchot has called 'unworking' (*désœuvrement*), referring to that which, before or beyond the work, withdraws from the work, and which, no longer having to do either with production or with completion, encounters interruption, fragmentation, suspension.[39] Herder already points to this unworking when he formulates the effect of church music as "an annihilation and melting away before God." Yet it is the writings of Wilhelm Heinrich Wackenroder that best evoke this sense of transindividual, quasi-mystical community in the experience of sacred music. As something sublime, it overpowers any concept of selfhood, it floods over the path to subjectivity. This is the case not only for the listener but also for the one who sings out the liturgy. With a voice before speech, the singular is heard before signification, before the articulation of meaning, and yet it is still heard, being shared in a community.

Of especial interest is the fact that Wackenroder deploys the resources of the sublime and the sacred in order to inscribe into his text aspects of life that might be believed to evade representation. His *Berglinger* novella, a highly autobiographical tale about an emotionally unstable composer, allows music and madness—as metaphors of nonrepresentability—to unwork the language of representation. Wackenroder has therefore set himself an impossible task: to write an autobiography that would save the self from autobiographical ensnarement, from reduction and falsehood. Are metaphors of nonrepresentability sufficient means for revealing aspects of the self that are taken to be unrepresentable, "before or beyond the work"? Or are they doomed from the very moment they are worked into a text? Then again, these questions may be too naive. Congruent with the Longinian sublime, even a failure is a success, as long as the failure is brilliant.

WACKENRODER'S *BERGLINGER* NOVELLA

In *Das merkwürdige musikalische Leben des Tonkünstlers Joseph Berglinger* (The strange musical Life of the composer Joseph Berglinger, 1797), Wackenroder liberally incorporates ideas and descriptions of the sublime inherited from Longinus, Burke, and Herder. His exploitation of the themes discussed so far (music's nonmimetic character, the loss of rational control in listening, the ecstatic community) formulates an important assessment of musical experience as something analogous to experiences of madness. His *Berglinger* therefore anticipates in many respects Kleist's *Heilige Cäcilie*, which portrays four brothers driven insane by the "power of music" (*Gewalt der Musik*). Both stories demonstrate a tension between verbal language, which abets reflective cognition, and music, which is grounded in immediate feeling. In this way, they bring out the ambivalent aspects of music's sublimity, as something both desirable and dangerous.

Beyond Kleist, Wackenroder's text played a considerable role in determining later philosophies of music, especially in the writings of Friedrich Schlegel and Arthur Schopenhauer, for its insistence on both the autonomy of art and music's capacity to articulate dimensions of human experience irreducible to verbal language. Although still grounded in the culture of *Empfindsamkeit* and its accompanying aesthetics of music as the expression of passions (*Ausdrucksästhetik*), Wackenroder's description of musical processes and effects already moves toward a new, nonrepresentational paradigm. Here music is less a "language of expression" and more an art of pure self-reference, what Berglinger refers to (in an allusion to Kant) as a "play of tones" ("Spiel der Töne" [*WW* 1.134/149]). The contradictory tension between expression and self-reference, between communication and noncommunication, rehearses the age-old *querelle* between the "melodists" and the "harmonists."[40] For the *Berglinger* novella, which is divided into two clearly demarcated parts, the terms and ramifications of this debate are concretely dramatized.

The tension polarizes the social world of productivity and the metaphysical sphere of art, which is essentially asocial. In short, the outer world is opposed to the inner realm of the imagination. This division engenders Wackenroder's figure of the isolated artist, who must struggle with the conflicting demands of expression, which is bound to the social world of communication, and the pure self-reference of his art. In this sense, Wackenroder's influence on literature was especially great. The disparity between a transcendent realm of musical fantasy and the quotidian world of noise represents a core feature of Hoffmann's versions of the composer-figure (for example, Ritter Gluck and Johannes Kreisler). The conflicts that the eccentric artist suffers in relation to the world around him reemerge in Grillparzer's mad violinist (*Der arme Spielmann*) and later in the mysterious association of music and death that structures the early work of Thomas Mann, from Hanno Buddenbrook's sickly fascination to Gabriele Klöterjahn's fatal Wagnerism (*Tristan*).

The Violent Power of Tones

The *Berglinger* novella relates the life of the young man as a kind of *Sonderling*: a misfit who fails to conform to his father's expectations and societal duties. Instead of following his father's wishes and studying medicine, he is compelled toward something "higher," that is, toward the religiously sublime art of music. "No one could fit into this family less than Joseph, who was always existing in a realm of beautiful fantasy ["in schöner Einbildung"] and divine dreams" (WW 1.131/147). The story is the final piece in Wackenroder's only published collection, the *Herzensergießungen eines kunstliebenden Klosterbruders* (Outpourings of the heart of an art-loving friar), which appeared less than a year before his untimely death at the age of twenty-four. Evidently, the pseudonymity of the stories, here attributed to a monk devoted to art, was also to characterize Wackenroder's second collection, *Phantasien über die Kunst* (Fantasies on art, 1799), the essays of which, on various topics in music, are put forward as Berglinger's own work.

The autobiographical gestures are highly pronounced. Like Berglinger's father, who "abhorred all the arts as servants of unrestrained desires and passions" (WW 1.134/150), Wackenroder's father had little respect for musicians, whom he regarded as base entertainers.[41] Wackenroder rejected his father's plans for him to study law and enter into a governmental career. Instead, he studied composition and associated himself with Berlin's musical circles, Carl Friedrich Fasch, Carl Friedrich Zelter, and Johann Friedrich Reichardt. Wackenroder's letters to his close friend Ludwig Tieck, who published the *Phantasien* posthumously, express a passionate love for music that closely corresponds with the statements of his fictitious composer. Thus Wackenroder legitimizes Berglinger's "fantasies" by putting forth a prefacing "recollection" (*Vorerinnerung*): "[Berglinger's] views on art agreed [*stimmten*] with mine most extraordinarily and, through frequent mutual confessions of our hearts ["Ergießungen unsers Herzens"], our feelings became more and more intimately allied" (*ww* 1.199/174). The hearts, attuned (*gestimmt*) like two instruments in unison, share their outpourings. The autobiographical gesture is unambiguous and in fact coercive: Wackenroder the anonymous writer should be heard in Berglinger: a textualized, pseudonymous self who himself writes. A semiotics of reflection is thereby established that not only allows Berglinger to refer to Wackenroder but also condones an eradication of the line that generally divides life from work. Incidentally, the uncanniness of this double is greatly augmented for us when we read at the conclusion of the *Berglinger* novella that Wackenroder foretells his very own fate in having his composer die "in the springtime of his years," also from a "nervous condition" (*ww* 1.144/159). As I shall demonstrate, the semiotics of reflection—including the metaphor of "tuning" (*stimmen*) and personal voices (*Stimmen*)—is aptly supported by romantic conceptions of what music means and implies.

In presenting the story of the composer's "strange life," the narrating friar has turned away from visual artists of the distant past (Raphael, Leonardo, Dürer, and so forth) to a contemporary musical artist. The emphatic shift from "past centuries" to "present times" (*ww* 1.130/146) underscores the relevance of music in conceiving a new, modern aesthetics that should be formulated in opposition to visual paradigms that are now somehow outmoded. As in Burke's reply to Dubos, aesthetic experience, from the point of view of both creation and reception, should be broadened to include a definition of the meaningfulness of art that rests not only on the basis of the clarity obtained by vision but also on the basis of the obscure. The eye should yield place to the ear. As a complement to beauty, which emerges in the space lying between the work and the observer, there is the sublime power of acoustic phenomena, whose nonsolid, invisible material resides internally in the listener's imagination.

Unlike the friar's essays on past masters of the Renaissance, the *Berglinger* novella is able to turn to personal testimony. The composer, the narrator explains, was his "closest friend" (*ww* 1.130/146). Despite this emphasis on present life and the living, however, the story is shaped entirely by an ascetic impulse that strains to escape the here and now. Accordingly, Berglinger's life begins in death: "His mother departed from the world while placing him into it" (WW 1.130/147). The detail may have been borrowed from Rousseau's autobiography: "I cost my mother her life, and my birth was the first of my misfortunes" (*Confessions*, ROC 1.7/19). Jean-Jacques's lifelong guilt over his mother's death—a judgment apparently promulgated by his widowed father—colors the writer's longing for maternal nature, which includes his obsession with an original unity of melody and speech. Analogously, Berglinger's uncontainable passion for music is directed toward sacred, feminine figures: Cecilia, the patron saint of music, and the Virgin Mary. Music becomes a project of retrieval, of return to a transcendent and redemptive place in the mother's presence: transcendent because it is a place before birth and redemptive because it marks a point before this life, that is, before the life that took his mother's life away. Consequently, the workaday world of the father is the site of the mother's absence. Music alone seems capable of bridging the divide.

While struggling with the medical textbook that his father forced on him, Berglinger dreams of the oratorio that had made an especially strong impression. It is the first piece of music he ever heard performed, and its melody never ceases to haunt. Tellingly, it sings of a mother's pain and a son's suffering: "Stabat Mater dolorosa / Iuxta crucem lacrymosa, / Dum pendebat filius" (WW 1.135/151). The narrator describes Berglinger's first musical experience in the cathedral as a transition from the "unmelodious" ordinariness of the gathered people to the beautiful heights of another realm:

Before the music started, when he was standing in the dense, softly murmuring crowd of people ["in dem gedrängten, leise-murmelnden Gewimmel der Volksmenge"], it seemed to him as if he were hearing the ordinary and commonplace life of men, bustling unmelodiously amidst each other and all around him like a large annual fair. . . . He expectantly awaited the first sound of the instruments;—and when it now broke forth out of the heavy stillness, mighty and sustained, like the blowing of a wind from heaven, and the full violent power of the sounds ["die ganze Gewalt der Töne"] passed over his head,—then it seemed to him as if suddenly huge wings were stretched forth from his soul, as if he were being lifted up from a barren heath, the gloomy curtain of clouds disappearing before his mortal eyes, and he floating up to the luminous heaven.

(WW 1.132/148)

Music removes the chosen one from the demotic morass. Typically, metaphors of darkness, desolation, and gloom provide a negative foil for the light of redemption. It is a description of spiritual transport directly aligned with the Longinian sublime but now reformulated in a decidedly Catholic environment.[42]

It is not fortuitous that Wackenroder set his story "in a little town in southern Germany" (ww 1.97/147) as opposed to the reformed, secularized milieu of his native Berlin. While studying jurisprudence in Erlangen, Wackenroder traveled throughout Catholic Franconia and Bavaria, including an impressionable visit to Bamberg in July 1793. In a report to his parents, Wackenroder confessed it was a "journey, in which [I] got to know what is especially for me an entirely new world, the Catholic world" (ww 2.194). The trip was occasioned by a mistake: he planned to attend the Feast of St. Henry to celebrate the Holy Roman Emperor, whose feast day, July 13, marked Wackenroder's own birthday (hence the author's middle name, Heinrich). When he arrived, however, he learned that, as usual, the procession had been postponed eight days to accommodate the cathedral clergy, who had to attend the feast in Würzburg. Despite the initial disappointment, Wackenroder eventually came to enjoy his stay, thanks to a chance encounter with a priest named Sauer, who generously accompanied the young student to all the sites of the city, which, like the eternal city, is built on seven hills. Wackenroder's report on this "German Rome" includes an extensive description of the cathedral, which contains the graves of Kaiser Heinrich and his wife, Kunegunde. It was here, while attending the mass for St. Henry's Day, that Wackenroder "fell to his knees" as he witnessed the Catholic celebration—the prayers, the hymns, and the music—in which "the entire world around [him] receded and everything disposed [him] to the utmost devotion"—"da eine ganze Welt um mich herum niedersank, und mich alles zur höchsten Andacht stimmte"—"here it seemed to me as though I did not belong to mankind"—"mir würde hier gewesen seyn, als gehörte ich nicht zu den Menschen" (ww 2.204). Thus, according to this piece of self-portraiture, the young law student arrived to commemorate his name day and ended up immersed in a sublime experience that obliterated the mundane and his connection to it.

It is this fundamentally Catholic experience that was reworked in the *Berglinger* novella, where the protagonist, "humbly on his knees in inward devotion [*Andacht*]," suffers the "violent power [*Gewalt*] of tones" that bears him to heaven's light. The identity between Berglinger and Wackenroder, which the author later promulgates, creates a mildly intertextual scene, which can be elucidated by the difference between mimesis and semiosis refined by Michael Riffaterre.[43] The mimetic narrative in *Berglinger* (a student from southern Germany travels to the bishop's see) may be interrupted by engaging semiotically with the author's letter (Wackenroder, a young man from Berlin, travels to Bamberg). In other words, the name Berglinger no longer functions transparently in the mimetic course of the story but rather becomes a sign that halts the narrative line and points the reader to the biography of the story's author. The mimetic flow is suspended, its direction is unworked, which allows the reader to see not meaning (as it transparently sits on the page), but rather the making of meaning. Specifically, Berglinger's rapture acquires further meaning when referred to the Protestantism of Wackenroder's birth. That is to say, the hero's religious ecstasy takes on the significance of a conversion.

Kleist formulates his own story on the "Gewalt der Musik" in terms of the hyperrationalized, iconoclastic fervor of the north in contrast to the immediate, musical force of Catholicism. Yet he does so by including the theme of conversion in the mimetic order of the narrative itself. What makes Wackenroder's *Berglinger* particularly striking, in my view, is that it energizes the literary form itself in order to unwork conventional modes of description. This process is accomplished in at least two ways: first, by coercively identifying the writer and the protagonist and, second, as I shall show presently, by turning to experiences generally regarded as nonrepresentational—nonverbal music and mad, inexpressible ecstasy. In both cases, the transparency of the written sign is blocked. In both, mimesis yields to semiosis, offering the reader an insight not only into what words mean but also how they mean.

A further look into the development of the novella illustrates the point. The *Gewalt* of the oratorio lifts Berglinger away from earth; it removes him from the dull circumstances of his existence, including his existence as a human subject in the world. The *unio mystica* eradicates the personal identity that his father hoped to give his son so that he might lead a productive life and be useful to the community. Yet, as Kleist's fraternal, iconoclastic horde will discover, the irresistible might of church music can rob one of one's mind and one's mission. Thus Wackenroder's enthusiast regards Saint Cecilia's power as inducing mental derangement, *Verrücktheit*:

> Siehe wie ich trostlos weine
> In dem Kämmerlein alleine,
> 　Heilige Cäcilia!
> Sieh mich aller Welt entfliehen,
> Um hier still vor dir zu knien:
> 　Ach ich bete, sei mir nah!

Deine wunderbaren Töne,
Denen ich verzaubert fröne,
  Haben mein Gemüt verrückt.

(Behold how I weep inconsolably
In my little chamber alone,
  Saint Cecilia!
Behold how I flee from all the world,
To kneel here silently before you:
  Ah, I pray, come near!

Your wondrous tones,
In which I indulge enchantedly,
  Have deranged my soul.)

(WW 1.136/152; TRANSLATION MODIFIED)

Berglinger's sanity is saved, we learn in the novella's second half, but only at the cost of losing touch with music's sublime power. Several years have passed. Thanks to the generosity of a close relative, Joseph was able to receive formal musical training and subsequently gain the post of conductor of the town's orchestra. In his letter to the narrator, Berglinger complains of his present, disenchanted situation. The mathematical rules that he was required to learn, the entire "grammar of art" that he was compelled to master, have created a kind of "cage" that prevents his spirit from flight. To use Herder's terms, the composer has been forced to spatialize his art. Music is no longer maddening but rather a servile means of entertainment, dependent on the vagaries of court patronage. As it follows, he is unable, as a musician, to stir the emotions, neither his audiences' nor his own. It seems as if the everyday world of productivity and usefulness— a world that had always been represented by the father—has now contaminated the realm of music, which once served as the single mode of escape. Tellingly, it is only when Joseph learns of his father's impending death that he is able to pour his heart out into a Passion Mass, which at last has a profound effect. The wished-for return of the sublime, however, is not without its fatal consequences. The mass is so demanding, so violently taxing on his nerves, that the young man soon succumbs to a fever that takes his life. The friar concludes his biography: "His lofty fantasy destroyed him" (WW 1.144/159).

Music, together with the madness it entails, is therefore ambivalent. It rids Joseph of his artistic impotence while consigning him to destruction. Optimistically viewed, the ecstasy of creativity saves him from an everyday existence that he considers to be no life at all. His revulsion from the "unmelodic" crowd is evident enough. From a more pessimistic point of view, however, his annihilation is presented as all too real. Analogously, Joseph is hardly indifferent toward his father's dying. On the contrary, he is profoundly saddened. The two men are reconciled at the deathbed—"they understood each other very deeply ["sehr inniglich"] without many words" (ww 1.143/158). The near-wordlessness, the inward exchange or the needlessness for outward forms of communication, in fact confirms the proximity of death, for it verges on the condition of art, which for Joseph, as for the friar, is always "unspeakable."

As the father's earlier position implied, art negates life. In passing his name on to the son, he set aside a possible life of societal value for him. What Berglinger discovers is that this possibility is conditioned by the absence of art. Accordingly, Joseph becomes successful only when art ceases to be art, that is, when it becomes a "grammar," a formalizable, rule-bound technique akin to language. But what kind of language? There are in fact many ways to conceive of language's work. For example, in an earlier essay from the *Herzensergießungen* ("Von zwey wunderbaren Sprachen und deren geheimnißvoller Kraft"), the friar writes on the "languages of art and nature," whose "mysterious power" distinguishes them from the "language of words": "We rule over the entire globe by means of words; with easy effort we acquire for ourselves through trade all the treasures of the earth by means of words. Only the *invisible force which hovers over us* ["*das Unsichtbare, das über uns schwebt*"] is not drawn down into our hearts by words" (ww 1.97/118; emphasis in original). The language of words allows us to govern and manipulate the world. This power is due to the fact that the words themselves are distinct from and transcendent to the reality they describe. As abstractions, words exist apart from the world to which they refer. Rather than viewing this rational control over the world as a benefit, the friar considers the disjuncture between words and things as a problem. The antiverbalism expressed here bemoans the implicit separation, namely, what divides his mind from his heart. Music, by contrast, promises a utopian nonverbal language: a language of immediacy, free of all the mechanisms that pose a barrier to one's experience, free of syntax, semantics, and grammar.

The *Berglinger* novella, however, as a piece of literature, seems to qualify this exuberance. The desire for "the invisible" (*das Unsichtbare*) threatens to render the enthusiast himself invisible. Indeed, at the story's conclusion, art, which had first taken him away from the father who lived, dispatches him to the mother who, from the beginning, is dead. His "lofty fantasy destroyed him."[44] The burning question that Wackenroder will impart to later forms of German romanticism is whether it is possible to devote oneself to art without exiling oneself from human society, either in the ascetic sphere of the friar or in death. In its capacity to represent the nonrepresentational (music and madness), literature appears to offer a solution.

The Manifest, the Latent, and the Hypogram

On the level of simple narration, the fatal danger of music and art questions the desirability of Berglinger's longing. Yet it also interrogates the benefits of a cognitively controlled language of words. Especially in the case of self-representation, there is the problem that the sign will never coincide with its referent. Music attracts Berglinger because it seems to overcome the gap endemic to the use of verbal signifiers, but it ultimately may also be the source of exile and madness. The dilemma is clear. Either the writer restricts himself to a manipulative process that subjugates the world—and thereby implicitly subjugates himself as well—or he effaces himself in a musical ecstasy that obliterates his relation to the world in which he lives. The Berglinger vita directly addresses this predicament, but not on the single level of the plot. Rather, music and madness disrupt the clear and clean working of plot-driven language and instead create a language that reaps the benefits of art without suffering the consequences. If the text achieves this ideal, it is, as I have already suggested above, because it disturbs the mimetic flow of representational language by introducing se-miotic forces. What I would like to concentrate on in this final section, then, is the particular kind of semiosis that is based on the tension between a manifest and a latent discourse.

In a later essay from the posthumous *Phantasien*, "The Characteristic Inner Nature of the Musical Art" ("Das eigenthümliche innere Wesen der Tonkunst"), Berglinger first chides those who approach music "scientif-ically": "Rather than welcoming that which is beautiful, like a friend, on all pathways where it presents itself to us in a friendly manner, they regard their art as a dangerous enemy instead, seek to subdue it in the most perilous ambush ["im gefährlichsten Hinterhalt"], and triumph thereupon over their own strength [*Kraft*]" (*WW* 1.217/189). As in Kant's scenario, such theorists counter the sublime with "their own strength [or power, *Kraft*]"; they attempt to use verbal language to master what they perceive to be an inimical encounter. Face to face with so dangerous a force, the scientific investigator is eager to prove the superiority of his rationality: the greater the threat, the more triumphant the victory. Through knowledge, the subject should verify its sovereign position. Yet, as Berglinger con-tinues, the power of music is not so easily subdued: "Whenever all the inner vibrations of the heartstrings—the trembling ones of joy, the tempestuous ones of rapture, the rapidly beating pulse of all-consuming adoration—when all these burst apart with *one* outcry the language of words, as the *grave* of the inner fury of the heart ["das *Grab* der innern Herzenswuth"]—then they go forth under a strange sky, amidst the vibrations of blessed harp strings, in transfigured beauty as if in another life beyond this one, and celebrate as angelic figures their resurrection" (*WW* 1.219/190–91; emphasis in original). The sublimity of music overpowers subjective integrity. The rational use of language, which grounds personal identity, is redefined as a tomb—*ein Grab*—that can barely contain the "fury" (*Wuth*) within. Instead of maintaining integrity before the violent power, the subject is consumed. The auto-da-fé carries the listener to a "life beyond this one."

The hymnal celebration of divine rapture and heavenly resurrection does not conceal the fact that we are dealing with a death, albeit metaphorical. Further in the essay, the ecstasy occasioned by music is therefore repeatedly coded as "mad": a "madly bold power" ("tollkühne Kraft"); an "almost mad pantomimic dance" ("fast wahnsinnigen pantominischen Tanz"); a "mad spontaneity" ("wahnsinnige Willkühr") (1.222/193). Despite Berglinger's enthusiasm, the sublimity of music either kills or drives one mad.

Wackenroder's version of musical madness unworks language in a way that is structurally similar to Diderot's. Both imply a power that does violence to the personal subject. Whereas the bizarre performances of the nephew broke apart identities to expose radical difference, however, Berglinger's experience of the sublime hurls formed identities into the flames of the supraindividual divine. In *Le neveu*, mere evanescent life is abstracted into a rational subject that endures across time, while in *Berglinger*, subjecthood is dissolved into an indefinable absolute. The implicit progression is in fact not far removed from Hegel's dialectic, which turns on representability. In the *Phenomenology*, the nonrepresentational immediacy of sense certainty passes through moments of figuration in various shapes of consciousness only to arrive ultimately at the nonrepresentable absolute. Why, then, does Berglinger emphatically describe this final step as a maddening experience?

The pathologization of divine rapture—written, we should recall, by a young Berliner fascinated with Catholic Franconia—registers a certain degree of resistance. It acknowledges that dissolution into the divine is no less a death than abstraction into representational form. The protest can only be expressed in writing, in "outpourings" that are, after all, literature. As an art of words, literature seems to allow the invisible to irradiate the language it shares with the quotidian. The language of literature—as a language of art—transforms the "heart's grave" into the heart's home. It is important to note that the essays that comprise the *Herzensergießungen* are devoted first to the visual arts and then to music, with no mention of the literary art to which they themselves belong. As pieces of literature, the essays seem incapable of turning literature itself into an explicit topic. Nonetheless, the opposition thematized by the *Berglinger* novella, between useful productivity and useless creativity, is overcome by writing, which enlists the mechanisms of language (its grammar, its lexicon, and so forth) for the higher aims of art.[45] In this way, literature resolves the fateful aporia facing the doomed composer, between a practical existence, which is no life at all, and a creative one, which kills. In pouring his heart out in music, Berglinger dies, while the friar who writes his "heart's outpourings" survives.

In Wackenroder's essays, literature may be said to be the latent topic beneath a manifest discourse devoted to visual art and music. It is important to note that the relation between the manifest and the latent is not one of synthesis but rather negation. The presence of one suppresses the presence of the other. On the grand level, we can either read the *Herzensergießungen* and *Phantasien* as essays manifestly about painting and music or as essays that latently refer to literature. The "Wesen der Tonkunst" essay quoted above already specified the relation as one of negation: the "language of words" negate the "language of the heart," and presumably vice versa.

This play of negation is also brilliantly carried out by the name Berglinger itself. I have already alluded to the coerced identity between Berglinger and Wackenroder, which forestalls the flow of mimetic narrative and thereby permits the text to acquire further meaning, as in my example, where an experience of ecstasy comes to be understood as one of conversion. This identity appears to be promulgated in yet another fashion, namely, in the semiotics of the hypogram elaborated by Ferdinand de Saussure. Alongside his lectures on language theory (*Cours de linguistique générale*), Saussure maintained notebooks that examined what he believed to be an organizing principle in Vedic hymns, Latin verse, and even early Germanic epic. These investigations, partially published posthumously in 1964, went on to motivate similar work in the poetic theory of Jean Starobinski, Roman Jakobson, Julia Kristeva, and others.[46] Without going into the complexities and distinctions of Saussure's terminology, I would like to mention the principal idea, namely, that in these ancient texts, there could be detected a theme word, usually left unsaid and primarily a proper name, say, of a divinity, an author, or a patron. That this kind of semiotic determination relies on a tension of manifest and latent discourse is clear. As Saussure's observations strive to demonstrate, the hypogram—literally an *Unterschrift* or "signature"—is an insertion into the text of what is outside the text, analogous therefore to the author's signature.[47] What I would like to suggest is that Wackenroder's text contains precisely this kind of determining sign, not in the author's own given name but rather in the magical name he gave himself.

Simply put, the written expression of a maddening (enervating, fatal) musical experience lets Wackenroder (the Protestant *Berliner*) *rescue* and *hide* himself—*bergen* and *verbergen*—in the Catholic figure of *Berglinger*. The semiosis moreover introduces the place of renewed baptism and conversion—Bam*berg*. Again, the plot-driven force of verbal language is made to decelerate or come to a complete stop. Its transparency as a signifier in the text—referring to the story's protagonist—is blocked and instead made to refer to a figure outside the text. The name Berglinger becomes a semiotic repository wherein meanings accumulate. It thereby becomes a sign that negates the name's function in the story's manifest plot. The "language of words, as the *grave* of the inner fury of the heart"— "als das *Grab* der innern Herzenswuth"—is literally reversed in its tracks. Wackenroder's emphasis—*Grab*—inversely spells out the radical of the hero's name (GRB/BRG) as well as the semiotic conglomeration of conversion, concealment, and Catholic Bamberg.

The name, materially composed of letters, engages a referent that always exceeds referential language. The expropriating threat of representation is defused by holding on to the letters as letters. It is as though the text wants to insist on the material ground of representation and thereby prevent that substance from moving to a second level of immaterial sense. It is a Marsyan strategy through and through that tries to import immediacy in the midst of mediation. The words are to be heard as tones whose sensuous presence is irresistible and possibly sublime. For the semiotic shift outside the text is not the same as the double articulation of symbols. The material sign does not transparently yield to meaning, but rather one sensuous presence is replaced by another. But how, one might ask, can this new language prevent itself from being reenlisted into yet another alienating scheme? Can writing be redeemed? Or is it only a fool's delusion?

The heart wants to be heard, but a heart poured out is no longer living. At the conclusion of the "Wesen der Tonkunst" essay, Berglinger despairs over the inadequacy of words as vehicles of reference. He prays for a sublime experience that would remove him from this world where high art all too readily becomes a mere product of exchange. In other words, he prays for an end to all representation, which always imports a gap and is moreover always a representation for others. "But why do I, foolish one [*Thörichter*], strive to melt words into tones? It is never as I feel it. Come, Thou musical strains, draw near and save me from this painful earthly striving for words, envelop me in Thy shining clouds with Thy thousand-fold beams, and raise me up into the old embrace of all-loving heaven" (*ww* 1.223/194). Wackenroder's *Berglinger* texts turn to the sublimity of madness-inducing music in order to appropriate verbal language. The essays strive to melt words, like the word "Berglinger" itself, into a single tone that may hold many meanings. In this way, the author should be able to place himself—his heart—into the text without the text betraying or mortifying his nonrepresentable life. It is the alter ego, the textualized self, that is to go mad and die in the author's place. Wackenroder seems to want to circumvent the problem of representation ("it is never as I feel it"). But is this project possible? It simultaneously desires a sublime, nonrepresentable music and a literature capable of representing the nonrepresentable. In the end, writing seems to consume itself. It is possible to regard the texts' semiotic energy as liberating some nonmediated mere life—understood as that which cannot possibly enter into writing—but then again it can also be seen as yet another name for the heart's grave.

5

With Arts Unknown Before

KLEIST AND THE POWER OF MUSIC

H EINRICH VON Kleist's haunting tale of music and madness *Die heilige Cäcilie oder die Gewalt der Musik* (*St. Cecilia or the Power of Music*, 1810–11) deftly rehearses the major motifs of the sublime. Four brothers arrive at a church, intending an iconoclastic riot at the height of the Reformation, and fall to their knees during the liturgical performance by an orchestra of nuns. Whereas the brothers originally came to the cloister armed with the Kantian *Gewalt* of reason, they leave dumbfounded, annihilated before the divine *Gewalt* of music. They spend the rest of their days confined to a mental asylum, where they sit in silence, forming crucifixes from pieces of birch. At midnight, every single night, year after year, they suddenly rise from their table to sing the very "Gloria in excelsis" that occasioned their descent into madness. Their individual, subjective existence has melted into the uncanny *communauté désœuvrée* of the madhouse. Despite the plurality of the protagonists, the autobiographical impulse (that is, as in Wackenroder, against autobiography) can be readily traced. In other words, Kleist's tale illustrates again how the unworking of language effects an eradication of the boundary between life and art. As I shall presently show, for Kleist, music and madness had always been synonymous with this unworking.

MUSIC, REFLECTION, AND IMMEDIACY
IN KLEIST'S LETTERS

A letter from Würzburg to his fiancée portrays the writer in a state of desperation: "And still no word from you, my *dear* friend? Is there then no messenger who could deliver [*herübertragen*] a line from you to me? Is there then no more connection between us, no paths, no bridges? Has an abyss caved in [*eingesunken*] between us...? Have you passed on from this earth, so that no further thought from you reaches [*herüberkommt*] me, as from another world?"[1] Kleist's theme of unbearable separation, underscored by the prefix *herüber-* (from over there), continues in this key. Complaints of hopelessness and distrust, bemoaning the gulf that has opened up between him and his beloved, are expressed in a series of frantic, self-conscious questions addressed to one absent, confided to a page that may or may not reach its destination. The anxiety abates only when Kleist recalls an experience three years past, as he journeyed across the Harz Mountains at night, "wandering lost in the darkness that prevailed over [him]" ("ich irrte nur, so lange die Finsternis über mich waltete"). The verb for "prevailing" (*walten*) lightly evokes the presence of the power (*Gewalt*) that hangs over him. As the sun began to rise from behind the mountains, as light "poured out over the friendly meadows," he "saw and heard, and felt, and now sensed with all [his] senses, that [he] had before [him] a paradise" (KSW 2.568). This morning paradise of sensory plenitude is what Kleist promises his Wilhelmine—"das *verspreche* ich Dir" (Kleist's emphasis). In this way, the nighttime wanderings serve as an allegory not only of the writer's distress but also of Wilhelmine's concern over her fiancé's absence. The letter adumbrates a dark night of the soul that promises to lead the couple to resplendent salvation.

At least initially, then, this letter of September 19, 1800, presents a brief narrative, from a night of errancy, loss, and anxious reflection to a dawn of redemption and clarity. Its coherence replicates the structure fundamental to Judeo-Christian myth. It alludes either to the story of Creation, to the beginning of history, where Edenic light dispelled the covering darkness, or to the Apocalypse, to the end of history, where the heavenly Jerusalem will receive the faithful. Thus anxiety yields to calm. Confusion is dissolved by reflection. The dark straying is overcome by a self-affirmation, by the establishment of an autonomous subject that rationally processes what it sees, hears, and feels.

The letter's continuation, however, opens up these narrative forms, these beginnings and endings, by turning to an experience of that which precedes the darkness, of something that comes before the beginning, and, for that reason, possibly after the end.

Sometimes—I don't know whether you've ever been fortunate to experience something similar and thus whether you're able to accept it as true. But, whenever I go off alone at dusk, against the blowing gust of the west wind, and especially when I then close my eyes, I sometimes hear entire, complete concerts, with every instrument from the tender flute to the booming [*rauschenden*] contrabass. Thus I recall one time especially, as a young man some nine years ago, when I walked up toward the Rhine and simultaneously against the evening wind, and so the waves of air and water resounded simultaneously around me ["mich umtönten"], I heard a melting Adagio, with all the magic of music ["Zauber der Musik"], with all the melodic phrases and the entire accompanying harmony. It was like an orchestral effect, like a complete Vauxhall ["wie ein vollständiges Vaux-hall"]; indeed, I actually believe, everything that the wise men of Greece wrote of the harmony of the spheres could not have been softer, more beautiful, more heavenly than this peculiar reverie ["als diese seltsame Träumerei"].

(KSW 2.568–69)

The crepuscular experience, together with the childhood reminiscence, represents a prehistory to the nighttime chaos of fear and worry. The "magic of music" ("Zauber der Musik") therefore also marks a posthistory to the redemption had by reflection. Dusk is a time before thought, before the reflection that always chases away the heavenly resonance heard in his inner ear: "I can repeat this concert, without orchestra, as often as I wish—however, as soon as a *thought* [*Gedanke*] intervenes, at once all is gone, as though spirited away [*weggezaubert*] by the magical: *disparois!* Melody, harmony, sound [*Klang*], in short, the entire music of the spheres" (KSW 2.569; emphasis in original). Thought is the magic word that dispels music's magic. Its return cannot be willfully obtained. Subjective intention, which is grounded in the mind's capacity to think, would by definition only block the reenchantment from occurring. For the music to return, it would appear necessary to enter a state prior to reflection, prior to yet another form, the form of subjectivity. Thus, Kleist goes on to report, he merely stands by the window at sundown with eyes closed, exposing his "breast to the evening breeze streaming in." His listening explicitly excludes thinking ("denke nichts, und horche"). Only then, perhaps, will there arrive "a sound [*Laut*] from *her*" (ibid.).

A series of emphatic questions, however, disrupts the silent attentiveness, disabling the readiness to listen: "*Does she live? Does she love* (me)?" The questions introduce both reflection and self-reflection—indeed, iconically so, by the slight but significant parenthetical insertion of the first-person pronoun. "*Does she live? Does she love* (me) ["*Lebt sie? Liebt sie* (mich)]? This is what I *think*—and gone is the entire resounding orchestra ["das ganze tönende Orchester"], nothing more can be heard save the ringing of the prayer bells from the cathedral's towers" (KSW 2.569; emphasis in original). It is the subject of thinking that authorizes the paronomasia ("Lebt *sie*? Liebt *sie*?") that signals the permutation from

the Rhine," and Wieland's own youthful collection, *Sympathies*. "My heart melted beneath so many inspiring impressions, my mind fluttered voluptuously, like a butterfly over honey-scented flowers, my entire being was driven by an invisible power [*Gewalt*], like a peach-blossom-apart [*Fürsichblüte*][3] of the morning air—It was as if I had earlier been a dead instrument, and now, suddenly presented with the sense of hearing, I would be enraptured by my own proper [*eignen*] harmonies" (July 28–29, 1801, *KSW* 2.673). Here sensory plenitude is associated both with music and invisible *Gewalt*. The letter rehearses the current idea, emphasized by Herder, that the human body is itself a resounding musical instrument. The statements also reflect a new assessment of wordless music, which the previous century had so regularly denigrated as senseless. Kleist's "butterfly" may in fact be alluding to a similar remark from Goethe's *Wilhelm Meisters Lehrjahre* (1795–96) that still insists, although not unambiguously, on the neoclassical demand that music play a role subservient to language. Goethe writes: "The instrument should only accompany the voice; for melodies, passages, and phrases without words and meaning [*Sinn*] seem to me to resemble butterflies or colorful birds."[4] For Kleist, it is precisely the wordlessness and senselessness that transform the Rhine valley into a "pleasure garden." The river passes through, creating two banks, "making two Paradises out of one." The description comes very close to the one written to Wilhelmine some months before: "Ah, I recall that sometimes in my rapture [*Entzückung*], when I close my eyes, especially one time, as I went strolling along the Rhine, as the waves of air and the river resounded simultaneously around me, I heard an entirely complete symphony, the melody and all accompanying chords, from the tender flute to the booming [*rauschenden*] contrabass. It sounded to me like church music, and I believe that everything the poets tell us about the music of the spheres was not as alluring as this peculiar reverie" (*KSW* 2.674). Here, too, natural sounds merge with an inner music. As in Herder's *Cäcilia* essay and Wackenroder's *Berglinger* novella, the sublime experience is associated with the sacred in contrast to the secular. The recollection from an irretrievable past therefore colors the present time of reflection as one of pain, separation, and fear—a fall from paradise. The implications of Herder's describing the reception of or participation in church music as an "annihilation and melting away" ("Vernichtung und Zerschmelzung") of the human subject is here made explicit: the secularized time of the present is grounded in an individual consciousness—what Herder names "character"—that introduces division and anguish. The "reverie" in which Kleist's heart once "melted" (*schmolz*) has been replaced by well-contoured and contour-forming ego. In a line from the *Cäcilia* essay that would not go unnoticed by Kleist, Herder denounces characterizing tendencies in modern church music as a "forbidden fruit."[5]

The opposition between paradisiacal grace and postlapsarian reflection is of course the central theme of Kleist's celebrated essay *Über das Marionettentheater*, first published in his *Berliner Abendblätter* in December 1810. The text is set up as a dialogue between a first-person narrator and a certain Herr C. that takes place in the winter of 1801 in the city of M—, referring perhaps to Mainz, the location of his adolescent reverie.[6] The conversation turns on Herr C., a professional dancer, who is obsessed by the marionettes that, in his opinion, display far more grace than the most proficient of human dancers. Moving under the puppeteer's control, the dolls are able to transcend "bare" gravitational force ("dem bloßen Gesetz der Schwere"), which impedes human performance (*KSW* 2.342). The puppets cannot know this higher power—they cannot be conscious of it—but it is precisely this lack of consciousness that allows them to exhibit incomparable grace. Hence the essay's striking conclusion: "We see that in the organic world, grace appears more radiantly and powerfully ["strahlender und herrschender"] in the measure by which reflection [*Reflexion*] becomes darker and weaker ["dunkler und schwächer"]" (345). Just as in the Wilhelmine letter thought obliterates the paradisiacal music, so is grace destroyed by the act of conscious reflection.

Gravity's bareness, or *Blöße*, which marks the human dancer's gracelessness, is a condition of the fall of mankind. Over the course of the dialogue, Herr C. makes two distinct references to the third chapter of the book of Genesis. Upon describing a dancer, whose gestures betray a soul pitifully located in the elbow, he comments: "Such mistakes [*Mißgriffe*] . . . are unavoidable, ever since we ate from the Tree of Knowledge. Indeed, Paradise is bolted shut, and the Cherub is behind us" (342). Further on, when his interlocutor seems to be losing the thread of the argument, Herr C. reproaches him, saying that he has not "read the third chapter of Moses' first book attentively" (343). The implication is clear: instead of receiving what the serpent had promised—to open their eyes, to make them equal to gods, to have knowledge of good and evil—Adam and Eve obtain only mortality, their eyes opened only to their own nakedness. Their having "taken" (*gegriffen*) the apple is a fateful, literal "mis-take" (*Mißgriff*), consigning them to the shame that is a testament both to their new capacity for self-reflection and their distance from God's grace.[7] Instead of knowledge of spiritual reality (immediate knowledge of a higher realm), mankind plummets into self-consciousness (the mediated knowledge of self-shame). Their eyes have simply been opened to their finitude, their definition, their death-bound subjectivity. God condemns mankind to live in labor, bereft of spiritual vision and consigned to the literalness of mere physical existence. Thus the serpent crawls henceforth on the ground, in stark contrast to the winged cherubs who guard the gates to Paradise.

Kleist frequently refers to man's fallen state, for example, in a letter to his stepsister, Ulrike: "Ah, there is a sad clarity that, for the sake of their happiness, nature has spared the many people who only see the surface of things. . . . [Nature] shows me everything around me and my own self in its entirely impoverished bareness ["in seiner ganzen armseligen Blöße"], and in the end the heart is sickened by this nakedness [*Nacktheit*]—To this is added an inexplicable embarrassment, which is unconquerable, probably because it has an entirely physical cause" (February 5, 1801, *KSW* 2.628). And then, in the letter to Rühle von Lilienstern that accompanied his manuscript of *Der zerbrochne Krug*: "Every initial move, everything involuntary, is beautiful, and all becomes askew and perplexing ["schief und verschroben"] as soon as it comprehends itself. O Understanding! Wretched Understanding! ["O der Verstand! Der unglückselige Verstand!"]" (August 31, 1806, *KSW* 2.769). As the German word may suggest, all understanding—Ver*stand*—evokes a kind of perversion (Ver*drehung*), dissimulation (Ver*stellung*), displacement (Ver*drängung*), or even mad dislocation (Ver*rückung*). "*Verstand*" is the mind's capacity to convert or divert the given into its own terms. The *Marionettentheater* essay and the relevant correspondence agree in recognizing mankind's cognitive capacities as an end to the spontaneity of grace. It is the bane of self-consciousness, the shame of seeing one's self in one's finitude, one's *Blöße*. It is precisely what the young man in the *Marionettentheater* piece suffers. According to the essay's narrator, he lost his innocence "by a mere observation ["bloße *Bemerkung*"]" before the mirror (344). Like Adam, the boy must live with the reflection that necessarily ruins the state of grace.

As shown, Kleist persistently portrays this state of grace in musical terms, however tentatively. His reminiscences of prelapsarian (and post-Apocalyptic) musical experiences are usually derived from early manhood. Among the testimonies of Kleist's acquaintances recorded by Helmut Sembdner, one finds repeated references to the author's early musical proclivities. Although the extent of his musical training is unclear, Kleist is said to have "composed dances, without knowing notes," to have "sung instantaneously everything that he heard." During his military service, including the time spent in the Rhineland, he regularly played the clarinet in a chamber quartet that he himself had organized, with many acclaimed performances in local villages—so many, in fact, that he was once arrested by the military police for neglecting his duties. After his death, Clemens

Brentano described him, albeit presumably with exaggeration, as one "of the greatest virtuosos on the flute and clarinet."[8]

Kleist shared Herder's belief that the Catholic vision of unity comes closer to the true idea of sacred music. In his letter to Wilhelmine of May 21, 1801, in the midst of reporting his concerns over the epistemological abyss that his reading of Kant has allegedly opened, Kleist turns to a musical-religious experience, whose sensory plenitude is opposed to mere cognition: "Nowhere have I found myself more deeply moved in the core of my being ["in meinem Innersten"] than in the Catholic Church, where the greatest, most sublime music still occurs with the other arts, violently [*gewaltsam*] moving the heart. Ah, Wilhelmine, our worship is nothing. It speaks only to the cold understanding ["zu dem kalten Verstande"], but a Catholic celebration speaks to all the senses. . . . Ah, just one drop of forgetfulness, and I would voluptuously ["mit Wollust"] become Catholic" (May 21, 1801, KSW 2.651). The violent power of music—*die Gewalt der Musik*—is not yet sufficient to obliterate the condition of the Fall. That is because "forget" is an impossible command; it would require that one remember to forget—to *think* it—"and gone is the entire resounding orchestra."

The double bind can only be handled by turning to a paradox. In the *Marionettentheater* essay, the narrator concludes with a provoking question: "Thus I said to him a bit absent-mindedly ["ein wenig zerstreut"], would we have to eat again from the Tree of Knowledge in order to fall back [*zurückzufallen*] to the state of innocence?" Herr C. replies: "Certainly . . . that is the last chapter of the history of the world" (KSW 2.345). History is the history of the Fall, it is the story of knowledge and self-consciousness. Kleist's own essay cannot escape mankind's fallen condition, which accounts for the multiple ambiguities and internal contradictions of the text. Paul de Man identifies the problem specifically as one of representational language: "From the moment the narrator appears in the guise of a witness and recounts the events as a faithful imitation, it takes another witness to vouchsafe for the reliability of the first and we are caught at once in an infinite regress."[9] De Man must conclude that the fall—including the "relapse" or "fall back" ("Zurückfall") that the narrator suggests might take man back to a state of innocence—are all, in the end, a textual "trap" (*Falle*) lying in wait for us who are condemned to a postlapsarian language, to a rational system built of grammatical "declensions [*Fälle*]" (290).

Innocence and grace therefore are posited as existing only when the forms of history, language, and self-identity dissolve, before the beginning and after the end, a timeless time that would be fully musical and entirely mad. "My most cheerful moments are those in which I forget myself"—"Meine heitersten Augenblicke sind solche, wo ich mich selbst vergesse" (May 4, 1801, *KSW* 2.648). Musical self-forgetfulness, however, does not necessarily imply a loss of what is properly one's own. We should recall how the Catholic chorale moved the writer "in the core of [his] being" ("in [seinem] Innersten"). Similarly, in the letter to Adolfine von Werdeck, Kleist referred to his "own proper [*eignen*] harmonies" as the means for enrapture. On many occasions he expressed the belief that each individual possessed his own "tone": he explains to Wilhelmine: "You *alone* sing but one *tone*, I *alone* also sing but one *tone*" (November 18, 1800, *KSW* 2.594; emphasis in original). Elsewhere he instructs her to think of each person she meets as a piano and then find out "the strings, the tuning, the tuner, the sounding board, the keys, the player, the notes, etc., etc." (November 29–30, 1800, *KSW* 2.606). This "musical" self can only manifest itself when the surface appearance of personal identity—*das Ich*—is penetrated, when one can get behind the mirror that only reflects our graceless nakedness: "Suppose you found the proposition that the *outer* (frontal) side of the mirror is not really ["nicht eigentlich"] the most important thing in the mirror, indeed, that it is really nothing more ["eigentlich weiter nichts"] than a necessary evil, in that it muddles the authentic image ["das eigentliche Bild"], that on the contrary what matters especially are the smoothness and polish of its *inner* (back) side, for the image to be pure and true ["rein und treu"]—what hint does that give us concerning our own [*eigne*] polish . . . ?" (November 18, 1800, *KSW* 2.596; emphasis in original). The conventional moral lesson, which reveals a gulf between outer appearance and inner truth, is transformed by Kleist to speak to a fundamental difference between a person's identity—formed and protected by one's subjective understanding—and what is properly one's own. The forms "muddle" (*verwirren*). The participation in music, however, may yield an experience that breaks through all obdurate forms and bridge all physical distances. The beloved's absence, which so grieved the author in Würzburg ("Is there then no more connection between us, no paths, no bridges? Has an abyss caved in between us?") is but another symptom of a fallen state, which can be corrected only by a music that would allow formed identities to melt away: "You alone sing but one tone, I alone also sing one tone; if we want to hear a *chord*, we must sing *together*"—"wenn wir einen *Akkord* hören wollen, so müssen wir beide *zusammen* singen" (*KSW* 2.594; emphasis in original). But how can the self sing selflessly? How can the participant evade the fact that it is he who is sounding the chord? How can one willfully forget one's subjective position? Does music occur before the beginning or does it simply mark the beginning of the end?

Just months before his suicide, Kleist confesses that he is "muddled by too many forms ["von zu viel Formen verwirrt"]," unable to arrive at any clarity concerning "inward intuition."[10] From the same period, in a letter to Marie von Kleist, he announces his plan to abandon art and turn instead to the study of music:

> I feel there may be various annoyances [or "discords," *Verstimmungen*] in my mind [*Gemüt*], which become ever more discordant in the impulsive, offensive relationships in which I live and which a simply cheerful pleasure in living would harmonically resolve, should that ever be granted to me. That being the case, I would entirely leave art alone perhaps for a year or longer and, except for a few scholarly areas ["außer einigen Wissenschaften"] in which I still have to catch up, concern myself with nothing other than music. For I regard this art as the root or rather, to express myself like a good schoolboy [*schulgerecht*], as the algebraic formula of all the others; and so, as we already have a poet—with whom, by the way, I do not dare compare myself—a poet who has related all his thoughts about art . . . to colors, so have I, from my earliest childhood ["von meiner frühesten Jugend an"], related to tones everything in general that I have thought about art. I believe that the most important disclosures [*Aufschlüsse*] in poetry are contained in the fundamental bass [*Generalbaß*].
>
> (KSW 2.874–75)

Although a decade has passed since his letters to Wilhelmine—ten years fraught with personal turbulence and professional failure, coming not least from the circle around the poet with whom he dares not compare himself—the utopian character of music still plays a consistent role. As before, the despair concerning social interactions and its relation to the problem of literary art are here presumed to find their solution in the art of music. Again the paradisiacal conception of music is colored by a notion of youth ("schulgerecht"; "von meiner frühesten Jugend an"). The statements, when taken as absolutely sincere, imply that music has always constituted the basis of Kleist's entire aesthetics.

The characterization of music as an "algebraic formula," however, points to a new conception. Whereas before music named an ideal of individual expression ("I alone sing one tone"), here the entire issue of expressiveness—let us call it art—seems to have been abandoned: "I would leave art alone . . . and concern myself with nothing other than music." Art, the *technê* of personal expression (of feelings, intentions, pain or pleasure), leaves the writer's "mind" (*Gemüt*) in an irredeemable state of discord. What this late letter in fact implies is that art, specifically the art of fiction, cannot be dissociated from what Kleist earlier described as thought, that is, from the reflection that immediately banishes the longed-for harmony: "as soon as a *thought* intervenes, at once all is gone." The disunity that necessarily haunts every representation, the division that makes every formed expression incongruent with its content, lies at the heart of the artist's anguish. It is true, art gives rise to a musical experience, but one that is horribly disharmonious, cacophonous, discordant. Here, at what will prove to be the end of his life, Kleist is reaching out for harmony, for an accord that would "resolve" or "dissolve" (*auflösen*) the conflict implicit in every artistic endeavor. The only choice, it seems, would be to abandon representation altogether.

Considered as an "algebraic formula," the music to which Kleist refers seems to be sacred or, more specifically, Catholic: the kind of music whereby the self is, according to Herder, "annihilated," wherein the ego "melts away." To abandon representation—that is, to renounce the representative logic that always yields discordance or disunity—it is necessary to annihilate the subject that occupies the grounding position of all representations. As Carl Dahlhaus has explained, Kleist's use of the term "fundamental bass" (or "thorough bass," *Generalbaß*) refers neither to the baroque and long-obsolete practice of the *basso continuo* nor to the system of abbreviation utilized to mark chordal relationships but rather to the harmonic theory of Jean-Philippe Rameau.[11] Rameau's approach was popularly received as a mathematization of song and thereby denigrated by Rousseau as a theory inimical to what he believed to be the true end of musical art: the melodic expression of individual feeling. In referring to music as "algebraic," Kleist turns away from this melodic conception and instead adopts the position of the so-called harmonists, where music—again, to use Herder's terms—"represents nothing." Indeed, Kleist's career-long critique against the divisiveness of reflection, his attraction to a Catholic unity that would override the "cold understanding" of his own reformed church, his longing to melt into a childlike grace that would redeem the fall into consciousness, readily put him on the side of the harmonists. Melody—as the expression of individuality, as the sign of personal character—only perpetuates the disunity, the anguish, and the pain: in general, the separation between him and the beloved. In music-historical terms: against the modern *seconda prattica* of monody, Kleist aligns himself with the *prima prattica* of polyphony, where words are subordinate to the music, where the individual voice melts into the voice of God.

DIE HEILIGE CÄCILIE ODER DIE GEWALT DER MUSIK

> The senses strongly affected in some one manner cannot quickly change their
> tenor. . . . This is the reason of an appearance very frequent in madmen; that
> they remain whole days and nights, sometimes whole years, in the constant
> repetition of some remark, some complaint, or song; which having struck
> powerfully on their disordered imagination, in the beginning of their phrensy,
> every repetition reinforces it with new strength, and the hurry of their spirits,
> unrestrained by the curb of reason, continues it to the end of their lives.
>
> —BURKE, *ENQUIRY*, 2.7

The theme of music and its manner of presentation receive their fullest
elaboration in Kleist's uncanny story about the ambivalent force of music
and the musical force of ambivalence: *St. Cecilia or the Power of Music.*
The story, originally published in Kleist's *Berliner Abendblätter* (November 15–17, 1810) on the occasion of the baptism of his friend Adam
Müller's daughter, Cäcilie. Müller, it should be noted, had converted to the
Catholic faith in 1805. Thus Kleist's story is given a dual, somewhat conflicting orientation: one grounded in name giving, that is, in the process of
coming into a personal, historical identity and the other directed by Catholicism, whose rituals were colored, at least in the Protestant imagination, as having the effect of dissolving the sense of individual selfhood.

Kleist expanded and revised the story the following year for the 1811
collection of the author's *Erzählungen.* The tale, subtitled "A Legend,"
takes place at the end of the sixteenth century, at the height of the Reformation's iconoclastic fury and Catholic defensiveness. It concerns four
brothers: one, a preacher in Antwerp, the other three, students from Wit-
tenberg, who have gathered together in Aachen to discuss an inheritance
from an unknown uncle. Over the course of a few days, the preacher so
incites his brothers that they decide to persuade a horde of young men to
attack the nearby convent of St. Cecilia and thereby provide the town of
Aachen with "the spectacle of an iconoclastic riot" ("Schauspiel einer
Bilderstürmerei" [*KSW* 2.216/217]).[12] The abbess, who has been warned of
the plan, becomes doubly distressed: not only do the local authorities
refuse to provide protection, but it also turns out that Sister Antonia, who
normally conducts the church orchestra, has fallen gravely ill and will not
be able to assure a suitable performance for the Feast of Corpus Christi.
Armed with axes and other instruments of destruction, the mob restlessly
awaits the signal, when entirely unexpectedly Sister Antonia appears,
holding the parts for the ancient Italian Mass originally proposed by the
abbess. Taking her seat at the organ, she leads the sisters through the

"Salve regina" and the "Gloria in excelsis." The music immediately silences the unruly crowd, not a stone is thrown, no window is smashed.

Six years later, the mother of the four brothers travels from The Hague in search of her lost sons. She has last heard from them on the eve of the would-be riot, in a letter that vaguely described their intention to act against the convent of St. Cecilia outside the city gates of Aachen. Eventually, someone recalls the four young men who, suffering from a strange "religious obsession," had been admitted some time ago to the "city asylum" ("Irrenhause der Stadt" [219/220]). Although the description of the men clearly refers to a Catholic disposition—one that is quite removed from the temperament of her children—she nevertheless visits the asylum, only to discover that the afflicted inmates are indeed her sons. As her initial shock dissipates, the warden informs her that the men barely sleep, eat next to nothing, and never utter a word. Only at the stroke of midnight do they rise from their seats in order to chant the "Gloria in excelsis" "in voices fit to shatter the windows of the house" (220/221). The next day, seeking more information, she consults the local cloth merchant, Veit Gotthelf, whom her son the preacher had mentioned by name in his letter six years before. He had been there on that fateful evening and can give the mother a full report: "As soon as the music began, your sons surprised us [i.e., those gathered to raze the cathedral] by suddenly, with a simultaneous movement, taking off their hats; slowly, as if with inexpressibly deep and ever greater emotion ["in tiefer unaussprechlicher Rührung"], they pressed their hands to their bowed faces, and no sooner had a few moments of moving silence passed than the preacher suddenly turned around and called to us all in a loud and terrible voice to bare our heads as he had done! . . . Whereupon he and his brothers, with their foreheads fervently pressed into the dust, recited in a murmur the entire series of the prayers he had mocked only a few moments earlier" (221/223). Hours later, Gotthelf returned to the now-empty church and saw the brothers still lying prostrate before the altar, as if "turned to stone." They spent the following days in their lodgings, tying birch twigs together into crucifixes, eating nothing and saying nothing until midnight, when they performed the "Gloria" "in voices that filled us with horror and dread ["mit einer entsetzlichen und gräßlichen Stimme"]" (223/225).

Upon hearing the terrible testimony, the mother proceeds to visit the convent itself and speak with the abbess. Beside her chair lies open the score of the "Gloria" that had been performed that evening for the Corpus Christi mass. The mere sight of the notes almost causes the mother "to lose her senses" (227/228). The abbess is not sure what confounded the minds the four young men. One might believe that it was simply the "power of the tones ["die Gewalt der Töne"]" that reduced the iconoclasts to such a humble state. The abbess's report, however, goes on to lend further mystery to the event. The sister who was ordered to attend the sick Antonia had testified that the latter never awoke, that she lay the entire evening in bed and in fact passed away on the very night of the mass. Under such circumstances, the archbishop of Trier later proclaimed that it was Saint Cecilia herself who must have conducted the music, a proposition just recently confirmed by the pope. In tears, the mother kisses the hem of the abbess's robe, deposits a sum of money to help care for her sons, and returns to the Hague, where she converts to Catholicism. Thus the legend ends.

As many scholars have pointed out, the legend's title—*Die heilige Cäcilie oder die Gewalt der Musik*—sets up the ambiguous mystery of the event.[13] Although most interpretations read the title's two terms as a choice concerning the cause of the brothers' fate, it is also possible to regard the "oder" as establishing an equation.[14] In other words, the interpretive decisions rest on the force of the coordinating conjunction, which may be taken as either alternative or explicative. In the first instance, we would recognize a disjunction and ask: Was it merely the natural "power of music" that induced the men's dementia (as Veit Gotthelf had speculated)? Or, following the abbess's story, was it St. Cecilia herself who took the dying sister's place at the organ and therewith struck down the enemies of the Catholic Church? In the second case, the title's latter half would simply specify the significance or strength of the saint named in the former. One part would be construed as a reformulation of the other. The difference, then, between the alternating or explicating function rests on the structural distinction between a relation of continuity or discontinuity. The acoustic phenomenon of music derives its power either from a transcendent source—as a hypostasis of the divine—or from its own immanent qualities. In both cases, however, the tension remains between the physical and the supernatural. They must be read together, split only by modality (in Scholastic terms, between a *causa transiens* and a *causa immanens*). In other words, the mass performed by the sisters may be powerful in itself or in its continuous participation in the divine. Likewise, Saint Cecilia may exert her influence from above, independent of the world, or she may only be effective insofar as her power is made manifest in the empirical realm.

That the physical "power of music" and the miraculous "St. Cecilia" must be read together is established by the addition of the subtitle, "Eine Legende," that stands in tensional opposition to the main title now taken as a set. Yet the subtitle, too, is not without ambivalence. On the one hand, as a generic marker, the term "legend" lends a certain fictiveness to the accounts that follow. The question of truth therefore begs credibility. On the other hand, in considering the force of the Latin periphrastic, the subtitle may be heard as an imperative, as presenting the story as that which "must be read" (*legenda est*). Accordingly, the novella's truth seekers follow the command and thereby, through the unfolding of the diverse narratives, contribute to the creation of the tale. The mother's inquiries best demonstrate this temporal movement, which ends with her acceptance of the abbess's miraculous explanation and the conversion. In this way, the subtitle's temporal axis intersects with the spatial axis evident in the main title between an immanent and transcendent cause, creating a schema that recalls the brothers' unceasing weaving and adoration of the crucifix—the literal crux of the story.

The cruciform pattern generates and perpetuates the ambiguities and ambivalences that course through the novella. More specifically, it gives rise to diverse conceptions of representation, music, and madness. To begin, the vertical axis reflects the classical distinction between a physiological madness and one sent from the gods, between a humoral melancholia and divine mania. Whereas in the former case there is a sickness that is immanent to the sufferer, the latter suggests that there is a condition, beneficial or punitive, that has a transcendent source. In Kleist's day, this opposition continued to shape psychological discourse: between the somatic psychiatry of the Viennese doctor Franz Joseph Gall, whose six-volume study *Sur les fonctions du cerveau* (1809) traced insanity to brain anatomy and phrenology, and the "psychism" of Karl Ideler, director of the psychiatric ward at Berlin's Charité Hospital, who insisted that madness was strictly a disease of the soul.[15] Concerning music, the vertical

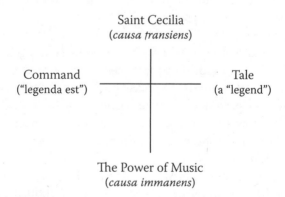

line marks the difference between performance, immanently bound to the choir and instrumentalists, and composition, which posits a transcendent cause independent of each execution. On the one hand, there is the "testing and tuning of the violins, oboes, and bass viols" (218/219)—that is, the physical means of producing sound—while, on the other hand, there is the score of the Italian mass, presumably carried in by Sister Antonia and then subsequently kept safe in the abbess's chamber (226/228).

Above all, however, the immanent-transcendent distinction touches on the division between the Protestant and the Catholic ideologies of the late sixteenth century. This division in fact rests on the issue of representation, which comes to a head in the Feast of Corpus Christi (*Fronleichnamfest*), a mass established by the Counter-Reformation in order to celebrate the mystery of Eucharistic transubstantiation. According to the general Catholic view, there is no representation taking place in the Eucharist. Through the priestly power of the word, the sacramental bread becomes the very flesh of Christ, that is, the divinity is immanent to the physical substance. The iconoclasts of course abhor this idea of "real presence." For them, there is only representation. The host is not magically modified material but rather a sign (*Zeichen*) that points to a transcendent source. In this sense, the Reformation goes past the Judaic *Bilderverbot* as conventionally understood: the problem with divine images is not simply that they seek to define (that is, render finite) what is in essence infinite; it is that they confuse the clear distinction between two modalities, between perception and intellection. At least since Augustine, the double articulation of the sign has been asserted: "Signum est quod se ipsum sensui et praeter se aliquid animo ostendit"—"A sign is that which shows itself to the senses and something else to the mind."[16] To return to Kleist's title, the Protestants read the "or" as an alternation (between this realm and the next), whereas the Catholics take it as an explication, disclosing a simple union. We should recall Herder's conclusion from his essay on sacred music: "The unity, for which the first church was so palpably and greatly set up, has more or less disappeared from our Protestant churches" (*Cäcilia*, 16.261). It is noteworthy that in Kleist's legend the iconoclastic conspirators explicitly wait for a "Zeichen" that never arrives (216/217). The double articulation, implicit in every semiotic operation, collapses into the singular presence of the Catholic communion.

Sign use is grounded in the capacity to hold together that which is dissimilar—say, the material sign and its immaterial signified—and therefore belongs to the power of reflection. As the letters reveal, it is precisely reflective thought and an adherence to the word that banish Kleist from the paradise of sacred music. As he wrote to his fiancée: "Ah, Wilhelmine, our worship is nothing. It speaks only to the cold understanding, but a Catholic celebration speaks to all the senses.... Ah, just one drop of forgetfulness, and I would voluptuously become Catholic." Herder's "palpability" is directly to the point. A creature of reflection, Kleist realizes that he will always find himself on this side of the Fall, dejected and alone. "Every initial move, everything involuntary, is beautiful, and all becomes askew and perplexing as soon as it comprehends itself. O Understanding! Wretched Understanding!"

In the *St. Cecilia* story, however, the brothers seem to accomplish what was at first denied to their original Protestant disposition. If they arrive in Aachen anxiously seeking an inheritance that never materializes and having no friends or relations to turn to, they end their days in the comfort provided by the mother's endowment, having lived long lives and dying "happily and peacefully." Initially disinherited, they come to enjoy what has been bequeathed to them. The asylum's warden assures the mother that the young men are "physically in perfectly good health" and that "they even undeniably possessed a certain tranquility [*Heiterkeit*] of mind, although of a very grave and solemn sort" (220/221). Opposed, then, to the brothers, Kleist the letter writer must accept a lack of happiness, peace, and tranquility as his lot.

Yet Kleist presents two main problems against reading the conversion in an unambiguously positive fashion. First, as he states in the letter to Wilhelmine, he expresses his wish for "forgetfulness," to relinquish his position as a thinking subject and thereby melt away into Catholic voluptuousness, while, according to his own logic, the wish itself is an expression of a subjective will that forever prevents him from reentering a prereflective state. The *Marionettentheater* essay, which dates from the same period, exposes precisely this double bind. Second, in *St. Cecilia*, the wretched condition of the brothers clearly puts into question the attractiveness of such a desire. Their sorry existence, wasting away as inmates in the asylum, severely qualifies the appeal of such "voluptuousness."

The issue becomes especially clear in the report offered by Gotthelf, who describes the brothers' mad chant as contagious, as that which threatens to unwork the very fabric of society.

> It was a sound something like that of leopards and wolves howling [*anbrüllen*] at the sky in icy winter; I assure you, the pillars of the house trembled, and the windows, smitten by the visible breath of their lungs, rattled and threatened to disintegrate, as if handfuls of heavy sand were being hurled against the panes. At the appalling scene [*Auftritt*] we scatter [*stürzen*] in panic, our hair standing on end; leaving our cloaks and hats behind, we disperse [*zerstreuen*] in all directions through the surrounding streets, which in no time were filled

At any rate, the ambivalence of Gotthelf's name is but one of the many ambiguities and confusions that course through Kleist's legend. For example, the brothers' bestiality ("like leopards and wolves") suggests how the line dividing mankind from wild animals is frighteningly porous. As something inhuman, their voices no longer communicate; their words no longer dissolve into immaterial sense. On the contrary, the sound that issues from their throats is all too material—a "visible breath" that strikes, harms, and destroys. Yet, as something human, their voices are also highly meaningful. As the warden reports, "they purport to realize better than anyone else that He is the true Son of the One God" (220/221). Possessed beasts or blessed seers, agents of fear or salvation, the brothers' character-ization demonstrates how the title's "oder" informs the entire narrative. As in the title, the conjunction's force may be discontinuous or continuous, either splitting apart what should be unified or collapsing together what should remain separate. The brothers' conversion, for instance, is and is not effective. Their iconoclastic will has been broken, but they are still iconoclasts: they entered Aachen wanting to give a "spectacle" (*Schauspiel*) against Catholicism and end up making a theatrical "scene" (*Auftritt*) that shocks the locals; they originally wanted to smash windows, and now the power of their lungs threatens to break them. Analogously, thanks to the "miracle," the cloister was saved, but, as the narrator reports, it soon would be secularized after the Treaty of Westphalia. The power of music van-quishes the order of the sign, and yet, during the episode in the abbess's chamber, the music itself is described as consisting explicitly of "signs."

There are in fact many consistencies where we would expect inconsis-tencies.[21] Conversely, discrepancies between the various testimonies are rampant.[22] For example, as his name's duplicity already suggests, Gotthelf is hardly a trustworthy witness. Unlike the brothers—who are fatherless, nameless, and without an inheritance—Gotthelf is married with children, having "taken over his father's prosperous business" (221/222). Upon ad-mitting that he, too, was one of the conspirators on that fateful evening, he pleads with the mother not to betray him and thereby threaten his comfortable position in life. In matching his statement to the narrator's opening remarks, one can note many contradictions. For example, whereas the narrator asserts that the imperial commanding officer refused to offer the church protection despite evidence of an impending iconoclastic riot, Gotthelf explicitly states that the imperial watch was there and made several arrests. All in all, the trustworthiness of his account is severely compromised. In describing the brothers' bestial, infectious performance, in consigning them to the pits of hell, he clearly wishes to distance himself as much as possible from his youthful fervor. Are we to believe the warden, who presents the afflicted ones as God-fearing and peaceful? Or the cloth merchant, Gotthelf, who insists that they induce among the city's population a panic reminiscent of St. Vitus's Dance?

Personal identities are difficult to grasp. Like the composer of the ancient Italian mass and like the uncle whose inheritance the brothers originally gathered to discuss, the true identity of most of the characters remains "unknown" (*unbekannt*). Despite the alleged realism or objectivity of Kleist's style, the names of the principal protagonists, the brothers and the mother, are never disclosed. The woman conducting the mass may be Sister Antonia or St. Cecilia. What it all amounts to is a critique of verbal representation, which always introduces a gap of uncertainty between description and referent. At best, words can approach their object by way of circumscription or figurative language. This is especially true when sound or music is depicted. For example, in Gotthelf's account, the brothers' maddening chant can only be depicted by way of similes—"like leopards and wolves," "as if sand were being hurled," "as if from the lips of sinners." The turn to these circumlocutions betrays the sublimity of the event, for, as Kant argued, the sublime is precisely the imagination's failure to find a concept for the phenomenon at hand.[23] In *St. Cecilia*, it is clearly musical experience that produces this sublime effect of incomprehension and frustrated rationality.

Kleist's letters, too, treat music in the same fashion, but with an added qualification. Here the general problem of representation (that is, the failure to represent music directly) touches on the problem of self-representation. Sublime is the self—an intimate, immediate experience of self-feeling, which eludes the grasp of words but may be heard in tones.[24] "I alone sing one tone." If, as Kleist's correspondence suggests, music occupies the "core of [his] being," if his selfhood could be regarded as his "own proper [*eignen*] harmonies," even if music is simply the "algebraic formula" from which all the other arts derive, then words are decidedly unable to find access to it. To use the terms from the letter of November 18, 1800, representative language is like the mirror's outer side that can only "muddle the authentic image"—"das eigentliche Bild."

Both Kleist the letter writer and Kleist the author of legends struggle with the problem of mediation in written expression. *St. Cecilia* features three specific pieces of writing—the uncle's will, the brothers' letter, and the written score of the oratorio—where the authors are explicitly described as "unknown"—*unbekannt*. The implication here is that the author in principle is unknowable. Knowledge presumably could be had if it were possible to ascertain a source or origin. Yet Kleist's novella, which indeed is about the quest for knowledge (for example, the origin of the brothers' madness: St. Cecilia or the power of music?), baffles every search. The untrustworthy string of testimonies and reports reveals the unfeasibility of such projects. A fourth piece of writing, a papal brief from Rome, does however have a father (*il papa!*) and for that very reason should carry the weight of legitimacy. The *Breve* that arrives to confirm the miracle of Cecilia's intervention may, on the one hand, act as a foil to the brothers' letter (*Brief*), which is only capable of perpetuating mysteries, while, on the other hand, it may be regarded as equally obscurantist.

As Socrates once warned Phaedrus, an orphaned writing is incapable of matching a statement with an intention. As the plot of Kleist's novella illustrates, acts, too, may proceed unintentionally. The brothers come to Aachen to discuss the inheritance but end up planning a riot. They march to the cloister, eager to carry out this plan, but instead suffer a conversion. Analogously, in considering the three "fatherless texts" in *St. Cecilia* (the will, the letter, and the oratorio), we see how each instance leads to a cognitive abyss. The skewed patrilineage marked by the uncle displaces the name of the father and leaves the young men wandering about in Aachen with no one to turn to. Like Jean-François Rameau, the brothers are specifically nephews, with apparently the same fate. One of the brothers, the preacher, addressed his letter to a friend—an unnamed colleague in Antwerp—but the document ends up somehow in the hands of the mother. The forwarded address would seem to aid the reader in the establishment of the man's identity: what origin is more certifiable than the mother? Not only is the family name never given, however, but the mother herself is portrayed in a way that, in the end, can only be understood as decidedly nonmaternal. Six entire years have gone by before she sets out to search for her own children. Moreover, Kleist—a master of the ironic detail—writes that it is three days after the mother has heard Gotthelf's terrifying account that she pays a visit to the cloister, and then only because the weather is nice—"weil eben das Wetter schön war" (225). Can a mother's concern afford such leisure? At the novella's end, she leaves Aachen, where her presence is described as "useless," and never visits her children again.

This portrait of possible negligence at least sheds a dubious light on the maternal and consequently on the power of music, which is specifically allied with the feminine. Personal identity may be unknowable, but the "feminine nature" of music is purportedly "known": "In convents, as is well known [*bekannt*], the sisters are practiced players of all kinds of instruments and perform their music themselves, often with a precision, intelligence [*Verstand*] and depth of feeling [*Empfindung*], which (perhaps on account of the feminine nature of that mysterious art) are not to be found in male orchestras" (217/218). Music is utopian, at once rational and sensual. As Kleist wrote to Wilhelmine (May 21, 1801), the "sublime music" of the Catholic Church moves the heart "violently [*gewaltsam*]" by speaking not merely "to the cold understanding" ["dem kalten Verstande"] but rather "to all the senses." This sublime music is also deadly, however, at least in a manner of speaking (which is the only way to speak about the sublime): during the performance of the "Gloria in excelsis," "it was, *as if* the entire population of the church were dead" (218/219; my emphasis). Similarly, as the mother gazes on the "unknown magical signs"—"die unbekannten zauberischen Zeichen"—she thinks she is "sinking into the earth" (225/226). The title's double articulation ("oder") contaminates all certitude: music either grants access to authentic selfhood or reveals how such access is forever blocked. Like the cloister of St. Cecilia, the brothers' souls may be saved or eternally cut off—secularized. Through the miraculous power of music, the church was spared the iconoclasts' attack— "right until the end of the Thirty Years War . . . when it was nevertheless [*gleichwohl*] secularized" (219/220). Music would remedy writing's failure to express authenticity were it not for the fact that music itself is a semiotic system, an art of "signs," however magical or unknowable. Ultimately, music turns out to be a representative art, which is to say it only produces misrepresentations. Its notes, like words, drive a wedge between the sensible expression and the *representandum*.

SELF-REPRESENTATION

Accompanying Kleist's career-long anxiety over writing is an obsession with music, including an attraction to the figure of St. Cecilia. Although the saint does not appear by name in any of the extant letters, there are many indications that he was quite familiar with Herder's *Cäcilia* and Wackenroder's *Berglinger*. One important allusion to the saint, albeit indirect, may be found in the letter to Wilhelmine of September 19, 1800, which I cited above. In comparing his musical hallucination on the banks of the Rhine to a "complete Vauxhall," Kleist lightly refers to the world of George Frideric Handel, whose compositions were regularly performed in the Vauxhall Gardens in London. Among Handel's works was of course his highly acclaimed oratorio *Alexander's Feast; or, The Power of Musick*, first performed in 1736. The piece is a setting of the poem written by Dryden—himself a convert to Catholicism—to celebrate the annual festival put on by the London Musical Society on November 22, 1683, in honor of St. Cecilia. Carl Wilhelm Ramler's 1736 translation of Dryden's ode (*Alexanders Fest oder die Gewalt der Musik*) not only pays homage to the London premiere of Handel's oratorio but also fixes the precise nature of music's "power" for the German tradition as *Gewalt* (and not, for instance, *Macht*). Devoted to the legend of Timotheus, whose music could both incite and calm the anger of the emperor, *Alexander's Feast* concludes with the arrival of St. Cecilia, who "with nature's mother-wit, and arts unknown before," provides humanity with the organ.

The name Vauxhall also touches on the idea of representation or, more specifically, the representation of the artist. In 1737 the gardens' manager, Jonathan Tyers, commissioned the French sculptor Louis-François Roubiliac to make a life-size statue of Handel that was erected the following year beside the performance rotunda.[25] The statue is the first recorded instance of a public monument made in honor of a living person. It depicts the German-born composer relaxed and collected, plucking the lyre—a clear reference to Orpheus and *Alexander's Feast*. The sunburst at the lyre's head also recalls Apollo, who so cruelly punished a satyr for his arrogant display of self-expression. Here the composer is in loving embrace with his god, their two faces gazing calmly out at the observer from a distance. A putto at Handel's feet sets the inspired tones down on the page, which completes music's transmission from heaven to the world. From behind, one can see that the composer is sitting on a short pile of bound scores, with *Alexander's Feast* on top. Thus the compositional paradigm sponsors the monumentalization of a living artist.

The statue of Handel raises issues of the representability of life, and Kleist's work interrogates precisely the epistemological presuppositions that would support such monumentalizations. Rumors of Handel's worry that Londoners meeting him in person would implicitly or explicitly compare him to his effigy express the fundamental anxiety before any mimetic doubling. In *Die heilige Cäcilie*, the ambiguity over Sister Antonia's identity—is it she? is it her ghost? is it Saint Cecilia herself?—feeds on the same anxious energy.

A noteworthy point is that the legendary figure of Cecilia as the patron saint of music has famously been regarded as a misrepresentation. Herder opens his *Cäcilia* essay by giving the hagiographical tradition, which demonstrates how the martyred woman was mistakenly assigned her saintly office. The *passio* introduces Cecilia as a young noblewoman devoted to Christ and only "listening to the voice of God" ("Dei vocem audiens").[26] A young man named Valerianus had fallen in love with her, but she prayed to God that he protect her virginity, since it was Christ alone whom she loved. Nonetheless, a marriage was arranged, and here is where the legend occasioned a misunderstanding. The crucial line describes the wedding day: "And with the instruments resounding, she chanted in her heart to the Lord alone" ("Et cantantibus organis, illa in corde suo soli Domino decantabat"). Herder's citation demonstrates how

Cecilia in fact turned away from the wedding music, how the later tradition mistook "instruments" for "organ," and how subsequently she was credited—"one does not know when and where"—with its invention, which blatantly contradicts the hagiography.

In a recent essay, Hans Maier has offered an explanation as to how the woman who explicitly rejected the *organa* could be later named the organ's inventor. He points out that, since the ninth century, the Latin liturgy for the Office of St. Cecilia gives an abbreviated version of the passion: "cantantibus organis, Caecilia Domino decantabat." Here the ablative absolute is particularly ambiguous, especially when one mistranslates the common Latin term for "instrument" with the medieval "organ"—"With the organs playing, Cecilia chanted to the Lord."[27] Kleist apparently turns to the ecclesiastical *Acta Caeciliana*, taking the saint as an ascetic renouncing worldly instruments and not as the patron of music or the inventor of the organ. He does so not in a direct portrayal of the legendary Cecilia but rather in his depiction of the brothers, who are possessed by some supernatural power, be it divine or demonic. In this sense, the brothers are mediators (or mediums) of the *Gewalt der Musik*. They are the plastic sign of some transcendent—inaccessible, nonascertainable—meaning. Three details demonstrate this function:

1. Cecilia's veneration is accompanied "by weeping" (*fletibus*; Herder: "mit Thränen"), and in Gotthelf's account the brothers specifically "wipe the tears [*Tränen*] from their eyes" (222/224).
2. Cecilia's prayers are silent ("in corde suo") and are complemented by days of fasting ("biduanis ac triduanis ieiuniis orans"); likewise, according to the asylum's warden, the brothers "hardly eat and never utter a word" (220/221).
3. The crucial liturgical line, which Herder emphasizes—"cantantibus organis, Caecilia Domino decantabat"—bespeaks an opposition between two types of singing: *cantare* ("to sing," "to resound") and *decantare* ("to sing something off," "to chant," often with the sense of mindless repetition and further associated with charms or bewitchment). Analogously, the brothers specifically perform the "Gloria" as a chant—*absingen*," which faithfully reproduces the Latin *decantare*"—as in the novella's final line: "they died happily and peacefully, after they had once more, as was their custom, chanted [*abgesungen*] the *Gloria in excelsis*" (228/230).

The idea of "chanting," or *Absingen*, can be understood as both mindless and strikingly mindful. The act of simple repetition suggests the absence of the cognitive processes generally associated with the linear progression of semantically endowed words. Indeed, what seems to take place in giving language over to song is a rejection of the double articulation basic to verbal communication. And yet the words are still words. The meaning is there, but the vehicle of that meaning becomes recalcitrant. It is as if the musicalization of a text helps to maintain the words' quality as words, that is, not as signs that point away from their sensible presence. Throughout his career, Kleist mistrusted the double move from material form to immaterial content. His concreteness demanded immediacy. Where others saw continuity between sign and referent, Kleist tended to spot a gap. Recognizing the disjuncture, he provided texts that exposed the noncoincidence of signifier and signified. In the end, writing could only be true when its truth became impossible. Since music could be understood "algebraically," that is, as circumventing the gaps latent in all attempts at signification, then it might offer a possible solution to this damning problem. In adhering to the words as words and not signs, incantation (*Absingen*) might allow a kind of salvation. But could Kleist, writing from this side of the Fall, have complete faith in this power of music? Is not every incantation a "swan song" (*Abgesang*)?[28]

Both Herder and Wackenroder presented Cecilia as an allegory of a sacred, sublime, transindividual art. As Herder reports, her feast day, November 22, is the day when "maestros and members of the music guild praise her in song."[29] During the course of his Italian journey, Goethe witnessed the festival in Rome at her church in Trastevere and commented on the remarkable crowd and the "effect" (*Wirkung*) of the musical performances.[30] November 22 was a day of celebration and harmony, a day when the sounds of voices from many mouths joined together in one single accord. For Kleist, however, the "cathedral's bells" would always be distant. His voice would find no concord. Instead he would remain apart and separate, not simply from others but from himself and from his words, literally profane. Music, the root of all the other arts, would continue to be inaccessible, having always come before the beginning and—now tragically— coming after the end. As agreed, on November 21, 1811, a day before St. Cecilia's Day, he accompanied Henriette Vogel to a quiet spot on the Wannsee and shot the young, terminally ill woman in the chest before taking his own life by placing the gun in his mouth and firing.

that there is no idea without the word.[1] Without examining the validity of so neat a claim, it is sufficient to recognize that, at least on a very basic level, these two differing conceptions of linguisticity, the designative and the disclosive, stand to qualify how verbal art is to be interpreted. Indeed, what results are two distinct notions of the mimetic enterprise: crudely put, either mimesis represents the world or it creates it; either it provides an adequate copy of the real or it reveals reality's inner, ideal truth. By taking language to be disclosive, one assigns a productive rather than a strictly imitative role to words and consequently blurs the opposition, especially operative in Kleist's work, between verbal reflection and nonverbal immediacy.

Andrew Bowie, who cites Taylor's account of this linguistic shift, has expounded its significance in relation to formulations of a new music aesthetics in the late eighteenth century while persuasively demonstrating this tradition's relevance for contemporary pragmatist thought concerned with the "'world-making' aspects of language."[2] At stake throughout is an emphasis on the constitution of human subjectivity. A purely designative language, in relation to personal selfhood, is ultimately regarded as constrictive or suffocating. By contrast, late-eighteenth-century theories of music's nonrepresentational quality open on to novel dimensions of consciousness and self-consciousness that move beyond linguistic reduction. As Bowie explains, music, and in particular so-called absolute music, becomes "the most symptomatic art form in this period because music exemplifies how our self-understanding can never be fully achieved by discursive articulation" (3). His reading of German romantic and idealist thinkers subsequently shows how music "reveals aspects of being in the world that verbal language is unable to reveal" and further how "the universalizing nature of verbal language is felt to be inadequate to the individual experience of the modern subject" (220). This judgment has important consequences for the ways music is thought to relate to language. When music is said to express what is otherwise ineffable, then it is generally opposed to a judgment that takes words to be a posteriori or simply designative. If, however, verbal language is appreciated according to a productive or disclosive principle—as a priori—then the stark distinction between words and tones begins to break down. No longer considered to be imitative products or works (*erga*), both music and verbal language emerge as processes that are better understood as energetic.

While I fully subscribe to this version of the unworking of language, I feel that Bowie's nearly exclusive emphasis on philosophical texts should be supplemented and qualified by an engagement with the epoch's literary production, especially with its obsession with the figure of the mad musician. His otherwise excellent reading of Hegel's analysis of music, for example, fails to consider the significance of Diderot's *Neveu*, which clearly plays a crucial a role in the philosopher's conceptions not only of musicality but, more important, of ideas concerning subjectivity and consciousness. What "aspects of being in the world," we may ask, does madness disclose? And how does a music explicitly coded as insane modify the nature of such revelations? In short, can the optimism that Bowie accords to romantic projects be rightfully maintained? Energetic art may indeed dissolve the designative forms that constrict authentic selfhood, but is this dissolution—or even liberation—always beneficial? The questions take us to the heart of aesthetic theory around 1800, especially in the realm of German letters, where projects of liberation were forever liable to suspicion, where revolution could always devolve into a new form of tyranny.

In taking Bowie's cue, it is readily apparent how the distinction between designative and disclosive paradigms of language has governed the varying conceptions that have shaped the history of music. In the *Affektenlehre* of the baroque period, musical material (melodies, harmonies, rhythms, and so forth) could be understood as representing a canon of general feelings and emotions, while the later "aesthetics of expression" (*Ausdrucksästhetik*) saw music instead as a means to articulate new emotions, emotions that are particular to each individual composer, performer, and listener (that is, not generalizable). On the basis of this change in interpretation, it becomes clear that the designative view necessarily subordinates music to words, insofar as words can denote general emotions in a way much less vague and ambiguous than a melody. (The fact that J. S. Bach could reutilize the same musical material for entirely different liturgical texts could point to this fundamental vagueness.) Bowie demonstrates the division between designative language and nondesignative music that underlies this historical practice. He subsequently broaches the possibility of bringing words and tones beneath a common function, precisely by emphasizing a disclosive view of language. As already suggested, if one admits that language constitutes the world as something meaningful, then music indeed can be taken as a language, revealing aspects or dimensions of the world that are new, neither pregiven nor preconstituted.[3] In a particularly illustrative and profound way, the writings of E. T. A. Hoffmann reflect on the ramifications of this significant shift. They do so, however, not merely by celebrating the beneficial results a disclosive art may hold concerning human subjectivity but also by offering a warning about the possibly baneful consequences that lurk behind the obliteration of forms of identity.

Hoffmann consistently opposed the straightforward, designative function of human communication to a truer, more musical idea of art as disclosure. Framed in terms of an opposition to the common and familiar, music's disclosive force invariably comes to be regarded as mad. In a key statement from his essay "Beethovens Instrumental-Musik" (1814), Hoffmann writes: "Music discloses to man an unknown realm ["schließt ... ein unbekanntes Reich auf"], a world that has nothing in common with the outer sensual world surrounding him, a world in which he leaves behind all definite feelings in order to devote himself to inexpressible longing ["einer unaussprechlichen Sehnsucht"]" (HW 2.1.52/HMW 96; translation modified). The musical transcendence described here is distinguished from the quotidian in three specific respects: the cognitive, the externally sensual, and the verbally expressible. The essay, ascribed to Hoffmann's fictional double, Johannes Kreisler—the mad musician par excellence— may be understood as a document on music's proximity to madness, insofar as it connects this art form with a detachment from the world all humans share. Instead it offers the listener the chance to experience something noncomprehensible, something that evades all conceptualizations. This formulation had already appeared in an earlier review of Beethoven's Fifth Symphony that Hoffmann published under his own name for the *Allgemeine Musikalische Zeitung* (April/May 1810). Here the nonconceptual nature of this disclosive experience is even more explicit: the listener approaches "a world in which he leaves behind all feelings ascertainable by concepts"—"in der er alle durch Begriffe bestimmbaren Gefühle zurückläßt" (HW 1.532/HMW 236). Unprotected by conceptual armor, the listener is prone to an experience that is penetratingly intimate, "that has nothing in common with the *external* world of the senses" ("die nichts gemein hat mit der *äußern* Sinnenwelt" [ibid.; emphasis in original]). This "independent" music, then, which "scorns the arts of poetry" (ibid.), is therefore irresistible—in a word, it is something sublime.

Hoffmann picks up on the early romantic notion of purely instrumental music as a free and autonomous art as developed by Tieck in his essay "Symphonies" from the *Phantasien über die Kunst* collection. What Hoffmann contributes to this burgeoning tradition is a deeper, more pronounced description of this autonomy, which he accomplishes by aligning it to the disclosive function of art. Furthermore, Hoffmann radicalizes the idea of independence, by specifying music as a creative origin distinct from the created realm. As that which gives rise to the world, transcendent music does not belong to the world. The origin is not included in what is originated. It is fundamentally out of place. With Kreisler, Hoffmann created an alter ego that could make manifest the inevitable pain that an artist must suffer in the world. As in Wackenroder, true music transports the initiate to a realm that is essentially asocial. Kreisler therefore is deemed mad by his contemporaries, insofar as he occupies a mental space unfamiliar in every sense. Like Socrates' mythic philosopher, he is suspected insane by those who dwell in the dark cave of everyday, commonsense reality. Despite his talent, he is relieved of his official post of Kapellmeister, simply because he refuses to work according to society's standards. He refuses to compromise his vision for the sake of the court. Thus Hoffmann introduces him as lacking the personal history that would ground a communicable, working identity. Like Kleist's brothers, in language borrowed from Diderot's *Jacques le Fataliste*, Kreisler is portrayed as decidedly "unknown" [*unbekannt*]— "Where is he from? Nobody knows. Who were his parents? It is unknown" (*HW* 2.1.32/*HMW* 79).[4]

In accordance with the poetics of genius that Hoffmann inherits from the eighteenth century, the erasure of models is a necessary gesture. Received ideas—that is, identifiable objects—are eradicated in order to make way for the nonidentifiable. More specifically, for Hoffmann, this idea of creativity is bound up with dismantling a particular notion of form, above all the concrete forms of linear narrative and personal identity. Here Hoffmann's debt to Herder, Wackenroder, and Kleist is especially evident, in that they all characterized sublime (in this case, sacred) music as producing an effect that was self-annihilating, as in Herder's "vernichten" and "zerschmelzen."

In his essay on church music ("Alte und neue Kirchenmusik," 1814), Hoffmann attributes the decline of the sublime style to the rise of the enlightened individual. Tellingly, the only piece worthy of the epithet "holy," "the highest achievement that the modern period has contributed to the church," is Mozart's *Requiem* (*HW* 2.1.523/*HMW* 370). Death and its structural counterpart, birth, are the limits that define the form of an individual life, conceived as a story line. Hoffmann's deeply ironic appreciation of life's complexities, its excesses and incongruities, its vague intentions and unwitting impulses, never allowed any linear sense to be left unquestioned. Consistently, his turn to music—which for him always implied an element of madness—reflects a writer's desire for a broader compass, a romantic absolute, that might disclose the infinitude out of which finite forms arise.

For Hoffmann, infinity—sublime and nonrepresentational—defies rationalization and therefore frustrates modes of subjectivity. Nonetheless, it is only out of this limitlessness that the self, usually associated with a singular voice, may materialize. In his short story "Das Sanctus" (1816), a fond homage to Kleist's *Heilige Cäcilie*, Hoffmann relates how a young woman, Bettina, mysteriously loses her voice after leaving the choir during a church performance of a Haydn mass. Her singing, which was capable of "brushing away all the earthly dirt of abysmal thoughts," would no longer be heard, because of her gross impiety" (*HW* 3.142). In abandoning the mass—on Good Friday, no less—she loses her sense of selfhood, not in the annihilating ecstasy of a Catholic celebration but rather by asserting her individual will. Only at the story's conclusion does Bettina realize that her voice is only secured by her capacity to melt before the transindividual realm of tones.

To return to the Beethoven essay, music is allegorized as "Orpheus' lyre," which "opened the gates of Orcus" (*HW* 2.1.52/*HMW* 96): music alone can break through the boundary that delimits the life of each individual mortal. As in Schopenhauer, Hoffmann affirms that music's "only subject matter is infinity," whereas the other arts represent the finite, that which has a beginning and an end, that which is born and will die (ibid.). Thus, like Orpheus, music is capable of transgressing the line that defines who we supposedly are. The inexhaustible forms of voice are not had by remaining in the form of personal identity but rather by relinquishing individual definition to the formless source.

Consistently, then, as a mark of the sublime, Kreisler refuses to give definite form to his musical experience: "So it was that his friends could not bring him to write down a single composition, or to leave it intact [*unvernichtet*] if he actually did write it down. Sometimes he would compose by night in the most exalted frame of mind. He would awaken his friend who lived next door in order to play for him, in a state of highest enthusiasm, everything he had scribbled down with incredible speed. He would weep tears of joy over the work he had produced ["das gelungene Werk"]. He would proclaim himself the happiest of men. And yet, by the following day, the splendid composition had been consigned to the fire" (*HW* 2.1.33/*HMW* 80). Kreisler's hesitation to write should be distinguished from Rousseau's, insofar as the latter recognizes in writing the gap between an individual subject and his words, while the former falls into anxiety over giving the exalted, inspired moment a fixed form. For Rousseau, musical expression is highly individual, while for Kreisler it is something transindividual, hence Kreisler's allegiance to the *prima prattica* of polyphony, which so upset the Genevan philosophe. In the introductory paragraph to the first series of *Kreisleriana*, the narrator informs us that the Kapellmeister would have been able to resume his position if only he had retracted his "eccentricities," namely, his offensive insistence that "true Italian music had disappeared [*verschwunden*]" (*HW* 2.1.32/*HMW* 79).

Moreover, Kreisler's art demanded the "annihilation" (*Vernichtung*) of the work and implicitly of the one from whom the work emerged: "Suddenly, nobody knew how or why, he disappeared [*verschwunden*]. Many thought they had observed signs of madness ["Spuren des Wahnsinns"] in him" (*HW* 2.1.33/*HMW* 80). Kreisler's work habits are the epitome of *désœuvrement*. An "intact" (*unvernichtet*) work is something his indefatigable creativity would not suffer.

For this reason, it would be a mistake to view Hoffmann's version of musical madness simply as a process of deformation and self-annihilation. Although it is true that Hoffmann's representation of Kreisler's character and thoughts shares many aspects with Kleist's depiction of the brothers in *Die heilige Cäcilie*, it is important to see that psychological dissolution in Hoffmann's fiction is not resultative but rather productive. Kreisler recoils from identifiable forms, he consigns what has been composed to the fire—in short, he has a tendency to "disappear," often to the asylum—but he does so in order to make room for more forms to appear. Whereas Kleist's brothers suffer an eventful conversion—say, from rational subjectivity to religious insanity—Kreisler undergoes none. His life is incessantly emptying out into forms and identities that are subsequently dissolved. The infinitude of which he speaks is an infinite set of finite works. Thus, unlike Kleist's anonymous master of the "ancient Italian mass," the composers listed in Hoffmann's analysis of church music bear the hallowed names of Palestrina, Scarlatti, Leo, and so forth. Rather than reject the notion of formed identity altogether, Hoffmann offers a dynamic conception whereby formlessness energizes form and creativity ignites what is created.

Accordingly, Beethoven discloses an infinite, unknown realm, precisely because he is a master of giving form. The "musical rabble [*Pöbel*]" complains of the composer's uncontrollable imagination; people doubt his ability to select and organize his ideas. In terms that are reminiscent of the narrator's introduction to Kreisler's writings, Beethoven is rumored to "follow the so-called genial method and dash everything down just as the feverish workings of his imagination ["die im Feuer arbeitende Fantasie"] dictate to him at that moment" (*HW* 2.1.55/*HMW* 98). Kreisler counters by proclaiming that this judgment of the Philistines entirely misses the mark. "In truth," Kreisler asserts, "[Beethoven] is fully the equal of Haydn and Mozart in rational awareness [*Besonnenheit*], his controlling self ["sein Ich"] detached from the inner realm of sounds and ruling it as absolute lord" (ibid.). The tension is between a selfless but internal realm and a sovereign sense of self that is implicitly external to the tonal source. To name that governing outer sense, Hoffmann uses the term "*Besonnenheit*," which immediately refers to the theoretical work of Herder, most notably to his essay on the origin of language. Here Herder uses *"Besonnenheit"* to specify the basic capacity of human reflection that allows verbal language to emerge out of the immediate feelings of "tones," which man shares with animals.[5] Along these lines, Kreisler describes Beethoven as a self-sacrificial hero or a kind of Orpheus, who loses himself in the nonreflexive, immediate realm of tones only to emerge, fully human and rational, in order to translate that experience into a communicable form. Hoffmann's writings therefore spur a reinterpretation of form rather than call for a simple obliteration.

THE USES OF FORM

Friedrich Schelling names music as the form that gives rise to and transcends finite forms. In his *Philosophie der Kunst* (1804), which Hoffmann studied, "musical form" consists of a nonconceptual, nondeterminant capacity to compose an aesthetic unity across a manifold of isolated, apparently discontinuous incidents. It involves a structure outside of time that is the precondition for—and disrupter of—that which is formed in time. In Schelling's terms, it is "the universal form of the informing of the infinite into the finite" ("die allgemeine Form der Einbildung des Unendlichen ins Endliche").[6] This "informing" (*Einbildung*) evokes the "capacity of imagination" (*Einbildungskraft*), the ground for all artistic creativity, that allows difference to emerge from nondifference, that is, from the absolute as pure identity.

In the discussion of Beethoven's Fifth Symphony, Kreisler reveals a debt to Schelling by employing a crucial contradiction: "All the phrases are short, almost all of them consisting merely of two or three bars, and are also constantly exchanged between winds and strings. One would think that such elements could result only in something disjointed and ungraspable ["etwas zerstückeltes unfaßbares"], but on the contrary it is precisely this overall arrangement ["Einrichtung des Ganzen"], as well as the constant, successive repetition of phrases and single chords, which intensifies to the highest possible degree the feeling of ineffable yearning ["das Gefühl einer unnennbaren Sehnsucht"]" (*HW* 2.1.56/*HMW* 99). The tension is produced by Beethoven's capacity for "arrangement" (*Einrichtung*), which implies an artistic control that somewhat contradicts the idea of "ineffable" or "unnamable" (*unnennbar*) "longing." Schelling, too, regarded artistic production as the result of two distinct aspects: the conscious planning that is free and the unconscious fortuity that is fated. This dichotomy is the motor of romantic "longing," or *Sehnsucht*. *"Sehnsucht"* is generally understood as that which is irreducible to conceptual determination—hence Hoffmann's recourse to the topos of ineffability—and yet as something consciously felt. At the core of Hoffmann's description is the cardinal paradox, common to formulations of romantic genius, for example, in Novalis, Wackenroder, Tieck, and even Jean Paul, whereby the genial composer operates on conflicting impulses, torn between unmediated experience and mediated articulation, between free reflection and fated perception. Kreisler's musicology thus rests on inconsistent bases, at once passive and active. On the one hand, reveling in his aversion to all mediation, in what amounts to a deep-seated antiverbalism, he describes Beethoven as a composer whose "fantasy has caught [*ergriffen*] a complete sound-painting [*Tongemälde*]," which "emerges from his inner world in shining colors" (*HW* 2.1.58/*HMW* 101). On the other hand, "he is fully the equal of Haydn and Mozart in *Besonnenheit*." Cognitive control is reinforced and shaken in one stroke.

To address this disparity, the musicologist Vladmir Jankélevitch distinguishes musical experience from other rational operations by focusing on notions of expression. For him, all theories of expression consist of instrumental or "utilitarian" approaches to the raw materials of art, approaches that "presuppose the precedence and the hegemony of guiding intellect" or what he calls "the logical and reasoning aspect of our soul."[7] The rational generation of meaning requires a rigorous distinction between the expressive subject and the medium of that expression. The intellect must deploy objective material, in order to impart a consumable, communicable message. That is to say, the ideational content of the representation is anterior or transcendent to the material means of representation. We are dealing, then, with a designative view of expression. Musical composition and poetry take, by contrast, a different approach: "The sounding material does not simply tag along after the human mind and is not just something at the disposition of our whims" (28). Musical composition is less a project of rational direction—be it intellectual intention or artistic expression—than an act that reveals the recalcitrance of the material. Although this material resistance displaces the directive powers of the intellect, however, it would be incorrect to think of it as a mere impediment. Musical material may block subjective control, but it is this very blockage that provides the ground for musical creation. Creativity takes place precisely because subjective intention has yielded its leading position. For Jankélevitch, then—in terms highly reminiscent of Kreisler's Beethoven essay—musical material is "neither a docile instrument nor a pure obstacle" (ibid.).

The phenomenon of improvisation strengthens this argument particularly well. As in poetry—which for Jankélevitch is more musical than linguistic—improvisation suffers "no gap between speculation and action, no distance, *no temporal interval*. To create, one must create" (29; emphasis in original). Musical creation is that pure spontaneity that Kleist painfully desired. By giving up the conscious desire to communicate or mediate meaning, music becomes stunningly significant: "Music means nothing and yet means everything" (11).

As I have already pointed out, Hegel speaks of an analogous situation, regarding not musical creation but madness. Consistently throughout the *Phenomenology*, verbalization—the mediated communication of ideational content—is the culminating point of self-fulfillment. That is, linguistic formulation represents the necessary means for bringing one's mere "life of feeling" (*Gefühlsleben*) to self-consciousness. For Hegel, rational subjectivity is grounded in the use of language, which alone permits consciousness to negotiate its inward sense of self with the outer realm of the nonself. Madness, then, is regressive, insofar as it fails to establish a relation to the external world. It is essentially a return to an original state of *Stimmung*, a withdrawal from reality, which has become a source of pain and impossible reconciliation for the psyche. The madman reverts to a preconscious stage of instinct and feeling, resisting the language of social convention. For Hegel, this spontaneity is deficient and must await mediation in public, communicable dialogue to acquire meaning. Here withdrawal into inwardness is a fall into madness, into a loss of consciousness. Jankélevitch's argument essentially reiterates this scene, but with an important reevaluation: this loss of consciousness, this derangement of subjective-subjugating control, is the beginning of musical creation, where the gap between "speculation and action" collapses into noncognitive spontaneity.

Musicologists have recognized in this idea of the spontaneous a key element for construing musical form as content. This approach first gained prominence in Hoffmann's reviews and continued to thrive throughout the nineteenth century. Referring to a historical shift around 1800, Frits Noske defines music grammatically as a "present participle": "what we hear, what we sing, or what we play is not the formed form, or the *forma formata*, but the form forming itself, or the *forma formans*."[8] Noske's modified allusion to Spinoza's *natura naturans* allows the issue of content to be circumvented altogether. Musical significance is not to be sought outside the single articulation of its material, sonic manifestation. Any semantics that would posit ideational content external to or distinct from its formal presentation is thereby falsified. On this basis, music exerts a strong attraction on poetry, at least in one particularly prominent, pan-European aesthetic tradition. Music, toward whose condition "all arts aspire" (Pater but with important echoes in Mallarmé, Verlaine, Stefan George, and others), becomes exemplary for poetry, which "should not mean / But be" (MacLeish and again with analogous statements from a host of poets from Valéry to Rilke). These poets are eager to borrow music's prereflexive, spontaneous power, which may short-circuit all rational processes intent on foreclosing sense.

Hoffmann's Kreisler is an initiate in the secret arts of improvisation, a rich blend of free fantasy and masterful command: "He was often content to play the piano for hours, elaborating the most curious themes with elegantly contrapuntal devices and imitations and most ingenious passages ["in den kunstreichsten Passagen"]" (*HW* 2.1.33/*HMW* 80). His "fatally inflammable imagination" actively and passively works with (not on) the material that arises from within and without: "Johannes was tossed back and forth by his inner visions and dreams as though on an eternally stormy sea, and he seemed to seek in vain the haven that would finally give him the peace and tranquility ["Ruhe und Heiterkeit"] without which an artist can create nothing. So it was that his friends could not bring him to write down a single composition or to leave it intact if he actually did write it down" (*HW* 2.1.33/*HMW* 79–80). Giving form to the improvisatory struggles would arguably offer respite from turbulent emotions, but only at the expense of seeing the music turn from a living creation into a fixed object of expression. To give form in this sense is to mortify.

The artist is therefore ultimately at odds with the communal sphere of cognitive manipulation, which demands set, identifiable works: "You have long been suspected of craziness [*Tollheit*], brought on by a love of art that rather too obviously exceeds the norm which the so-called rational [*verständige*] world preserves for measurements of that sort" ("Letter from Baron Wallborn to Kapellmeister Kreisler," *HW* 2.1.362/*HMW* 125). For Hoffmann, authorial production is but one-sided, for it neglects to appreciate the recalcitrance that madly grounds musical creation. Baron Wallborn is a pseudonym for Baron de la Motte Fouqué whose letter, cited here, was first published in *Die Musen* (1814). In the editorial note to the second part of his *Kreisleriana*, where this letter is reproduced, Hoffmann reports: "Baron Wallborn was a young poet who succumbed to insanity and a merciful death as a result of unrequited love, and whose story de la Motte Fouqué has told in a novella entitled *Ixion*" (*HW* 2.1.360/*HMW* 123). Like Hoffmann's Kreisler, Fouqué's Wallborn goes mad in the author's place. In other words, madness precedes and gives rise to the work that the author accomplishes in narrative form. In order to ensure the future of such work, the composer must continually regress, unworking what has been achieved and reanimating what has been formed.

This idea of reanimation has broad, philosophical ramifications. In reaction to a Cartesian reduction of music to the status of a lifeless *res extensa*, Hoffmann shared with his age the desire to elevate art by giving back its soul. The shift, discernible across the late eighteenth century, moved from mechanistic to biological representations of the body. Hoffmann's writings accordingly reevaluate musical experience as a living voice of nature that resonates with the inner voice of the self. The *harmonia mundi* is no longer an expression of a Platonic realm of transcendent forms but rather, following Schelling and Johann Christian Reil, an immanent, vibrant manifestation of a life force, or *Lebenskraft*.[9] Fraught with organic connotations, the notion of *Lebenskraft* alludes to the active productivity of nature (*natura naturans*) as opposed inertness as an accumulation of products (*natura naturata*). Subjective understanding may grasp the finite objects of nature by means of concepts but fails in its encounter with the infinite potential of nature's creativity. Infinitude, like infinite yearning, remains inaccessible to cognitive, appropriative strategies. For Schelling, musical experience is a privileged arena wherein this nondeterminate relation to the natural may occur. As a temporal art that loses none of its immediacy in its unfolding, music provides the "form of succession" whereby the infinite emerges.[10] In this light, music is directly opposed to scientific knowledge, which, by dealing with the finite objects of understanding, by applying conceptual form to experience, robs nature of its free potential.

EMPTYING OUT INTO FORM: JULIA MARK AND THE "BERGANZA" DIALOGUE

Hoffmann turns to metaphors of nonrepresentational music and madness in order to recuperate the referent, that is, the life that always exceeds or withdraws from representation. In this sense, he develops the lines drawn out in *Le neveu de Rameau*, a book that he persistently mentions in both his fiction and his letters. In Diderot's dialogue, the referent—the nephew's musical madness—comes into constant conflict with the narrator's representational strategies. The bizarre performances are of such presence and immediacy that they are registered as forceful intrusions within a society grounded in mediations of convention. The fact that all the nephew's scenes take place at the Café de la Régence before a group of chess players is telling, in that they stand in for city dwellers who interact according to a set of conventional rules. Music, as Lui presents it, is bestial because it upsets a civilized sense of order, because it interrupts the "game." The "exclamations" and "interjections" act as savage assaults on mediated forms of communicative interaction. The cloth of cognitive mastery, which is woven by the civility of linguistic mediation, is ripped apart by his fierce, piercing "animal cry of passion." As I have commented, it is the nephew's lung power that leads Hegel to the philosophical notion of a *Zerrissenheit* that lurks within modern, civilized consciousness. The works of Hoffmann, which are so often structured on the antithesis between the conventional and the eccentric, pursue precisely this Hegelian line. Hoffmann gives repeated expression to the rupture that divides subjective consciousness from itself. The splits that occur from without and within mark his stories, both on the level of content and on the level of style, by means of a thorough irony, which Baudelaire will duly note and name a *dédoublement*—a doubling.

I have discussed how doubling effects energize Kleist's *Cäcilie* novella. There the alternatives, mirrorings, and divisions—as well as the bestial nature of the brothers' voices—occasion a general interrogation of representation. For Hoffmann, the idea of doubling, including his famous *Doppelgänger*, also turns representation into a problem. Hoffmann's method, however, is more explicitly engaged with a notion of form. An understanding of doubling is grounded in the idea of form, considered as a defined shape that permits a double to be recognized as such. For Hoffmann, every form has a beginning and an end, like the form of personal identity, which can be said to take shape between a birth and a death. In this conception of form, it becomes evident that the doubling inherent in self-rupture creates a pair of defined shapes that, having a beginning and an end, point to the possibility of something before the beginning and after the end: a place outside of form that permits a form to take place.

According to Hoffmann, music is what comes before the beginning and after the end of the forms established by language. Herein lies its madness. Although the object of Hoffmann's fiction is the recuperation of the referent (that is, life), music is persistently distinguished from referential, discursive language, which is now regarded as the intellect's tool for shaping experience into comprehensible and signifiable concepts (*Begriffe*), into a form that can be grasped (*gegriffen*). Paradoxically, reference is gained by relinquishing referential means. The nonrepresentability of music—its madness—allows life—for example, Hoffmann's life—to escape a representational logic that would rigidify it into a cold, lifeless form. In many respects, then, Hoffmann's aesthetics coincide with Adorno's characterization of nineteenth-century "autonomous" music, which demonstrates the possibility of a nontotalizing "cognition without concepts"—"eine begriffslose Erkenntnis."[11] For Adorno, too, Beethoven stands as a high point of bourgeois culture, where convention coincided with the individual.[12] Hoffmann participates in the same philosophical legacy—instigated by Kant, tracked by Hegel, and eulogized by Adorno—where objective form comes into dialectical confrontation with individual freedom. In this sense, Hoffmann's fiction turns to musical metaphors, in order to suggest an experience beyond the conceptual, in order to introduce the superfluous into writing. Music allows one to "devote oneself to the inexpressible" precisely because it cannot be placed, because it stands in relation to language as the formless to the formed.[13]

A brief text from his diary serves to illustrate the issues of formlessness and form, of life and work, in direct relation not to music but rather to madness. The first entries of the year 1811 show that Hoffmann's interest in his one-time vocal pupil Julia Mark had escalated into a feverish obsession. He first met her in Bamberg in 1809, when she was just twelve years old. Now, within two years, despite his intense work schedule, his passion had overtaken him so entirely that he characterized it repeatedly as a kind of *Wahnsinn*. On January 6, 1811, he writes: "Why do I think of madness so often, sleeping and waking?—I should think that mental purgation ["geistige Ausleerungen"] would work like a blood-letting" (*HW* 1.377). The intellectual excretions or evacuations (*geistige Ausleerungen*) refer to Hoffmann's indefatigable writing and composition habits, work that would presumably distract him from thinking about Julia and therefore alleviate his incessant fears of going mad. Apparently, however, even after submitting his inventions to the symbolic orders of language and notation, after translating manic, inspired moments into discursive logic, madness persists, as source and aftermath, "sleeping and waking," before writing and after.

In further considering the biographical context, Hoffmann's "mental purgation" here alludes to work on either music or musical themes. His magnificently rhapsodic opera *Aurora*, sketched just days before this diary entry, would center on the power of music deified as Dawn herself, who fell unexpectedly and insanely in love with the shepherd Cephalus. Simultaneously, he was at work on the short prose texts destined for his first collection of *Fantasiestücke*, pseudonymously ascribed to Johannes Kreisler, the brilliant, extemporaneous performer and "deranged musician par excellence." The persistent anxieties over madness, then, are also associated with concerns about putting music or musical experience into some kind of form. His impossible infatuation with Julia Mark, a girl with a peerless voice, lay at the heart of this almost neurotic will to form. Unlike Rameau's nephew, whose figuration Foucault regarded as the "absence of work," Hoffmann, the prolific writer, composer, artist—not to mention his future activities as one of Berlin's top jurists—redefines madness as the "absencing" of work already accomplished.

In order to conceal his "imagined adultery" ("geistiger Ehebruch") from his wife, who often peeked into the writer's diary, Hoffmann entered Julia's name in a private code. Specifically, he introduced Julia into his journals by alluding to Kleist's fifteen-year old protagonist Käthchen von Heilbronn. Hoffmann, who organized one of the first productions of Kleist's play in Bamberg, confessed to his friend Julius Hitzig that, in addition to Calderón's *La devoción de la cruz* and Shakespeare's *Romeo and Juliet* ("Romeo und Julie"), *Käthchen* counted as one of the three most important pieces in his life: "they put me into a kind of poetic somnambulism, in which I thought I vividly perceived and recognized the essence of romanticism in various, gloriously illuminating shapes [*Gestaltungen*]."[14] Again, we see how, with perfect consistency, Hoffmann described the emergence of forms (*Gestaltungen*) from a state of mindlessness. A young girl of graceful innocence and a somnambulist in her own right, Kleist's Käthchen served as an ideal figure for Hoffmann's Julia, who thereby first enters the diary as "KvH," "Kthch," "Kth," and "Ktchn" before finally being fixed as "Ktch."[15]

The monogrammatization of the beloved is polyvalent. In addition to concealing the true name, it imports the affair into the realm of fiction. Moreover, although Hoffmann turns to Kleist's *Käthchen* in order to deal with his infatuation, this reliance on theatrical representation also breaks the mechanism of representation. Monograms essentially stop the unidirectional movement of a verbal text. They collapse the time of the narrative into single, lapidary moments that pull out of the represented scene. In other words, the condensed letters escape from representation and return back to the life outside the text. Hoffmann's fragmentation of the fictive name therefore bears the marks of this violence aimed at bringing life into writing. I shall demonstrate below how the author's monogrammatical practices strive to accomplish the same in the fictional works.

As life continued in Bamberg, the consul's wife, Julia's mother, eventually began to sense Hoffmann's feelings. Then Johann Gerhard Graepel arrived from Hamburg to wed Julia, as had been prearranged. Later in the year, there was an outing to the country, where, after much wine, Hoffmann loudly berated his rival, who had fallen to the ground. His scandalous passion for a girl twenty years younger, which many had already quietly suspected, was now exposed before Bamberg society. Upon leaving to assume a new post in Dresden, Hoffmann made good on his promise to his publisher and friend Carl Friedrich Kunz, namely, that he would shape his Bamberg experience into an "admirable book" that would "astonish the world."[16] Hoffmann's "Nachricht von den neuesten Schicksalen des Hundes Berganza" ("News of the Latest Fortunes of the Dog Berganza") appeared in 1814, in the first volume of the author's *Fantasiestücke*. In this piece of "mental purgation," set as a dialogue between a first-person narrator and a talking dog, the name that stands in for the consul's daughter, whose voice has a "magical effect," may come from Kleist: not "Käthchen" but, more tellingly, "Cäzilia."[17]

"Berganza" opens with a highly romantic tone, as the narrator emerges from the tobacco smoke of a tavern, "like Ossian's spirits out of the thick mist." Music infuses the story from the start, as usual with Hoffmann's distinctions between high and low, exterior and interior, the eccentric and the conventional, and so forth. Thus the narrator comments how he was held up by his "thoughts, ideas, and plans," which "ran like an inner melody across the harmonic accompaniment of the guests' loud conversation" (*HW* 2.1.101). Moreover, in the silent moonlight the narrator crosses before a statue of St. Nepomuk, the patron of Bohemia but also a name full of contemporary musical references, including the composer Johann Nepomuk Hummel (b. 1778) and Johann Nepomuk Maezel, whose newly developed metronome was celebrated by Beethoven. It is from behind this statue that an anxious sigh is heard. The narrator tries to ascertain the source of the "tones" and discovers Berganza, a black bulldog endowed with the faculty of speech. As Hoffmann alerts us in a footnote, Berganza is one of the two dogs who engage in a learned conversation in Cervantes' "Coloquio de los perros" from the *Novelas ejemplares* (1613). In Hoffmann's parody, the Cervantean text is recharged by Diderot's *Neveu* and thereby yields a digressing dialogue on the topics of poetry, the theater, music, and madness. We eventually learn that Berganza lived in a number of homes, including the homes of the composer Johannes Kreisler and the young woman Cäzilia.

As in the diaries, Hoffmann has recourse to a literary subterfuge in order to bring life into his work. "Berganza" is replete with references to the Julia affair, often featuring lines lifted directly from the writer's journal. Hoffmann allows himself to vent all his hitherto constrained feelings, his frustration and anger. As expected, Graepel, Julia's fiancé, receives especially harsh treatment in the figure of Monsieur George, a fundamentally unmusical philistine whose "fumbling manners" and "nauseatingly repetitive storytelling" make him a particularly bad match for the angelic Cäzilia. Hoffmann therefore employs a traditional means—a speaking animal—both to voice a critique of the unartistic masses and to secure a place for his own isolated station in life as a creative person.

"Berganza," however, is not simply a vehicle for expressing lived experience in novelistic form but rather also takes the distinction between life and work as a principal theme. That theme, we should recall, played a prominent role in Diderot's text, where the first-person narrator attempted to define his position against the "bestial" utterances of Lui. There, when the topic of life and work arose in relation to Racine, Moi took the side of culture, whereby the artist's morality should be judged from the point of view of eternity. By contrast, Lui argued for the here and now: Racine's great artistic accomplishments cannot and should not erase the fact that he was a horrible husband, a miserable friend, and a deplorable citizen. Lui's position, in other words, is congruent with a performative paradigm: it is the singularity of this life that counts, and any attempt to pull it toward a universal justification is plainly a falsification.

> MOI: But don't you see that with such a line of argument you overturn [ren-versez] the universal order of things [l'ordre general], and that if everything were excellent here below nothing would stand out as excellent?
> LUI: You are right. The main thing is that you and I should exist, and that we should be you and I. Apart from that let everything go as it likes. The best order of things, to my way of thinking, is the one I was meant to be part of, and to hell with the most perfect of worlds if I am not of it. I would rather exist, even as an impertinent arguer [raisonneur], than not exist at all.
>
> (NR 14-15/42–43)

The ego or self—Moi—has good reason to insist on the universal, since personal identity, as Hegel demonstrates in the *Phenomenology*, is itself a universal. So much already seems to have been accomplished through Diderot's textualization of the first person by lifting mere biological existence into a communicable identity both for contemporaries and for readers to come. The nephew, both unproductive and unwilling to produce, resists this pull by insisting on an existence outside the work. The mad musician rejects the philosopher's universal judgment by turning to a radically existentialist argument. Nothing could be clearer. Strange, then, that in Hoffmann's parody, the positions are explicitly reversed:

> I: But what does the private life matter, if a poet is and remains [ist und bleibt] simply a poet!—To speak honestly, I uphold the opinion of Rameau's nephew, who prefers the poet of *Athalie* to the good father.
>
> (HW 2.1.175)

Hoffmann, who confessed to have read Diderot's dialogue dozens of times, could hardly be accused of misreading. On the contrary, there is a very good reason for his conflation of the two positions. It is still the ego that speaks, still taking the side of the universal ("ist und bleibt"), but now the notion of textualization is broadened so as to include the nephew's insistence on mere existence—"Le point important est que vous et moi nous soions, et que nous soions vous et moi." In reversing the argument, in giving Moi's opinion to the nephew, Hoffmann effects a synthesis of the concrete and the abstract. Berganza concurs, distrustful of any attempt to disassociate the artist from the existential conditions of his life.

The infuriated and embarrassed Hoffmann wanted to give blood—his blood—to his textualized forms, but the madness always returns: "Why do I think of madness so often, sleeping and waking?—I should think that mental purgation would work like a blood-letting [Aderlaß]." Berganza recognizes his interlocutor to be a poet and feels compelled to warn him: "Your blood flows too hotly in your veins [Adern], your fantasy in its playfulness often bursts open magical circles [Kreise] and hurls you unprepared and unarmed into a realm, whose enemy spirits can one day annihilate [vernichten] you" (HW 2.1.105). The magical "circles," or Kreise, of the narrator's fantasy are the forms he imports from another realm, like the autobiographical form of Kreisler, whose power as an uncanny double threatens to annihilate.

As an artist himself, whose "fantasies" at the piano "disclose the innermost sanctum of this most mysterious art" (HW 2.1.124), Kreisler is equally vulnerable. In a stunning gesture of irony, Kreisler is turned into an autobiographer of sorts, relating a story about a mad artist and his terrible fate.

Once in my presence Johannes Kreisler told a story about a friend, how the madness [Wahnsinn] of the mother once formed [gebildet] the son into a poet in the most pious manner.—The woman imagined herself [bildete sich ein] to be the Virgin Mary and her son the unrecognized Christ, who wandered on earth, drank coffee, and played billiards, but soon the time would come when he would gather his congregation and lead them directly to heaven. The son's active fantasy found the hint of his higher vocation in the mother's madness. He considered himself one of God's chosen ones, who was to proclaim the mysteries of a newly refined religion. With an inner power [Kraft] that let him put his life into this recognized vocation, he might have been able to become a new prophet or I don't know what, but given his inborn weakness, given his attachment to the everyday matters of the common life, he found it more comfortable to indicate his vocation only in verse, even well nigh to deny it, whenever he believed his bourgeois existence was in danger.

(HW 2.1.176)

The anecdote does little to hide Kreisler's own fears of an imminent madness. The forms that emerge in the realm of fantasy are inimical indeed, especially when one wants to maintain one's position in this world. In the great traffic pattern charted out by Hoffmann, the threat freely circulates, from lived experience to a fictional form that inevitably circles back to life.

Through Berganza's reports we learn that the source of Kreisler's mad flights is Cäzilia herself, a story that doubles Hoffmann's infatuation with the teenage Julia. Once Berganza hears Cäzilia's voice, he realizes that "it only could have been she whom the Kapellmeister Johannes Kreisler meant when he spoke of the mysterious, magical effect of the singer's tone" (HW 2.1.129). As in Kleist's story, the *Wahnsinn* is saturated with the sacred. During a staged performance, Cäzilia strikes the exact image of Carlo Dolce's portrait of the patron saint of music at her organ, which both Kleist and Hoffmann had admired in Dresden. The girl's playing conjures for Berganza a vision of the *harmonia mundi*: "The simple and yet strangely wondrous progression, the chords of this choir of cherubim and seraphim, resonating down as though from another world, vividly reminded me of some church music that I heard two centuries before in Spain and Italy, and I felt the same holy shudder ["denselben heiligen Schauer"] shaking through me as before" (HW 2.1.150). The passage conflates the saint's martyrology (Cäzilia is unfit for worldly marriage) and Kleist's *Gewalt der Musik,* which is due cause for shuddering. Arguably, what saves Hoffmann from the fate of Kleist's brothers—and perhaps Kleist himself—is a will to form, a capacity to survive the inimical, tonal realm of selflessness and, like Beethoven, to circle back, bearing the work by means of *Besonnenheit.*

EUPHONY AND DISCORD: "RITTER GLUCK"

Hoffmann's literary career began in 1809 with the publication of his story "Ritter Gluck" in the pages of the *Allgemeine Musikalische Zeitung.* In the cover letter addressed to the paper's editor, Friedrich Rochlitz, Hoffmann acknowledged that his "composition" was in fact inspired by a tale that Rochlitz himself wrote and published some years before: "Der Besuch im Irrenhause" (The visit to the madhouse, 1804). Hoffmann cordially expressed his admiration for Rochlitz's piece "about a madman who used to fantasize at the keyboard" and clearly regarded it as an appropriate precedent for his own "Ritter Gluck."[18]

Rochlitz's "Besuch im Irrenhause" posits itself as an anthropological-psychological study of madness as a musical obsession. Intent on conducting a kind of anatomy of the living, the author states his scientific desire to "grab the soul with the forceps and bring it beneath the microscope."[19] The analysand is a young man named Karl whom the narrator discovers at the piano while visiting a local asylum. Karl's account of his previous life in the outside world reveals a dour existence with a tyrannical father, remedied only briefly by an ecstatic love for sacral music. These details alone already betray Rochlitz's debt to Wackenroder's Berglinger. Tellingly, when asked about his art and life, Karl openly declares his propensity for "pouring out his heart" ("Herzensergießungen" [13]). As he reports, following a nervous collapse, his mother, Julie, provided him with a piano, on which he indulged his hypersensitivity to tones. Having received no formal training, the autodidact was given exclusively to improvisation, which he continues to this day in the *Irrenhaus*, producing chords "without connection, without rhythm" (9). Karl looks back to his first communion, which took place on Good Friday. He remembers with sadness how he entered the church unaccompanied. Upon hearing the choir sing of Christ's passion ("He was the most despised [*der Verachtetste*] and the most worthless [*der Unwertheste*)]" [19]), he immediately recognized his own dejection as well as the possibility of glorious justification. His encouraged but nearly somnambulist state caused the preacher to take him for a fool, "unworthy" ("nicht werth") to receive the host (20). Nevertheless, the harmonies and text of the closing hymn—"His God Called Him from His Holy Heaven"—sufficiently strengthened and refreshed his spirit (21).

Musical experience continued to guide Karl's existence. Consigned to a small room, apart from the family, he one day heard the girl next door sing to her guitar. "From this moment on he developed a burning love for music in his innermost heart" (35). This *innamoramento*, however, led to neither ideal nor carnal love but rather precipitated his downfall. He had difficulty hearing the human voice. To him, Lottchen's song sounded like "held-out chords from an organ" (36). As his mental state worsened, he turned more and more to piano fantasies, ultimately conceiving a hatred not only for words but for all vocal expression. Harmony was all, the triad representing for Karl a symbol of the Holy Trinity. By contrast, simple melody had become a cause for distress and Lottchen a source of despair. He eventually entered the asylum, where visitors could hear him murmur in phrases that were for the most part incoherent yet on occasion punctuated by moments of stunning acuity. The narrator concludes by relinquishing his analytical forceps, confessing his incapacity to comprehend: "Whether his movement was entirely arbitrary, for example, like the rapid blinking of the eyes often observed in other impetuously emotional persons ["heftigen Menschen im Affect"], or whether shapes [*Gestalten*] of his then-heated fantasy hovered before him, to whom he believed he was really speaking in a private language and speaking understandably, whether by confusing "language" and "music"—(e.g., "music," "language of the heart," "without words," and the like), he mixed both up whenever he was inflamed, first conceptually and thereafter in execution; or what it otherwise meant: I do not know" (54).

Hoffmann's "Ritter Gluck" plays on the same incomprehensibility, not by introducing an unknown, deeply disturbed young man but rather by presenting—however elusively—a famous historical figure, the composer Christoph Willibald Gluck. As in Rochlitz, this tale relates a chance encounter that touches on the aesthetics of music and, implicitly, the nature of madness. Rochlitz's division between the world of the sane investigator and the realm of neurotic fantasy reappears in Hoffmann's distinction between the norm of quotidian society and the exotic deviance of a higher, more romantic sphere. Hoffmann, however, increases the bizarre effect by subtitling his story "A Recollection from the Year 1809": the fact that Gluck passed away in 1787 points to the profound ambiguity of the story, the very oscillation that Tzvetan Todorov regards as the earmark of the fantastic.[20] Indeed, although the narrator is portrayed as fairly rational— quite similar on the surface to Rochlitz's forceps-bearing scientist—that judgment is severely qualified by the possibility that he may be speaking with a ghost.

Hoffmann opens by conjuring urban Berlin as a place of cacophony, which spans from the harsh dissonance of a badly tuned café orchestra to the soulless noise of humdrum routine. The highly ironic depiction of the capital in late autumn eventually directs us to the first-person narrator, who is seeking asylum in a quiet corner of a café. Precisely like Diderot's Moi at the Café de la Régence, he withdraws from the crowd, presenting himself as a paradigm of constancy and self-sufficiency, oblivious to the everyday bustling outside: "nothing disturbs me, nothing can scatter my imaginary companions ["meine phantastische Gesellschaft"]" (*HW* 1.500).[21] Yet, again like Diderot's philosophe, he freely "abandons [himself] to playful reveries in which sympathetic figures [*Gestalten*] appear with whom [he] chats" (ibid.). With this assertion, Hoffmann effectively combines Diderot's libertine thinker and Rochlitz's mad pianist who—we should recall—also spoke with imaginary *Gestalten*. Through this quick marriage of intertexts, Hoffmann demonstrates that the border between madness and sanity is impossible to maintain.

Nor is the boundary between the self and the outside any easier to uphold. As in *Le neveu*, abandoning oneself freely to one's thoughts introduces an aspect of vulnerability. While Hoffmann's narrator is enjoying his internalized, phantasmatic soliloquy, he is brusquely interrupted by the sudden appearance of a man seated at his table. "I had never seen a face, never a figure [*Gestalt*], which had made such an impression on me so quickly" (*HW* 1.501/50). Hoffmann's language perpetuates the ambiguities that will course through the tale: Is this a real man? Or simply yet another *Gestalt* produced by the narrator's imagination? Is this bizarre man the one who is mad? Or is the madman the narrator himself, obsessed by a debilitating idée fixe ("I could not take my eyes off him" [ibid.]). The reader's questions circle back to the tale's sphinxlike riddle: who is (this) man? Someone who merely fancies himself to be Gluck or the ghost of a composer, dead some twenty-two years? Or is he, again, simply a figment of an overactive imagination? The story's final line of personal identification—"Ich bin der Ritter Gluck"—finalizes nothing.

Indeed, the problem of personal identity constitutes one of the story's main themes. The two interlocutors explicitly decide not to exchange names. As their conversation unfolds, the stranger suggests: "We will not ask each other's name; names are sometimes a burden [*lästig*]" (503/52). The implication is that designated names would impede a more profoundly disclosive communication. Whereas it could be claimed that identity should be the very ground for intersubjective exchange, here it is that which frustrates a truer communication. The ambiguities of "Ritter Gluck," which are all essentially ambiguities of identity, establish an ideal space in which the limits of subjectivity might be transcended. Given the Hoffmannian separation between the quotidian and the romantic, one could consider the burdensome (*lästig*) quality of names to be based on the very weight (*Last*) that threatens to keep the interlocutors down to the mundane.

In preserving their anonymity the two men augment their capacity for mystical transcendence. The stranger recognizes a kindred spirit and therewith relates his experiences of ecstasy, namely, how he is one of the elect few who has passed through the "gates of ivory" to enter the "realm of dreams" ("Reich der Träume" [505/53]). What is being offered is an account of inspiration: how one comes to compose. Here, so the stranger asserts, one encounters "mad figures"—"Tolle Gestalten"—and frightening monsters who block further passage. Even among the few who gain access

to this magical kingdom, "many dream away the dream ["viele ver-
träumen den Traum"] . . . they dissolve [*zerfließen*] in dreams, they
become incorporeal [*körperlos*]" (ibid.). These creatures who "lose their
shadows" are presumably incurably mad: those who are unable to depart
from the dream realm. Those, however, who awaken from the dream
discover "the highest moment," a *visio intellectualis* that establishes
"contact with the eternal, the ineffable [*dem Unaussprechlichen*]" (ibid.).
The difficulty of the path and the suddenness of the culminating vision
clearly allude to the Platonic allegory of the cave.[22] Thus the stranger exclaims: "Look at the sun; it is the triad from which the chords, like stars,
shoot out and entwine you with threads of fire" (ibid.). Thus the helio-
tropic path—leading from the noise of Unter den Linden to the resplendent harmony of the heavens—rehearses the age-old philosophic
journey from *doxa* to *epistêmê*.

Like Kreisler, the stranger is prone to enter this oneiric state where he
loses himself or his personal identity in sublime rapture. The anonymity
of the hero corresponds to the unnamable nature of his adventure. As
"Berganza" warned, and as the stranger confirms, it can be a terrible place,
where the individual suffers the pain of dissolution: "When I was in the
realm of dreams, a thousand aches and worries tortured me. It was night
and I was terrified by the grinning larvae of the monsters ["die grinsenden
Larven der Ungeheuer"], who dashed out at me and sometimes dragged
me into the ocean's abyss, sometimes carried me high into the air" (505–
6/53–54). The anxiety is due to the fundamental ambivalence that
Hoffmann persistently viewed as the source of great art. As in Hegel, this
source is understood as an experience of immediacy, a withdrawal from
the everyday world of temporal progression, and an immersion into pure
simultaneity. Accordingly, Gluck's fantasy moves to convert the time-
bound art of music into timeless vision. The ear is replaced by the eye,
only to return, ultimately, back to the ear. "Melodies streamed back and
forth, and I swam in this stream and was about to drown. Then the eye
looked at me and sustained me above the roaring waves. It became night
again: two colossi in gleaming armor strode towards me: the Tonic and
the Fifth. They snatched me up ["sie rissen mich empor"], but the eye said
smiling, 'I know what fills your heart with yearning. The gentle, soft Third
will walk among the colossi, you will hear his sweet voice; you will see me
again and my melodies will be yours'" (506/54). At first, the subject loses
himself in the heteronomy of aural engulfment. The climax of inspiration
and concomitant selflessness is represented by the colossi, allegories of
the perfect concordance of the tonic and fifth. The *unio mystica* promises
the disambiguating third, whose movement will define the triad as major

or minor. This movement moreover symbolizes the composer's own personal "yearning," his desire to return to himself and to the sensible world, where he can be author of his own work. The task, which relies on the composer's *Besonnenheit*, will be to retain the immediacy of this high point, while rendering it into the linear form of a musical piece. The stranger closes his colorful account of musical inspiration by leaving the image of himself in the calyx of a great sunflower. At this point, the odd man suddenly dashes from the room and does not return. Later, the narrator runs into the man again on the streets of Berlin and receives an excuse, albeit obscure: "It got too hot and the euphony began to sound" (507/54).

Without entering into the complicated critical discussion of what in fact this "euphony" is, I would like to return to the two colossi, the tonic and fifth, of the first vision. It is possible—however speculative—that Hoffmann has set up these monuments as a magical allegory of the historical composer's own self. C and G, the paradigmatic tonic and fifth, strikingly offer an (incomplete) monogram of the story's protagonist, Christoph Gluck. The tonality may also refer to Gluck's famous "reform" opera, his *Orfeo ed Euridice* of 1762. A great measure of that opera's unity consists in setting the opening sinfonia of mourning in C minor and then the glorious finale, the "Triumph of Love," in C major. It is undecided, in the vision Hoffmann relates in "Ritter Gluck," whether the "longed-for third" will be the E of C major or the E flat (*Es* in German notation) of C minor, whether the vision will lead the initiate back to the light of selfhood, as promised ("my melodies will be yours") or the madman will drown in the darkness of self-loss.

The inscription of a proper name by means of the musical alphabet was of course a well-established practice of the baroque that continued throughout the Western tradition. Perhaps the most famous example is Schumann's *Carnaval, scènes mignonnes . . . sur quatre notes* (Op. 9). Here the four notes A-(E)s-C-H (A-E flat-C-B in English notation) encipher the name of his fiancée's hometown, Asch, in addition to alluding lightly to the composer himself, *Sch*umann, the German word for the carnival preceding Lent (*Fasching*), and a host of other possibilities.[23] Thomas Mann organizes a good deal of material in *Doktor Faustus* on the cryptogram h-e-a-e-es, which Leverkühn uses to memorialize his "Hetaera Esmeralda," a name that serves as a determining leitmotif throughout the novel. Mann's narrator, Serenus Zeitblom, comments: "Leverkühn was not the first composer, nor will he have been the last, who loved to insert secret messages as formulas or logograms in his work ["Heimlichkeiten formel- und sigelhafter Art in seinem Werk zu verschließen"], revealing music's innate predilection for superstitious rites and observances charged with mystic numbers and alphabetical symbols."[24]

Lending narratives to tonal intervals and patterns is one of Kreisler's favorite pastimes. It constitutes an obsession for the madman Karl in Rochlitz's "Besuch" and is also pursued at length in the neo-Pythagorean elaborations performed by Hoffmann's beloved Johann Wilhelm Ritter, whose *Fragmente aus dem Nachlasse eines jungen Physikers* (1810) contains an entire series of complex metaphysical explanations for all the major and minor keys.[25] Monograms, however, are not simply an esoteric means to inscribe latent significance beneath a manifest narrative. As suggested above, they collapse the time of verbal transmission into a single moment. In the terminology of Lessing's *Laokoon*, the "succession," or *Nacheinander*, of poetry turns into the "simultaneity," or *Nebeneinander*, of vision. One could say that temporal reflection, which collates and mediates verbal elements as they appear and vanish in their unfolding, gives in to a spatial immediacy or vividness. This process pertains especially to the romantic concept of music, insofar as music was regarded as immediate (or instantaneous) but nevertheless appreciated as an art that progressed linearly.

The monogram therefore reinforces Hoffmann's general theory of music as a combination of immediacy and reflection, as in the tension between the instantaneous vision and the "rational awareness" (*Besonnenheit*) that underlies the account of inspiration both in "Ritter Gluck" and in the famous review of Beethoven's Fifth Symphony. The latter, published the following year, speaks explicitly of the power of Orpheus's lyre to open "the gates of Orcus." One reason for the extraordinary significance of Beethoven's Fifth for Hoffmann may in fact be the selfsame modulation that arches across Gluck's *Orfeo*, from the forcefully dark first movement in C minor to the brilliant concluding movement, whose finale consists of twenty-nine fortissimo bars of C major.

Particularly strong corroborating evidence for reading the colossi in "Ritter Gluck" as a monogrammatic figure of the hero's struggle between expropriation (C minor) and reappropriation (C major), between self-annihilation and *Besonnenheit*, may be found in a brief text that Hoffmann entitled "Kreislers Musikalisch-poetischer Klubb." Here, the E flat (Es) explicitly carries with it the threat of madness. In this text, from the second set of *Kreisleriana* (1814), the composer offers a dual narrative at the piano in words and chords. He accompanies his verbal descriptions with a harmonic progression, beginning with A flat minor and ending in C minor. The first triad (A flat–C flat–E flat; German: As-Ces-Es) sets the tone for infinite longing, rapture, and the self's painful fight to break free in a quasi-religious ascesis: "A flat minor chord (*mezzo forte*): 'Ah! They carry me to the land of eternal yearning, but as they take hold of me, pain awakens and tries to burst from my breast by violently rending it asunder ["gewaltsam zerreißt"]'" (*HW* 2.1.372/*HMW* 133). The *Gewalt der Musik*, with its attendant *Zerrissenheit*, is followed by a modulation to E major (that is, the A flat and C flat are enharmonically interpreted as G sharp and B, respectively, while the E flat rises to E). With this introduction of the E (here the tonic but still the longed-for major third in "Ritter Gluck") comes new strength: "E major, first inversion chord [German: Gis-H-E] (*ancora più forte*): 'Stand firm, my heart! Do not break under the searing heat that suffuses my breast'" (ibid.) How distant is Hoffmann from this passage? Just as the outer elements of the C major triad yielded the Christoph Gluck monogram, so the E major triad (E–Gis–H) reveals the initials of Ernst Hoffmann, another perfect fifth. Kreisler's accompanying narrative begins to be reflected in a narrative composed of the triads' notes. Returning to the opening chord (A flat minor = As-Ces-Es), we can perhaps detect the ascesis that tears the spirit from the body. Reinterpreted as H (for Hoffmann), the Ces (C flat) also hints at the self-assertive power that is checked by the Es of expropriation. The move from A flat minor to E major changes the Es to E and thereby firms the heart of E.H. The author himself seems to steal into the text that he signs. The question posed by the colossi scene of "Ritter Gluck" then becomes the following: is the "longed-for third" the E of Ernst Hoffmann, or is it the neuter, depersonalized pronoun "*es*"?

The "Musikalisch-poetischer Klubb" continues along similar lines, staging the same drama by means of an encrypted progression based on the disappearance and reemergence of the threatening E flat (Es). In other words, it may be read as an oscillation between the self-affirmation of E and the self-loss of Es. Uncannily, the passage ends in C minor (C-Es-G), which drives Kreisler into a violent hallucination: "C minor chords (repeated *fortissimo*): 'Don't you recognize him? Don't you recognize him? Look, he clutches at my heart with red-hot talons! . . . Do you see it lying in wait, the ghastly apparition with its flashing red eyes? Stretching out its claw-like skeleton-hands [*Knochenfäuste*] towards you from its tattered [*zerrissenen*] coat? Shaking the crown of straw on its smooth bare skull?— It is madness ["Es ist der Wahnsinn"]'" (*HW* 2.1.374/*HMW* 134–35). The same panic—and arguably the same tonality—overcomes the strange musician of "Ritter Gluck." After giving his account of this moment of enthusiasm, the man brusquely abandons his newfound friend. Later, at the Brandenburg Gate—a negative colossus, dedicated to the vulgar city—the narrator spots him and questions his sudden departure. The stranger's excuse: "It got too hot and the euphony began to sound" (HW 1.507/54). Like Rochlitz's Karl and Wackenroder's Berglinger, the heated state of the musical sublime renders the individual impersonal and asocial. Worldly communication becomes a source either of indifference or of hatred. The drowning formlessness, which for Hoffmann is always a prelude to accomplished work, cannot bear the presence of external identities. Subjectivity must be relinquished. In both "Ritter Gluck" and the "Musikalisch-poetischer Klubb," the individual subject—perhaps the E of C major (as in *Orfeo*'s "Triumph of Love") or perhaps the "e" of ego and Ernst—must yield to the "it" or the E flat (Es) of dementia: "*Es* ist der Wahnsinn."

POSTSCRIPTUM: "RAT KRESPEL"

Hoffmann repeatedly thematized the dialectical relationship between madness and creativity. Outside the limits of this model of inspiration—a model of loss and return, of expropriation and reappropriation—lie two mute alternatives: quotidian banality (where one never leaves the mundane, where one never risks self-loss) and complete insanity (where one never comes back from the realm of dreams).

A useful illustration may be found in the story entitled "Rat Krespel," together with the long letter that accompanied its submission. The letter dates from the fall of 1816, the year Hoffmann was appointed to the supreme court in Berlin. It was addressed to his friend and sometime collaborator the baron de la Motte Fouqué. At the outset, Hoffmann apologizes for his incapacity to provide a story for the upcoming *Frauentaschenbuch*—a collection of pieces that Fouqué published annually for the entertainment of Prussian society. By way of an excuse, Hoffmann refers yet again to Diderot's mad musician, offering a self-portrait of despairing frustration: "I've just been knocking on my forehead, like Rameau's splendid [*famoser*] nephew, in sheer despair certainly, though pleading lightly and asking very courteously: Isn't anyone, anyone at home?—But no answer!—They have all gone out [*ausgegangen*], the masters and the servants. Heaven knows if anyone will ever return or otherwise if at least some good people will move in" (HW 4.1271). As earlier in Bamberg, Hoffmann's head has again been emptied out—*ausgeleert*. His skull has been dispossessed of its inhabitants. It is a disembodiment frightfully devoid of any spiritualization. This idea of evacuation is one of Hoffmann's favorite tropes for literary impotence: having written, he now writes only of his inability to write further. The vacant mind therefore likens itself to Diderot's idle madman who was unable to accomplish anything at all.

The allusion may be to the episode when Moi asks Lui why he has been so unproductive, why he has never created a work of beauty. In response, the nephew bemoans his fate, stating how nature denied him the kind of fixed identity that his uncle enjoys, how she repeatedly "misdressed" (*fagota*) him in giving him not a single "face" but rather a series of contradictory "faces" (*NR* 96/114). The composer's identity, stable over time and space, may produce works by imitating nature in artistic form, but the figure born under the influence of inequality can only be lazy, *désœuvré*, unworked. Imitation, which functions on the premise of equivalence or *vraisemblance*, cannot take place under the nephew's peculiar, unequal disposition. In an apparent non sequitur, the nephew proceeds to tell an odd anecdote about one Abbé Le Blanc, who was once escorted to the Académie Française. At the threshold to this place of productive poets, artists, and scientists, the abbé fell, breaking both legs. A "man of the world" suggests that he should knock the door down with his head. The crippled abbé replies that he has already tried but only received a bump. At this point, the nephew unexpectedly interrupts himself. He abandons the abbé knocking at the Académie's door and begins instead to rap violently against his own blank forehead. "Sighing, weeping, lamenting, he lifted his hands and eyes, beat his head with his fist hard enough to break his skull or else his fingers, and went on: 'And yet I think there is something [*quelque chose*] in there, but bang and shake it as I will nothing comes out.' Then he fell to shaking his head and banging it harder than ever, and said: 'Either there is nobody at home or he won't answer ["Ou il n'y a personne, ou l'on ne veut pas repondre"]'" (*NR* 97–98/114–15). Violent emotions ("sighing, weeping, lamenting") have pushed rationality out of the head. The shift from metaphorical object ("quelque chose") to personification ("personne," "on") is telling. Would-be genius fails to produce. Its legs are broken. It goes nowhere. In short, genius unworks itself and discovers itself a "mad fool" (*fou*)—"I had persuaded myself I was a genius, and at the end of the first line I can read that I'm a fool, a fool, a fool" (ibid.). The nephew thereby offers a comic illustration of Hegel's notion of "tornness" (*Zerrissenheit*): in knocking on his own head, he splits himself between active and passive subjects. The violence of the gesture moves in both directions: either the acting fist or the passive skull is on the verge of breaking.

Hoffmann, however, may be thinking of another episode, for this is not the only place where the nephew suffers a self-afflicted strike. Elsewhere, he bangs his head as he complains of his poverty and of losing favor with those who once supported him.[26] Mindful of Hoffmann's scandalous attraction to Julia Mark, it is noteworthy that at this point in Diderot's text the nephew, a music instructor, imitates a pimp, desperately trying to seduce a teenage student. Pounding his forehead, he remarks that at least he can enjoy regular bowel movements: "The important thing is to evacuate the bowels easily, freely, pleasantly and copiously every evening. *O stercus pretiosum!*" (NR 25/52). Hoffmann internalizes his literary impotence by transforming it into a psychological allegory: the empty home of his own mind. Hoffmann's evacuation, intellectual rather than fecal, is hardly a benefit at all, leaving the artist quite literally de-mented.

This scene from Diderot's *Neveu* contributes further details to Hoffmann's self-description in the letter to Fouqué. Directly after beating his skull and then commenting on his metabolism, the nephew forges ahead by turning to music, imitating Pietro Antonio Locatelli, the violin virtuoso who, incidentally, first secured his reputation in Berlin. In Hoffmann's letter, too, the gesture of exacerbated frustration includes a kind of music. For the knocking on the forehead arguably creates a pattern, a rhythm. This rhythmic performance, however faint, splits the subject into an I that knocks and an uncanny space within. It fractures the integrity of the subject who would write. The strange, percussive pattern and the self-styled dementia mark off a space of subjectivity only to call attention to its vacancy and division. Hoffmann therefore concludes the letter in somber resignation. There will be no new story to submit. "Excuse me this time, most honorable Baron, and my own imbecility, for which I blame only myself ["deren ich mich selbst anklage"]. . . . Your most devoted servant, E. T. A. Hoffmann" (HW 4.1271). The closing *Klage*, or complaint, reinforces the subjective split, now emphasized in the reflexive division between "*ich*" and "*mich selbst*." Whereas Hegel regarded the nephew's *Zerrissenheit* as a source of volubility, Hoffmann's tornness results only in wordlessness.

But then there comes a postscript:

Postscriptum: Has it not, Baron, already happened quite often to you, that out of the gray, gloomy, shadowy clouds that hung deep in your life, there suddenly flashed out in colorful fire all sorts of friendly, heavenly shapes [*Himmelsgestalten*]; and that after such illumination only a blacker night enveloped you? But then in the far, far distance a pale shimmer rose, and it spoke in your breast, ah, that is indeed the beloved image, but only pain recognizes its magnificent, heavenly traits. Now, as the shimmer began to take form [*gestalten*], with more and more fiery beams, then you become aware that what appeared to you as a shimmering, radiant image was but a reflex [*Reflex*] of the heated, ineffable longing ["unaussprechlichen Sehnsucht"] that has risen inside your very own self ["die in Ihrem eigenen Innern aufgegangen"].

(*HW* 4.1272)

Hoffmann goes on to report how various shapes appeared and disappeared in rapid succession until—he now shifts to the vivid present tense—"a clear tone breathes forth, as though from a woman's breast." The divine voice is of a familiar singer, perhaps reminiscent of his Julia, who is now so painfully distant in the past. A tiny devil then appears on the scene, an inimical spirit, mocking the poet with an evil laugh. But the heavenly voice draws him back to his rapturous experience: "From deep within [his] breast," he responds to the tone, sighing, with a name: "Antonie!" The name, pronounced in isolation, will occupy the inaccessible center of the narrative here taking shape. It is literally the *Reflex*, or reflection, of the author's own yearning, having "risen inside [his] very own self." The writer's name appears inversely, as through a glass: An*Toni*E. The devil departs, and in his place emerges an older man, haggard and dressed in gray. His hairstyle is as ancient as his clothing. Hoffmann recognizes him at once. He is the counselor Krespel.

It is a this point, still within the letter's postscript, that Hoffmann begins the tale that is commonly referred to as "Rat Krespel." An impassioned violinist given to hopping about on one foot, Krespel bears a close resemblance both to the Ritter Gluck and to the Kapellmeister Kreisler and is therefore yet another of Hoffmann's mad musicians. At the story's conclusion, Hoffmann presents a second postscript—a *postscripti postscriptum*—where he asks if the foregoing tale may make a suitable contribution for his correspondent's collection. Needless to say, Fouqué published the story together with the frame narrative of the letter in the 1817 issue of the *Frauentaschenbuch*.

Since Hoffmann later inserted the Krespel story into the first volume of his *Serapions-Brüder* collection, this original epistolary frame has been neglected in the critical tradition. In my estimation, however, analyzing the story precisely as a postscript reveals crucial elements that are otherwise ignored. The insanely musical figure of Rat Krespel perpetuates the dementia that Hoffmann evokes in the accompanying letter, before the tale began, where rhythms, however crude, were played out against an empty skull. The letter's literary allusion to *Le neveu de Rameau*, where the empty-headedness of the misfit is replenished with the figure of the virtuoso, Pietro Antonio Locatelli, nearly perfectly anticipates the reoccupation of Hoffmann's mind with an eccentric violinist and his Antonie, who shares Locatelli's name. Musical madness is pre-scriptive (though not in the categorical, regulative sense) and post-scriptive as well. The form of Hoffmann's narrative, defined by its beginning and its end, receives its shape from mad music, which reaches before and after, "sleeping and waking." In being both prior and posterior, mad music passes through the narrative, breaking apart the discursive order it defines. As something itself written, Hoffmann's musical madness opens up within writing a new dimension, a new relation to what falls outside the narrative form.

Whereas the vacancy of Rameau's mind functions within a performative paradigm, providing a critique of authorial identity and cognitive control, Hoffmann's self-evacuation essentially reflects a process of composition. The intellectual emptiness marks a phase before and after language is put to use. Yet to say that Hoffmann simply adopts a mode of naive authorship is to miss the significance of these periods of blankness. The passivity described in the letter, where the would-be author is accosted by flashing shapes, is indicative of the writer's qualified relation to compositional control. The dementia that precedes literary creation suggests a different encounter with the narrative materials that, as reflexive, are—paradoxically—both internal to the writer and external.

The story of "Rat Krespel" revolves around the figure of Krespel's daughter, Antonie, who has been endowed with a "surpassingly beautiful voice." Sadly, the unmatched splendor of her tone, which "transcends the sphere of human song," derives from a fatal defect in her chest. If she continues to sing, a doctor warns, she will certainly die within months. For her, shaping expression into song would be the worst and most decisive emptying-out of all. Antonie's potential for song must resist formation. In order for art to remain possible, artistic production must be prohibited. Antonie therefore belongs to the ranks of Hoffmann's other female singers, whose pure voices must avoid public exposure. For Amalie ("Musikalische Leiden"), Donna Anna ("Don Juan"), as well as the disembodied voice of "Ombra adorata," the divine gift of song becomes deadly when compelled to enter the profane zone of the quotidian.[27]

Hoffmann thus advances the opposition of determinate knowledge and open potential only to complicate it by placing each pole into dynamic relation. The opening episode introduces the eccentric Counselor Krespel as he builds a new home "without once consulting an architect or thinking about a plan." When the builder arrives at the site, asking for the blueprint, he is shocked when Krespel replies that none would be necessary, that "things would turn out all right in the end, just as it should be ["wie es sein solle"]" (*HW* 4.40). Krespel's house, in other words, is to be formed only in the act—a *forma formans*. The house therefore is in Hoffmann's logic essentially musical. Like the "disjointed" movement of Beethoven's C minor symphony, the building, in its thorough asymmetry, has the "maddest appearance ["den tollsten Anblick"]" when viewed from the outside, but upon entering the "interior arrangement [*Einrichtung*]" gives one a deep sense of "well-being."

Whereas Hegel's *Aesthetics* will place the purely temporal, immaterial art of music at the furthest remove from the purely spatial, material art of architecture, Hoffmann effortlessly conflates the two by considering music as both immediate and linear. To underscore this conflation, Hoffmann emphasizes the materiality of the building process: we see Krespel buying all the necessary materials, slaking lime, sifting sand, piling up bricks, while the townspeople look on. Hardly an ideal structure hovering in some metaphysical realm, this architectural music is thoroughly sensory and thoroughly in the world.

The incongruity of the building's ordered interior and mad exterior serves as a metaphor for Krespel himself—another *homo inaequalis* who speaks erratically, flitting from one topic to the next, without any apparent direction—"in allerlei wunderliche Irrgänge": "His tone was sometimes rough, harsh, and screeching, sometimes low, drawling [*gedehnt*], and singing, but at no time did it match the content of what [he] was saying" (*HW* 4.43). In addition to prefiguring the inadequacy of Krespel's tone to his intention, the house further points to the counselor's madness. When Krespel commands the laying of the foundation and the erection of four solid walls, he again causes the master builder to pause: " 'Without windows and doors, without partitions?' broke in the builder, as if shocked by Krespel's madness [*Wahnsinn*]." "Ohne Fenster und Türen, ohne Quermauern?" The *"ohne"* ("without") emphasizes the lack of an architect's plan but may also reveal the nature of Krespel's madness. In Old High German, the adjective *"wan,"* cognate with the Latin *"vanus,"* signifies "empty" or "lacking." *"Sinn"* is cognate with the French *"sens,"* which means "sense" but also "direction" (from the Latin *"sentire,"* *"sensus,"* "to feel one's way"). Johann Christian Adelung, the great lexicographer of Hoffmann's day, goes so far as to suggest an etymological connection between *"Wahn"* ("delusion") and the preposition *"ohne"*—the Old High German *"wan"* being further derived from the Gothic adverb *"an"* ("without"). Thus the builder's reply—"*Ohne* Fenster . . . *ohne* Quermauern"—implies *"Wahn-sinn," "ohne Sinn,"* "without sense," "without direction," "without plan."

The theme of directionlessness or the incalculable is modified, however, by notions of improvisation, where forethought is unnecessary, where accomplishments are coincident with processes, where things turn out "as they should." This idea persistently marks Hoffmann's depictions of a true, as opposed to a philistine, musical experience—for example, Ritter Gluck's piano performance read explicitly off blank staff paper—hence the theme of intellectual vacancy—"die geistigen Ausleerungen," which Hoffmann associates with thoughts of madness, "sleeping and waking." Indeed, the dementia described in the letter to Fouqué, likening the author's head to a house emptied of masters and servants, posits the epistolary frame as a mad exterior, out of control and unproductive, that nonetheless conceals a brilliant tale, the story of "Rat Krespel," within.

Hoffmann's penchant for complexity subsequently turns the narrative into another madhouse, which invites the curious narrator (and with him the reader) to penetrate its inner secrets. Tellingly, many commentators insist on the sheer anecdotal quality of the story: a loose collection of episodes from varied points of view in no chronological order, held together only insofar as they contribute to the portrayal of the peculiar counselor. This judgment perpetuates the traditional view of the Hoffmannesque style, established in the first series of *Kreisleriana*, whose collection of wildly staggered and discontinuous thoughts and motifs so captivated Schumann, George Sand, and others. In contrast to this conventional view, Benno von Wiese's explication of "Rat Krespel" persuasively demonstrates that Hoffmann's control of narrative is much tighter than generally presumed.[28] This is not to say that the anecdotal aspect is falsely read. On the contrary, the ruptured, episodic narrative is crucial to perpetuating the tale's nonpredetermined form. It gives the impression that the story, like Krespel's house, emerges without plan, without concept, without template: extempore and unexpectedly perfect, "wie es sein solle."

The story's form is musical insofar as the breaches in linear development impel the reader to seek significance in a nonlinear but also nonconceptual structure. Again, the essay on Beethoven offers a decisive metaphor for this theme. Music disrupts the world of sensory perception in the same way that musical form destroys the linear development of plot. The Orphic lyre provides access to the infinite in contradistinction to the finite but also in opposition to what is expressible in concepts. The implication is that there are aspects of human experience—for example, affective or emotive qualities—that elude cognitive, plot-driven approaches. The "idea of absolute music," as Carl Dahlhaus explains, is historically founded on the desire to articulate such irreducible experience in the wake of Kant. Accordingly, Dahlhaus characterizes Hoffmann's review of Beethoven as "one of the charters of [a] romantic music aesthetics" that "consists of the conviction that instrumental music purely and clearly expresses the true nature of music by its very lack of concept, object, and purpose."[29] Along these lines, Hoffmann's notion of musical form has to be distinguished from common ideas of linguistic form, in that it strives to give access to an experience that evades verbal expression. The essential quality of music, once presumed by eighteenth-century moral philosophy as a deficit (as an incapacity to represent like language), leads to Hoffmann's nineteenth century, where instead language is regarded as deficient, as incapable of revealing aspects of experience transmissible through music alone.[30]

"Rat Krespel" pursues the ramifications of this theory and complicates it in significant ways. The postscriptive setting that Hoffmann designed is decisive. In the letter, he complains to Fouqué that, despite his grandest plans and resolute intentions, he is incapable of writing a single word. In this self-representation, all plans and intentions belong to the kind of cognitive approach that is doomed to come to naught. It is presented as a subjective mode that poses obstacles to creativity. By planning, by "having" something "before" one's mind (*vor-haben*), Hoffmann confesses that he can achieve nothing. Only when he relinquishes the will to write do the forms approach. The tale itself is a postscript, because it manifests itself only after what has been "scripted" fails. Writing is shameful, in much the same way as it was for Rousseau, who despaired over the way mediated articulation destroyed an originally immediate accent.

A written text against writing, "Rat Krespel" is ultimately a story that exemplifies the acquisition of knowledge from indeterminate particulars. In Kant's terms, the process is closer to "reflective judgment," as opposed to "determinant judgment": "Judgment in general is the faculty of thinking the particular as contained under the universal. If the universal (the rule, the principle, the law) be given, the judgment which subsumes the particular under it . . . is *determinant*. But if only the particular be given for which the universal has to be found, the judgment is merely reflective" (emphasis in original).[31] Accordingly, along with the story's narrator, who tries to uncover Krespel's secret by thinking through various events and statements, and along with Krespel himself, who builds houses and violins without any predetermined plan, the reader does not set out from a general law.

The fact that all of this is highly wrought, fictive writing, the fact that brilliant interiors may become insane exteriors, is not simply an instance of romantic irony. More important, it is a demonstration of how all artistic expression inevitably marks out the end of art. Antonie is the doomed Eurydice, the *puella moritura* ("the girl about to die") in Vergil's rendering of the Orpheus myth. Once grasped, she must by law pass away forever. Krespel, then, is an Orphic figure, able to listen for and harmonize nature's powerful music, but after he discovers the secret of Antonie's otherworldly voice, after he learns that with each performance she arrives closer to death, Krespel makes a decision to master the situation. He keeps the child locked up in his home and prohibits visitors from goading her to sing. He is pleased when her fiancé re-forms the girl's name into a categorical prescription: "daß *NIE EIN TON* über *ANTONIENS* Lippen gehen solle" ("that a tone should never cross Antonie's lips"). With the Gothic *"an"* (*"ohne,"* "without"), the name Antonie can be deciphered as literally meaning "without tone"—a name that nearly monotonously declines the notion of negation and evacuation: AN—O(H)N—NIE.

Like Hoffmann's ego, split between being knocked upon and willful knocking, Krespel is divided between a romantic receptivity and a craftsman's tireless activity. He builds houses like he "builds" violins ("Violinbauen"):

> Once he has finished a violin, he plays on it himself for one or two hours, truly with remarkable power and with captivating expression ["mit hinreißendem Ausdruck"]; then he hangs it up beside the rest and never touches it again or suffers anybody else to touch it. If a violin by any of the eminent old masters comes up anywhere, the counselor buys it immediately, no matter what the price put upon it. But he plays it as he does his own violins, only once; then he takes it to pieces in order to examine closely its inner structure, and should he fancy he hasn't found exactly what he was looking for, annoyed he throws the pieces into a big chest, which is already full of the remains of broken violins ["voll Trümmer zerlegter Violinen"].
>
> (*HW* 4.45)

Opposed to his architectural-improvisational project, Krespel's approach to violin building is nothing if not scientific. It is analysis in the most literal sense of the word. A renowned lawyer, he tears apart violins like he prosecutes defendants, mercilessly eager to reach some truth. His desire to find the secret, however motivated by a love for music, is a quest that spells the end of art. Ultimately, Krespel is left with a wall of unplayed violins and a drawer full of splintered wood.

Krespel's scientificity works at cross-purposes with his artistic temperament. His desire for mastery results in a world of silence. His attraction to his wife Angela, a popular operatic performer, betrays his love for the public production of song. In Hoffmann's bizarre allegory, Angela, too, pays the price for emptying herself out onstage: she dies after contracting a cold during a theatrical performance. It is precisely Krespel's lust for realized music—his obsessive need for musical pieces, for *formae formatae* with defined beginnings and ends—that must be renounced in order to preserve the life of his daughter. Likewise, Antonie's love for her father causes her to pledge never to sing again. Instead, she assists with the disassembly of precious instruments. The father-daughter couple has acquired a concept that maintains life, but a life without music. One night, in half delusion or perhaps in a dream, Krespel hears Antonie's voice, he sees her embracing her fiancé: "terrible anguish [is] mingled with a delight [*Wonne*] he never experienced before" (*HW* 4.63). When he rises from his bed, he realizes that Antonie is dead.

Hoffmann's introductory letter to Fouqué presents the same predicament. As long as he desires cognitive mastery over his art, art remains inaccessible. The fiction of spontaneity or prereflective simultaneity, expounded in the letter, is a masterful tale of abandoning mastery. All the same, liberation from a desire for conceptual control may lead to becoming conceptualized oneself. The subject of science, which aims to subjugate the object of research, may itself become vulnerable to subjugation. The curious narrator, who displays the same eagerness for scientific mastery, happens on the counselor Krespel on his way back from his daughter's funeral. The bereaved madman remarks: "Now you imagine my sentence is pronounced, don't you, my son? But it's nothing of the kind—not at all! not at all! Now I'm free—free—free—hurrah! I'm free! Now I shall make no more violins—no more violins—Hurrah! No more violins!" (*HW* 4.54). The German is particularly parodic in its sing-song effects, alternating between /ich/ and /ei/ in staccato figures: "Mit nichten, mit nichten, nun bin ich frei—frei—frei—Heisa frei !—Nun bau ich keine Geigen mehr—keine Geigen mehr—heisa keine Geigen mehr." In abandoning his violin-building obsession, Krespel regains his freedom, albeit madly. He reverts to the disposition in which we first encountered him, when he built his home without blueprint. He can only live *wahnsinnig*—without sense, but only insofar as sense exhausts itself.

Krespel's tragedy remains real, even if musical form provides him with a way for stepping out of what he himself identifies as the "insane asylum" of our world. In the end, the tale suggests that Krespel demonstrates precisely the kind of romanticism that Hoffmann was always able to resist. Krespel's tune may be "mirthful" (*lustig*), but it is also "horrible" (*schauerlich*). As a corrective, Hoffmann offers a musical experience that remains prereflective but postscriptive—a musical approach to the world that folds itself back into the world without eradicating it, without rejecting it. Musical form emerges through a method that remains nonviolent and nonsubsuming, while achieving a formal condition nonetheless. It unworks the very forms it proffers. As a postscript, it simply sounds out—or sings—something more, after all has been said.

PRAESCRIPTUM: *KATER MURR*

Autobiography is perverse. In turning his own life into a text, the autobiographer impossibly attempts to articulate a life in a form that can never be adequate. Thus Rousseau, on presenting himself exhaustively "in all the truth of nature" in his *Confessions*, was compelled by that very nature to continue the project in the *Rêveries*. After all has been said, there is always more to say. If the autobiographer began with faith in the working of language as a means of representation, he soon realized how well indeed language worked in setting up a self-definition and consequently a mortification. Such a delimitation could only betray the self that produced it, for in writing a life the writer had to remain outside it. This is the problem of mimesis. It provides a similarity that can only ever be a dissimilar similarity.

Yet the problem of autobiography is not restricted to the impossibility of giving form to the formless or to the difference implicit in every representation. In giving oneself over to the semiosis of language, in transforming oneself into a textualized figure, the writer invariably suffers an alienation, an expropriation—certainly, one of Rousseau's greatest fears. The mimesis proffered in a story line of one's life is always liable to semiotic disruptions. Misreadings and misunderstandings, both honest and malicious, plague the autobiographer, who feels he has fallen into dangerous hands. The so-called play of the signifier becomes a source of grave concern. In the end, it is the reader, or rather the infinite set of possible readers, that determines the direction of any given form. This idea of unworking representational, communicative language generally preoccupies the writer, who obsessively strives to control the contents of what is being transmitted.

Nonetheless, it is also possible to regard the unworking of language as a way of allowing the excessiveness of life to reenter and break open the verbal forms that invariably limit life. In other words, the problem of semiosis may solve the problem of mimesis. If life is understood as something excessive, if one feels—iconoclastically—that the fullness of existence can never be represented in all its truth, then anything that challenges representational language can serve to reintroduce life, whatever that may be, into a text that would otherwise compromise it. It has been a principal contention of this study that writers who turn to the topic of music and madness do so in order to unwork the limitations endemic to the language of representation. In referring to aesthetic and psychic experiences that are conceived as fundamentally nonrepresentable, music and madness, as metaphors, open a text up to what no text can properly contain.

If we are to trust his statements, Hoffmann was greatly affected by his early reading of Rousseau's *Confessions*, which he claimed first inspired him not to literature but rather to musical composition.[32] As for autobiography, Hoffmann seemed from the beginning of his writing career to find such a project both highly attractive and terribly problematic. The creation of an enduring alter ego, Johannes Kreisler, points to the desire and the anxiety of putting his life into a work. Despite the wonderfully rich development of this character across a number of published texts, Hoffmann admitted that it was only his last novel, *Die Lebensansichten des Katers Murr*, that would finally show his full self, actual and potential— "what I now am and can be *pro primo*."[33] The book does indeed pose itself as an autobiography, but neither in Hoffmann's name nor in Kreisler's. Instead, the task of self-portraiture is assigned to a cat. Kreisler's biography is nonetheless included, but only by way of a printing error. For blotting paper, the well-educated, bourgeois feline tore pages from a Kreisler biography, which were accidentally published together with the memoirs. *The Life and Opinions of the Tomcat Murr, Together with a Fragmentary Biography of Kapellmeister Johannes Kreisler on Random Sheets of Waste Paper* thus confuses two distinct life stories and in this confusion unworks the very premise of a coherent autobiographical work.

To begin, whereas Murr's story runs in strict chronological order, despite the interruptions, the Kreisler sections move in reverse, beginning with the chronologically last scene and ending with the first. At the book's conclusion, Kreisler receives an invitation to the name-day festival whose proceedings are related at the novel's opening. The line of Murr's autobiography is therefore countered by the inversion of Kreisler's journey, which, as should be expected, "circles" (*kreist*) back on itself. Although the two lives take different paths, there are enough shared experiences to relate the two together, either in simple reflection or in ironic conflict. Like the inverse image that appears on the blotting sheet, Kreisler's inverted tale supports and undermines Murr's otherwise straightforward narrative. Likewise, the cat's confessions destabilize and reinforce the mad composer's escapades. Hoffmann of course is present throughout, both in the biographical details that he always shared with his double and, more surreptitiously, in the aspirations and ideals of the tomcat Murr, whose species name faintly "murmurs" monograms of both the author and his alter ego: K-*ATE*-r and Kate*R*. Ultimately, it is Hoffmann's life that latently determines the manifest discourses. It cleverly surfaces as the work of autobiography, narrative, and representation breaks down.

Hoffmann participates in the same double game that structures his ironic novel. In signing the cover of the book, Hoffmann exiles himself from the work as the one who is necessarily outside the text. Yet by inscribing himself as a latent, semiotic force he strives to reappropriate the writing. Even on the level of manifest discourse, Hoffmann breaches the book's limits by adopting the role of an editor who provides a brief account of the autobiography's strange configuration. I have already mentioned, in the introduction, how Hoffmann's coupling of the "scurrilous" (*Skurrilität*) and "the serious" (*das Ernste*)—derived from the caricatures of Jacques Callot—allow his own name, Ernst, to slink, catlike, into the text. Thus Hoffmann makes every gesture to indicate the veracity of what will unfold in the narratives. As he confided to Dr. Speyer in Bamberg, the novel is dedicated to his cat, Murr, "*a real cat* ... [who] gave me the opportunity for this scurrilous joke, which weaves through a truly very serious [*ernste*] book" (*HW* 5.913; emphasis in original). Moreover, Hoffmann himself signs, dates, and concretely situates this "foreword": "Berlin, November 1819." He refers to his own writings, for instance, the *Nachtstücke*, and names his actual publisher, Ferdinand Dümmler, whose office may be found in Unter den Linden. In other words, Hoffmann coerces the reader to consider this foreword as a document grounded in the real world. In fact, the foreword presents itself as belonging to the true circumstances that produced the book to be read. It is, in every sense, a *Vor-wort*, a *praescriptum*, that which comes before the beginning of the story lines.

Still, the foreword remains an integral part of the work. The transcendent origin is materialized on the immanent plane of the pages. Hoffmann therefore insists that this origin must be read—"Daher bittet der Herausgeber den günstigen Leser, wirklich zu lesen, nämlich dies Vorwort" ("The editor ... begs the kind reader really to read, namely this foreword" [*HW* 5.11/*KM* 3]). To read—"really ... namely." It should be noted that in Latin legal terminology, certainly familiar to one of Berlin's most prominent jurists, a *praescriptum* is an "objection." It interrupts the court's proceedings and begs (technically, "pleads") that there be a delay, giving time for further consideration to stop and really read what comes before the word. Thus the tomcat Murr, too, demurs in providing two prefacing remarks. The first clearly tries to set a sentimental, romantic tone, a plea for an understanding, sympathetic soul. The second, "suppressed by the author," boastfully and more coercively attempts to orient the upcoming account with a moral direction typical of the conventional *Bildungsroman*, the genre that portrays how one's identity came to be "formed" (*gebildet*). The editor then adds a "postscript," in which he regrets the inclusion of what should have been suppressed. These paratexts not only protect and legitimize what follows, they not only pull the text back into the world from which it presumably emerged, they also establish the game of latency and suppression, which will persist beneath all the manifest plots and descriptions.

———⟨∞⟩———

The profound complexities and manifold details of the novel prevent me from giving any adequate account, but a simple list of the main characters will help to navigate my brief comments below. The tale of Murr's "exemplary career" moves through all of life's stations—from childhood, through marriage, to contemplative resignation—in a style that is wholly derivative and subtly satirized. As in Hoffmann's piece on Jacques Callot, the conflation of the bestial with the human introduces a fresh means for exposing conventions and disclosing higher truths. Murr's disenchantment with a number of society's institutions—marriage, the fraternity club (*Burschenschaft*), and the beau monde—systematically reveals their vacuity.

The fundamentally private, bourgeois world of Murr is contrasted with Kreisler's attachment to life at the court of Sieghartsweiler. The latter is reigned by the dull prince Irenäus, who in fact is no longer sovereign of his petty realm. His son, Ignaz, is an imbecile who has been contracted to wed Julia in a mismatched matrimony that recalls Cäzilia's union with the dim-witted Monsieur George in "Berganza" (or Julia Mark's marriage to Graepel in Bamberg). Julia is the daughter of Madame Benzon, who was once Irenäus's mistress and now deviously controls the action at court through her intimate conversations with the prince. She is leery of Kreisler, who barely hides his affections for Julia. Hedwiga, the daughter of Irenäus, is also attracted to Kreisler, even though he frightens her. It was the organ builder, Meister Abraham, who invited his former student, Kreisler, to Sieghartsweiler, ostensibly to help deal with the headstrong Benzon. Thus Kreisler unwittingly becomes entangled in the court's intrigues. Tension rises when Prince Hector, Hedwiga's fiancé, arrives and conceives a passion for Julia. Kreisler intervenes to protect the young woman and ends up fleeing the court for the monastery at Kanzheim.

The title's explicit reference to Sterne's notoriously disruptive *Life and Opinions of Tristram Shandy* (1759–67) opens the floodgates of allusions, quotations, and parodies.[34] Sterne of course is a nearly perfect anagram of Ernst, whose earnestness should nowhere be trusted. The *Lebenansichten*, like Sterne's novel, fail to be what they purport to be. Promising to be an intellectual biography of Shandy, Sterne gives us instead the erratic events of Uncle Toby. Likewise, although the Kreisler biography is but mentioned in the subtitle—appearing on wastepaper no less—the composer's life outweighs the cat's by nearly half.

In addition to what Jean Paul derided as Hoffmann's "plundering,"[35] *Kater Murr* rehearses the entire tradition of music and madness. Murr's swipes at bourgeois society are highly reminiscent of the unmasking effect of Diderot's bizarre nephew. Indeed, allusions to *Le neveu* are scattered throughout the novel. Kreisler, whose disruptive power is equally great, is often described in the same terms of astonishment and repulsion that the *philosophe* expressed. Tellingly, we hear how the young Kreisler was initiated into music's secrets by his uncle. At one point, his early precociousness causes the older man to comment: "Oh yes, my little *neveu* is sufficiently foolish" (*HW* 5.113/*KM* 75). Beyond Diderot, Kreisler's frustration in the Kanzheim abbey readily recalls Berglinger's dissatisfaction with his work as the cathedral's Kapellmeister. His dream of immediacy echoes Herder's nostalgia for Catholic unity.

Once, on a walk through the village grounds, Julia and Hedwiga happen upon a chapel, where a choir is performing. Both are struck down by the power of sacred music. As they kneel at the prie-dieu, the strains of Kreisler's "Ave maris stella," which Hoffmann himself once set to music, begins to suffuse the evening air. Lost in "fervent devotions," they try to rise after the piece is over but fall into each other's arms. "A nameless melancholy, woven of pleasure [*Entzücken*] and pain, seemed to be trying to wrench itself violently [*gewaltsam*] from their breasts; the hot tears that flowed from their eyes were drops of blood gushing from their wounded hearts" (*HW* 5.216/*KM* 149). Madame Benzon recognizes the infectious threat of Kreisler's maddening music. She is troubled by Hedwiga's recent neurosis, which was to all appearances caused by the composer, and is seriously concerned over his effect on her daughter. In a heated altercation with Meister Abraham, she complains of the deleterious presence of the composer, "that unlucky man who brings nothing but distress and mischief wherever he goes" (*HW* 5.255/*KM* 180). Madame Benzon defends her so-called coldness: the woman, she proclaims, "who has more strength of mind will raise herself up by force and give . . . ordinary circumstances of life a form [*Gestaltung*] which offers her peace and repose" (*HW* 5.258/*KM* 182). Her faith in form and formalities, her trust in the straight path, causes her to entrench herself against the confusingly vicious circles that Kreisler brings on. She lightly alludes to her prior waywardness (the affair with Prince Irenäus) and now stands among the penitent strong. The semiotic pull of her own words, however, still shows signs of infection: "I put my mind wholly to the sphere [*Kreis*] of ordinary life, and if much happened even within that sphere [*Kreise*] to lead me, unobserved, off the straight and narrow path, if I can excuse much that might seem blameworthy only by the pressure of circumstances at the time, then let the first stone be cast by the woman who, like me, has fought the hard battle leading to the entire renunciation of all higher happiness, even if that happiness be nothing but a sweet, dream-like delusion [*Wahn*]" (*HW* 5.258/*KM* 182). The repudiation of "delusion" [*Wahn*] and its "madness" [*Wahnsinn*] sets her on a path that is apparently straight but indeed overturned by an unavoidable circularity. Diachrony, however strictly maintained, is always liable to the pull of synchrony, "the higher happiness" that reveals the vertical determinacy of every horizon.

In giving the autobiographical project to a cat and the composer's life to scrap paper, Hoffmann interrogates the viability of all forms as well as the sovereignty of rationality. If a cat has language, then the classical, Aristotelian definition of man—as the animal who possesses the *logos*—is annulled.[36] Beasts are to be regarded as rational creatures and humans are to be viewed as bestial. This holistic view is but an expression of the romantic longing for the absolute, for a broader view that realizes the determining force of bestial impulses and instincts that lie latent below rationalized forms. Hoffmann's reassessment of madness strives to demonstrate that personal identity does not result from the renunciation of the formless but rather from an acceptance of the formlessness that underlies (and overturns) who we are and where we are going.[37] Hoffmann therefore rewrites Rousseau's nostalgia for an original, musical language. In this respect, again, he comes very close to Diderot's misgivings. Music, Hoffmann suggests, does not name an ideal speech that would immediately express our individuality but rather some mad force of difference that divides us from others as well as from ourselves. It is that which comes before the beginning of both verbal and personal forms. Hardly a paradisiacal notion, it is also that which will come after the end: "Kreisler stood there shaken to his depths, unable to utter a word. He had always been obsessed with the idea that madness lay in wait for him like a wild beast slavering for prey ["wie ein nach Beute lechzendes Raubtier"], and one day would suddenly tear him to pieces" (*HW* 5.172/*KM* 117).

Hors d'œuvre II

Doch es kehret umsonst nicht
Unser Bogen, woher er kommt.
—HÖLDERLIN, "LEBENSLAUF"

HOW LONG is it possible to resist the work of language? The madman may call in sick, the musicians may be on strike, but in the end—in the *end*—they will all be back on shift. To speak with Deleuze and Guattari, language may initially be a deterritorialization of the mouth, tongue, and teeth (which are meant to eat rather than speak),[1] but invariably—as humans defined rationally (as those animals who possess *logos*)—our mouths water for the main course, if not for the postprandial conversation. The digestive system is but a metaphor for a working-through, for a reterritorialization in meaning. "Der deutsche Geist ist eine Indigestion, er wird mit Nichts fertig"—"German spirit is indigestion, it is never finished with anything" (*NW* 6.280/*EH* 86). Nietzsche's accusation (like all his accusations) should be heard with the ambivalence of one who painfully tried to stay out of work by putting his life in the work.

Nietzsche's case is therefore emblematic in the strongest sense of the word. His philosophy (that is, his life and work) begins and ends with music and madness. The ecstatic pages of the *Geburt der Tragödie* (1872), devoted to the shattering, form-breaking effect of Dionysiac music, find their fateful echo in the sheer abandon of the "Dionysos-Dithyramben" (1888), written in Turin on the eve of the writer's collapse. The "Bacchic choirs" that disrupt and dissolve the *principium individuationis* in the early essay "Dionysische Weltanschauung" (1870) return in Nietzsche's final work, *Ecce Homo* (1888), in the "Gondola-Lied" that accompanies the complete loss of rational control. These examples are simply end points of a life's work replete with musical references and metaphors, with themes of madness and a series of mad figures.

What distinguishes the beginning and end from the rest of the philosophical œuvre, however, is the curious collocation of cognitive breakdown and aural art. It is as if the isolated topics of music and madness that are dispersed across the writings join together at either extreme, as origin and telos, thereby defining the philosophical project as an unfolding of what this pairing implies. The linking of music and madness, then, both at the start and finish of Nietzsche's thought, could be taken as a summons and a retreat, an instigation and a renunciation, an expression of hope and a cry of despair.

For this reason especially, from the biographical point of view, one could say that music and madness come after the end of philosophy and before its beginning. While still a student of classical philology at Bonn, Nietzsche wrote to his mother and sister, informing them that he was still composing "with energetic fury [Wuth]," most recently "a song in the highest style of the future ["im höchsten Zukunftsstile"], with a natural scream and suchlike ingredients of a silent madness [Narrheit]."[2] Nearly twenty-four years later, when Franz Overbeck arrived in Italy to rescue his deranged friend, he found him at the piano wildly improvising melodies, sublimely powerful and frighteningly disconcerting, "in brutally immediate attacks of raving madness."[3] The hagiographies that quickly emerged in the wake of Nietzsche's death were fond of perpetuating the portrait of the mad musician, which inscribed the philosopher into the standard romantic tradition of coupling musical experience and mental illness. In this way, the erstwhile philologist and seething Antichrist could join the ranks of Wackenroder's Berglinger or Hoffmann's Kreisler; he could be understood as having succumbed to the fate of Kleist's fraternal band of iconoclasts. Thus Nietzsche entered the space of high modernism that postdates him, particularly by way of Thomas Mann, either as Gustav von Aschenbach, whose faith in literary discipline was unworked by the Dionysiac "drum rattles" and the "deep, alluring tones of the flute" of his Venetian nightmare,[4] or as Adrian Leverkühn, the protagonist of Mann's "Nietzsche-Book," whose final Umnachtung falls upon the composer as he sits on the piano stool.

Ernst Bertram's Nietzsche: Versuch einer Mythologie (1918), which Mann acknowledged as a key source for Doktor Faustus, suggests that the philosopher's descent into musical madness was but a return. In an allusion to Hölderlin's ode Lebenslauf, Bertram writes, "the arc of this strange life turned back to the point from which it came":[5] after the end of philosophy and before its beginning. The legend of Nietzsche's madness therefore raises the same issues that have coursed through this study. Is his fall into insanity yet another instance of a romantic convention? Or does the legend itself, with all its implications, promise to articulate something crucial to philosophy itself, to the processes and consequences of thinking? How should we account for Nietzsche's consistency, which brings together musical and mad experience at either end of a writing career, which indeed reveals music and madness to be there before and after philosophy, that is, before the beginning and after the end of thought in philosophical form—a consistency all the more noteworthy given Nietzsche's notorious capacity and self-avowed proclivity to contradict himself, to break apart any formalizable identity for his thinking?

It is important to interrogate the persistent tendency in Nietzsche studies to confuse text and author. Certainly, Nietzsche's writings, which insist that "there are no philosophies, only philosophers," readily invite a conflation of the man and the work. Yet other comments seem explicitly to disparage such a method: "I am one thing, my writings are another" (NW 6.298/EH 99). Nonetheless, we read the chilling validations of derangement (for example, in section 14 of Morgenröthe: "Ah, give me but madness, you heavenly ones! Madness, that I may finally believe in myself!" [NW 3.26]), we observe the repeated flirtations with insanity, and we find it difficult to divorce such statements from the later image of the demented, godless prophet sitting in the Carignano Opera in Turin incapable of holding back his tears.

The idea that Nietzsche's work could have induced his madness is further corroborated by his pervasive allusions to the danger of his thinking. Moreover, in the same aphorism from Die Morgenröthe, "The Significance of Madness in the History of Morality," Nietzsche explains the indispensability of madness for thinking: "almost everywhere it is madness that blazes the path ["den Weg bahnt"] for new thoughts, that breaks the spell [den Bann] of venerated custom and superstition" (NW 3.26). As he famously proclaims toward the conclusion of Ecce Homo: "I know my lot. One day my name will be connected with the memory of something tremendous ["etwas Ungeheures"],—a crisis such as the earth has never seen, the deepest collision of conscience, a decision made against everything that has been believed, demanded, held sacred so far. I am not a human being, I am dynamite ["Ich bin kein Mensch, ich bin Dynamit"]" (NW 6.365/EH 143–44; emphasis in original).

The aural shock of Nietzsche's detonations reaches back to the imperative "Listen to me!" that opens his autobiography. "Above all," Nietzsche explains in reference to his Zarathustra, "you need to listen properly to the tone coming from this mouth, the halcyon tone, so as not to be miserably unfair to the meaning of its wisdom ["um dem Sinn seiner Weisheit nicht erbarmungswürdig Unrecht zu thun"]" (NW 6.259/

EH 72–73). We recall that, since antiquity, music and acoustical phenomena have been regarded with suspicion by those eager for philosophical reflection. The ordered speeches regulated by Phaedrus in Plato's *Symposium* proceed smoothly once the flute girls have been banished but are subsequently upset by disturbing sounds: first, mildly, by Aristophanes' loud hiccups and then, crucially, by Alcibiades' uncalculated intrusion, which leaves the door open for the seductive flautists' return. Hence Kant's distaste for music, which, like a strong odor, "extends its influence further . . . than is required." In a brief essay from his *Parerga und Paralipomena*, Schopenhauer similarly complains against "noise" (*Lärm*), which "is the most impertinent of all interruptions, since it even interrupts our own thoughts, indeed destroys them."[6] Nietzsche's philosophy does not merely face up to musical distraction and acoustic disturbance; it is itself an explosion—"dynamite"—whose deafening noise, far from destroying our capacity to think, urges us to think further.

Music, however, need not be shrill and abrasive like Zarathustra's "halcyon tone." The Italophilia that pervades *Ecce Homo* is also accompanied by a sweeter, more serene art that is not without a threat to subjective control: "I will say another word for the choicest of ears: what I really want from music. That it be cheerful and profound ["heiter und tief"], like an afternoon in October. That it be distinctive, exuberant, and tender ["eigen, ausgelassen, zärtlich"], a sweet little female, full of grace and dirty tricks. . . . I will never admit that a German could know what music is. . . . And when I say 'beyond the Alps,' I really am only saying Venice. When I look for another word for music, I only ever find the word 'Venice.' I cannot tell any difference between tears and music. I know the happiness of not being able to think of the South without a shudder of apprehension" (*NW* 6.290–91/*EH* 94–95). As I have reported, music's propensity to relax the will, to induce hypersensitivity and cause sexual licentiousness, immorality, and even madness has, at least since the eighteenth century, posed a threat to those intent on maintaining rational sobriety. At the end of the nineteenth century, the agent most responsible for music's harmful effects was Richard Wagner. Nietzsche's contemporary Ferdinand von Saar expresses in his novella *Geschichte eines Wienerkindes* (1891) some of the fears that still made the gleeful Antichrist shudder. At a dinner party toward the story's end, Elsa, the protagonist who has stumbled into a string of adulterous affairs, pleads with a musician guest to play the "Liebestod" from Wagner's *Tristan und Isolde*. Despite the reservations voiced by the somewhat prudish Frau von Ramberg, the young man turns to the piano: "Thus again there arose a silence, full of expectation, and soon thereafter, out of evenly trembling waves of sound, in gradual, cruelly voluptuous crescendi, continually sinking back into themselves, there developed the most violent [*gewaltsamste*] attack on human nerves known to music. . . . Everyone, in their own way, felt gripped, overwhelmed, tortured, delighted, disheveled. Even Frau von Ramberg could not maintain her dignity; she began to writhe on her chair like a snake. . . . Elsa lay leaning back in the low fauteuil. She was pale, and quick, even tremors shook her body. Suddenly she uttered a piercing cry."[7] The irresistible, penetrating effect of Wagner's music is a contagion that dissolves self-composure and decency; even the morally upright Frau von Ramberg undergoes a transformation into the very symbol of evil and sexuality. Contributing to the popular imagination was the fact that the tenor Ludwig Schnorr, who played the role of Tristan in the premiere performance, died soon thereafter, after suffering a violent bout of delirium; his wife, Malwina, who played Isolde, would experience wild, terrifying hallucinations for the remainder of her life.[8] Nietzsche himself had promulgated such fantasies when he presented the Wagnerian example and asked "true musicians"

> whether they can conceive of any person capable of perceiving the third act of *Tristan und Isolde* purely as a vast [*ungeheuren*] symphonic movement, with no assistance from words or images, and who would not then suffocate as their soul attempted, convulsively, to spread its wings. How could anyone fail to be shattered immediately, having once put their ear to the heart of the universal Will, so to speak, and felt the raving desire for existence ["das rasende Begehren zu Dasein"] pour forth into all the arteries of the world as a thundering torrent or as the finest spray of a stream? Is such a person, trapped within the miserable glass vessel of human individuality, supposed to be able to bear listening to countless calls of pleasure and woe re-echoing from the "wide space of the world's night," without fleeing, unstoppably, with the strains of this shepherd's dance of metaphysics in his ears, towards his first and original home [*Urheimat*]?
>
> (*GEBURT DER TRAGÖDIE*, NW 1.135–36)[9]

Somber or cheerful, violent or serenely seductive, the mad and musical content of Nietzsche's thought may have driven the thinker out of his mind and may be striving to do the same for those of us who have the right ears. Indeed, once the line separating Nietzsche's life and work has been breached, we are faced with the terrifying, or perhaps exhilarating, prospect of having his philosophy—his music and madness— explode or melt our own sanity. If Nietzsche's mental state was truly a consequence of his philosophy—and not, say, merely the result of a syphilitic infection—then we are justified in considering what in fact this mad thought may possibly be. Can we suffer a philosophy—a love of knowledge—without a rational subjective ground? Thought without a thinker? Even if we were to allow the possibility of an obscure clarity or a lucid darkness, what kind of significance or truth could we grant it?

—❧—

As throughout this study, all speculation on an author's madness and on its possible link to musical experience must of course remain conjectural. Nonetheless, the line between life and work that critical interpretation invariably must draw can never be rigorous, at least in the case of Nietzsche. On the one hand, any attempt to give a strictly philosophical reading to his writings—and this is especially true of his autobiography, *Ecce Homo*—is compelled by the very content of the text to explode the border that would separate the author's words from the living being that produced them. Nietzsche's corpus is never easily distinguishable from his corpus, as his frequent references to his own health and physiology, to his headaches, his diet, and digestion, readily make clear. Here Nietzsche belongs to a long preidealist tradition, reaching back to Hamann and Herder, that refuses to separate thinking from sensuousness (*Empfinden*). As Herder expresses it in his essay "Vom Erkennen und Empfinden der menschlichen Seele" (1775): "Das Denken ist im Empfinden verwurzelt"—"Thinking is rooted in Sensing." Along these lines, a rigorously immanent reading of Nietzsche's philosophy would fail to respect the terms of that philosophy. This interpretive decision continues to shape Nietzsche studies. Christoph Türcke, for example, begins his analyses of the philosopher's late works with a representative caveat, based on his author's own methodology: "With philosophers, may one make a clean separation between the work and the person? . . . Nietzsche's answer is: no."[10] On the other hand, however, a solely biographical approach, where the philosophical system is derived exclusively from psychological or even psychoanalytic investigations, cannot be adequate. The sheer rhetorical force of Nietzsche's *Ecce Homo*—the rampant metaphors, the plurality of personae, not to mention the blatant contradictions and reversals—reminds the reader of the textualized nature of all references to a living being and furthermore discourages the desire to consolidate and ground the autobiography in a single, identifiable, historical person. Nietzsche, and this name could be taken with or without its original bearer, is not a "Mensch"—neither measurable nor measured (*mensus*)—he is rather "Dynamit," a power or a potential (*dynamis*) that blows to pieces all the philosophemes that are fragilely held together in the term "autobiography": "autos," "bios," "graphein": We read what Nietzsche is only by examining and questioning the rubble: What is writing? What is life? What is a self? How do they relate?

The preface to *Ecce Homo* declares it will inform those listening who "I, Friedrich Nietzsche, am." "Listen to me! I am this one and this one"—"Ich bin der und der." The text goes on to introduce chapters primarily organized around this "I am": "Why I am so wise," "Why I am so clever," "Why I am a destiny." The duplicity or multiplication, already signaled by the "ich bin der und der," culminates in the doubled, antagonistic, and somewhat insane signature that concludes the book: "Dionysus versus the Crucified"— "Dionysus gegen den Gekreuzigten." Throughout *Ecce Homo*, multiplicity pervades and intensifies the self-representations. Semiosis overloads any simple reading along the lines of a mimetically true life story. The philosopher's self-styled doubled ancestry tears the self between the antithesis of life and death, between the father who is dead and the mother who survives, between the affirmative power of Bizet and the sickly decadence of Wagner. "Ich bin der und der": I am alive and I am dead. As Jacques Derrida conjoins us: "Must one not take this unrepresentable scene into account each time one claims to identify any utterance signed by F. N.?"[11] Clearly, the self, the writing, and the life fail to coincide but instead demand a particular kind of revaluation, an *Umwertung* that every reader with the right ears must perform. The reader, who would remain comfortably outside of the text, is by the very act of reading—or listening—already implicated in its action. Nietzsche indulges in an autocitation from the *Zarathustra*: "Now I call upon you to lose me and find yourselves; and only after you have all denied me will I want to return to you" (*NW* 6.261/*EH* 73).

The noncoincidence that is revealed by Nietzsche's explosive text opens up a space outside but also constitutive of the philosophical project. This nonconceptualized, nonmoralized, nonindividuated space is in fact an obsessive theme that extends throughout Nietzsche's writings—and, I should now add, his life. It is, moreover, consistently presented in metaphors of music. Already, in the passage on Wagner's *Tristan* from the closing pages of the *Geburt der Tragödie*, the space is named as the "first and original home"—the *Urheimat*—of the soul, as that which comes before and after all (Apolline) form, including not only the form of thinking but also the form of individuality that authorizes the text. Earlier in the book, Nietzsche further legitimizes his position, which he borrowed almost entirely from Schopenhauer, by turning to the authority of Schiller, who explained: "In my case the feeling is initially without a definite and clear object; this does not take shape until later. It is preceded by a certain musical mood ["eine gewisse musikalische Gemüthsstimmung"], which is followed in my case by the poetic idea" (*NW* 1.43).[12] The musical metaphor is apt for Schiller's age, which developed the notion, positively or negatively, of music as a nonrepresentational art form. Filtered through Schopenhauer's description of the Will, which underlies all representations, and of music's privileged access to this Will, the nonrepresentational quality of music furnishes the young Nietzsche with an art that can articulate dimensions of existence that elude representation, aspects that play out an "unrepresentable scene." Nietzsche, whose writing demanded to be heard rather than read, may be offering us a language beyond words, a language that is either musical or mad or both.

To musicalize or dement language, however, often enough means to demusicalize music or render madness sane. Nietzsche the writer faced this problem in an especially acute fashion. The expression of his thinking requires the adoption of a lexicon that necessarily harbors its own contradictions. Rational language, which is based on fixed identities and conventional agreement, belongs to the herd: "We no longer sufficiently value ourselves ["wir schätzen uns nicht genug mehr"], when we communicate. Our true experiences [*Erlebnisse*] are not garrulous ["nicht geschwätzig"]. They could not be communicated even if they wanted to be. This is because the right words for them do not exist. The things we have words for are also the things we have already left behind. There is a grain of contempt in all speech. Language, it seems, was invented only for average, mediocre, communicable things. People *vulgarize* themselves when they speak a language.—Excerpts from a morality for the deaf-mutes and other philosophers" (*Götzen-Dämmerung*, *NW* 6.128/*EH* 205; emphasis in original). Thus, along with Wackenroder and Kleist, Nietzsche perpetually tried to bring the power of music into language only to experience, painfully, the evanescence of music and the pathologization of madness.

Spontaneity, immediacy, prereflexivity—all these notions are implied by the romantic idea of music as a purely self-referential sign system. Semiotic, rather than semantic, musical significance rests on the indissociable (immediate) identity of what in discursive practice is divided into sign and referent. And it is precisely this immediacy that invariably characterizes the phenomenology of insanity. Historically, the nonrepresentational qualities of music have been held in a positive light, most notably by proponents of so-called absolute music, while the speech of madmen has been identified in general as a deficit or failure. The ineffable heights of musical experience seem to stand in starkest contrast to the piteous babblings of lunacy or the sorry delusions of delirium. For the romantic authors discussed above, however, both consistently enjoyed the privilege of transmitting something that resists appearance in and through words. From the nephew's deracination of the self-identical subject to the anagrammatical interruptions of Wackenroder and Hoffmann, the machine of representation is sabotaged. But for how long? The disruptive semiotic play that permits the author's name to become manifest within the discourse is always thereby reinscribed into another discourse, equally referential, equally mimetic. The recalcitrant, intractable aspects of life—beautifully troped in terms of music and madness—are eventually brought into line with a program. The mad and the musical may speak language's silence, they may interrupt the work process, they may indeed be heard or seen, but only like Eurydice, at the very moment of vanishing, of being reabsorbed into text.

Notes

INTRODUCTION

1. For early modern Europe, the overwhelming power of music was generally understood to be due to the musical proportions said to underlie and order both the human and the cosmological realm. For a useful discussion and bibliographical references, see Timothy J. Reiss, *Knowledge, Discovery and Imagination in Early Modern Europe: The Rise of Aesthetic Rationalism* (Cambridge: Cambridge University Press, 1997), 169–87.

2. Jacques Lefèvre d'Étaples, *Musica libris quatuor demonstrata* (1496; reprint, Paris: Cavellat, 1552). Along similar lines, Abraham Cowley in a note to his *Davideis* (1640–42) clarified the point made in his biblical epic: "That *Timotheus* by *Musick* enflamed and appeased *Alexander* to what degrees he pleased, is well known to all men conversant among Authors" (*Davideis: A Sacred Poem of the Troubles of David* [London, 1677], 34 n. 32).

3. See Gary Tomlinson, *Music in Renaissance Magic: Toward a Historiography of Others* (Chicago: University of Chicago Press, 1993).

4. See Pascal Fournier, *Der Teufelsvirtuose: Eine kulturhistorische Spurensuche* (Freiburg im Breisgau: Rombach, 2001).

5. Franz Franken, *Die Krankheiten grosser Komponisten*, 4 vols. (Wilhelmshaven: Noetzel, 1986–97).

6. For an overview, see Ruth Padel, *Whom Gods Destroy: Elements of Greek and Tragic Madness* (Princeton: Princeton University Press, 1995).

7. A by no means exhaustive list would include Kay Redfield Jamison, *Touched by Fire: Manic-Depressive Illness and the Artistic Temperament* (New York: Free Press, 1993); Arnold Ludwig, *The Price of Greatness: Resolving the Creativity and Madness Controversy* (New York: Guilford, 1995); Stephen Diamond, *Anger, Madness, and the Daimonic: the Psychological Genesis of Violence, Evil, and Creativity* (Albany: State University of New York Press, 1996); Philippe Brenot, *Le génie et la folie en peinture, musique, littérature* (Paris: Plon, 1997); Leo Navratil, *Manisch-depressiv: Zur Psychodynamik des Künstlers* (Vienna: Brandstätter,

1999); Michael Fitzgerald, *Autism and Creativity: Is There a Link Between Autism in Men and Exceptional Ability?* (New York: Routledge, 2004); and Nancy Andreasen, *The Creating Brain: The Neuroscience of Genius* (New York: Dana, 2005). For a critical discussion, see Silke-Maria Weineck, *The Abyss Above: Philosophy and Poetic Madness in Plato, Hölderlin, and Nietzsche* (New York: State University of New York Press, 2002), 2–3.

8. Two typical, representative examples: Wilhelm Heinse, Hoffmann's older contemporary, defines music as the art "that universally expresses what language can often only roughly and obliquely indicate"; later, Grillparzer confesses that "tones speak where language can no longer suffice" (cited in Corina Caduff, *Die Literarisierung von Musik und bildender Kunst um 1800* [Munich: Fink, 2003], 44).

9. From *Either/Or* (1843), trans. David F. Swenson and Lillian M. Swenson (Princeton: Princeton University Press, 1959), 1.68–69.

10. George Steiner, *Language and Silence: Essays on Language, Literature, and the Inhuman* (New York: Atheneum, 1967), 43.

11. Pamela Potter, ed., *Most German of the Arts: Musicology and Society from the Weimar Republic to the End of Hitler's Reich* (New Haven: Yale University Press, 1998), ix.

12. Eric Prieto, *Listening In: Music, Mind, and the Modernist Narrative* (Lincoln: University of Nebraska Press, 2002), 19. For a full discussion with relevant bibliography, see Prieto's section "Beyond 'Musico-Literary' Studies," 16–25. Also see Susan Bernstein's probing chapter "The Musical Alibi in Theories of Performativity" in *Virtuosity of the Nineteenth Century: Performing Music and Language in Heine, Liszt, and Baudelaire* (Stanford: Stanford University Press, 1998), 36–57.

13. See Shoshona Felman, *Writing and Madness: Literature/Philosophy/Psychoanalysis* (Stanford: Stanford University Press, 2003); also, Jean Rigoli, *Lire et délire: Aliénisme, rhétorique, et littérature en France au XIXe siècle* (Paris: Fayard, 2001).

14. Carolyn Abbate, *Unsung Voices: Opera and Musical Narrative in the Nineteenth Century* (Princeton: Princeton University Press, 1991), 18.

15. Jacques Derrida, "Cogito and the History of Madness," in *Writing and Difference*, trans. Alan Bass (New York: Routledge, 2001), 36–76.

16. Recently, however, studies among Germanists have begun to treat this theme. See, for example: Christine Lubkoll, *Mythos Musik: Poetische Entwürfe des Musikalischen in der Literatur um 1800* (Freiburg im Breisgau: Rombach, 1995); Corinna Caduff, *Die Literarisierung von Musik und bildender Kunst um 1800* (Munich: Fink, 2003); and Nicola Gess, *Die Gewalt der Musik: Literatur und Musikkritik um 1800* (Freiburg im Breisgau: Rombach, 2006).

17. Slavoj Žižek and Mladen Dolar, *Opera's Second Death* (New York: Routledge, 2002), 19.

18. Michel Poizat, *The Angel's Cry: Beyond the Pleasure Principle in Opera*, trans. Arthur Denner (Ithaca: Cornell University Press, 1992), 45.

19. See Julia Kristeva, *La révolution du langage poétique: L'avant-garde à la fin du XIXe siècle. Lautréamont et Mallarmé* (Paris: Seuil, 1974), 17–22. After distin-

guishing within language both a symbolic and a semiotic modality, Kristeva refers to music as exclusively semiotic (22) and then proceeds throughout her book to depict this preverbal "semiotic chora" with metaphors of musicality.

20. See Adriana Cavarero, *For More than One Voice: Toward a Philosophy of Vocal Expression*, trans. Paul A. Kottman (Stanford: Stanford University Press, 2005), 131–38.

21. Roland Barthes, *The Pleasure of the Text*, trans. Richard Miller (New York: Hill and Wang, 1975), 63.

22. Philippe Lacoue-Labarthe broaches the connection among music, madness, and autobiography in "L'écho du sujet" (1979), translated as "The Echo of the Subject" in *Typography: Mimesis, Philosophy, Politics*, ed. Christopher Fynsk (Cambridge: Harvard University Press, 1989), 138–207.

23. See Philippe Lejeune, *Le pacte autobiographique* (Paris: Seuil, 1975), 14.

24. Philippe Lacoue-Labarthe and Jean-Luc Nancy, *The Literary Absolute: The Theory of Literature in German Romanticism*, trans. Philip Barnard and Cheryl Lester (Albany: State University of New York Press, 1988), 57.

25. In his later work, Lacoue-Labarthe will turn to a more pronounced reflection on music's relation to verbal language. Specifically, he pursues the tradition of subjugating music to the word, which he designates, with reference to Adorno, as *musica ficta*, precisely as a reaction to music's insubordinate resistance to such objectification. See *Musica Ficta (Figures of Wagner)*, trans. Felicia Mc-Carren (Stanford: Stanford University Press, 1994).

26. Maurice Blanchot, *L'espace littéraire* (Paris: Gallimard, 1955), 229; idem, *The Space of Literature*, trans. Ann Smock (Lincoln: University of Nebraska Press, 1982), 174.

27. Maurice Blanchot, *L'entretien infini* (Paris: Gallimard, 1969), 524; idem, *The Infinite Conversation*, trans. Susan Hanson (Minneapolis: University of Minnesota Press, 1993), 357.

28. See the *Tagebuch* entry for February 8, 1812 (*HW* 1.397); and the letter to Julius Hitzig, April 28, 1812 (*HW* 1.243).

29. Paul de Man, *The Rhetoric of Romanticism* (New York: Columbia University Press, 1984), 69; emphasis in original.

30. Letter to Julius Hitzig, January 8, 1821 (*HW* 6.202).

1. HEARING VOICES

1. Speaking of Diderot's paradoxical style, Jay Caplan points to the irreconcilability of the standpoints presented: "Diderot's work does not easily fit into a single, coherent frame. Instead it continually shifts between mutually exclusive dialogic positions, neither of which provides an entirely satisfactory answer to the question at hand and yet neither of which can be disregarded, either." (*Framed Narratives: Diderot's Genealogy of the Beholder* [Minneapolis: University of Minnesota Press, 1985], 4).

2. Jean Starobinski, "Diderot et la parole des autres," *Critique*, no. 296 (1972): 3–22. For an overview and discussion of this line of interpretation, see J. Creech,

"Diderot and the Pleasure of the Other: Friends, Readers and Posterity," *Eighteenth-Century Studies*, no. 11 (1978): 439–56.

3. Cited in Starobinski, "Diderot et la parole des autres," 10.

4. Ibid., 9.

5. Arthur Wilson, *Diderot* (New York: Oxford University Press, 1972), 24. Most of the biographical information in this section comes from this comprehensive and eminently readable work.

6. Julia Kristeva pursues the theoretical ramifications of Diderot's use of pronominal forms in *Le neveu*, with ample reference to Lacan and Benveniste, broaching many provocative issues that would take the present reading too far off course: See "La musique parlée; ou, Remarques sur la subjectivité dans la fiction à propos du 'Neveu de Rameau,'" in *Langue et langages de Leibniz à L'encyclopédie*, ed. Michèle Duchet and Michèle Jalley (Paris: Union Générale d'Éditions, 1977), 153–206.

7. Littré includes the Pascal citation. *Dictionnaire de la langue française*, 4 vols. (Paris: Hachette, 1889), s.v. "Moi" (sec. 27).

8. Jean Fabre's critical edition is especially useful in collating the dialogue's passages with Diderot's œuvre (*NR* 111–242).

9. René Descartes, *Discours de la méthode*, ed. L. Renault (Paris: Flammarion, 2000); idem, *Discourse on Method and the Meditations*, trans. F. E. Sutcliffe (New York: Penguin, 1968), 54.

10. Lacanian psychoanalysis, with its theory of the object voice, consistently interrogates what Derrida has famously dubbed "phonocentrism." Mladen Dolar comments: "For psychoanalysis, the auto-affective voice of self-presence and self-mastery was constantly opposed by its reverse side, the intractable voice of the other, the voice one could not control. . . . We could tentatively say that at the very core of narcissism lies an alien kernel which narcissistic satisfaction may well attempt to disguise, but which continually threatens to undermine it from the inside" (*A Voice and Nothing More* [Cambridge, Mass.: MIT Press, 2006], 41; see also 36–42).

11. See Bernard Sève, *L'altération musicale* (Paris: Seuil, 2002), 22–29.

12. Michel Foucault, *History of Madness*, trans. Jonathan Murphy and Jean Khalfa (London: Routledge, 2006), 351.

13. Adriana Cavarero, *For More than One Voice: Toward a Philosophy of Vocal Expression*, trans. Paul A. Kottman (Stanford: Stanford University Press, 2005), 42–46.

14. *Encyclopédie; ou, Dictionnaire raisonné des sciences, des arts, et des métiers*, 17 vols. (Paris, 1751–72; facsimile reprint, New York: Pergamon, 1969), 7.42–43.

15. See Thomas Christensen, *Rameau and Musical Thought in the Enlightenment* (Cambridge: Cambridge University Press, 1993), 291–306.

16. Diderot, *Leçons de clavecin et principes d'harmonie*, in *Œuvres completes*, ed. J. Varloot (Paris: Hermann, 1975), 19.378.

17. The Marsyas myth, variously interpreted, has often been used to introduce decisive strands in the history of music as well as in the analysis of so-called musico-literary studies. See especially John Hollander, *The Untuning of the Sky:*

Ideas of Music in English Poetry, 1500–1700 (Princeton: Princeton University Press, 1961); and Daniel Albright, *Untwisting the Serpent: Modernism in Music, Literature, and Other Arts* (Chicago: University of Chicago Press, 2000). The negative prefix in my term "unworking" is in part a grateful acknowledgment of my debt to these studies. For a broad account of the myth in the European classical tradition, see Edith Wyss, *The Myth of Apollo and Marsyas in the Art of the Italian Renaissance: An Inquiry into the Meaning of Images* (Newark: University of Delaware Press, 1996).

18. See Ruth Padel, *Whom Gods Destroy: Elements of Greek and Tragic Madness* (Princeton: Princeton University Press, 1995), 120–28.

19. Apollodorus, *The Library*, 1.4.2, trans. J. G. Frazer, Loeb Classical Library (Cambridge: Harvard University Press, 1921), 28–29 (translation modified).

20. Apollodorus may have invented the story of the inversion, which is later picked up by Hyginus (*Fabula* 165).

21. Later developments increased the lyre's strings to seven, thereby aligning a heptatonic scale with the seven planets. See Pliny, *Natural History*, 2.20. For further aspects of Pythagorean correspondences through to the Renaissance, see Wyss, *Myth of Apollo*, 27–33.

22. Diodorus, a Sicilian presumably well acquainted with Pythagoreanism, further reports that Apollo, regretting the cruelty of his acts against Marsyas, broke the strings of his lyre and thereby destroyed the *harmonia*.

23. See Dolar, *A Voice and Nothing More*, 14–19.

24. Wilhelm von Humboldt, *Werke*, 5 vols., ed. Andreas Flitner and Klaus Giel (Darmstadt: Wissenschaftliche Buchgesellschaft, 1960–81), 3.418.

25. Seth Benardete, *The Rhetoric of Morality and Philosophy: Plato's* Gorgias *and* Phaedrus (Chicago: University of Chicago Press, 1991), 104.

2. UNEQUAL SONG

1. See Avital Ronell's insistent interrogation of philosophy's compulsion to wed music to some discursive system. "Finitude's Score" in *Finitude's Score: Essays for the End of the Millennium* (Lincoln: University of Nebraska Press, 1994), 19–40.

2. For an extended discussion in relation to the broader historical context, see Wolfgang Promies, *Die Bürger und der Narr; oder, Das Risiko der Phantasie* (Munich: Hanser, 1966), 14–51.

3. Johann Christoph Gottsched, *Versuch einer Critischen Dichtkunst* (1751; facsimile reprint, Darmstadt: Wissenschaftliche Buchgesellschaft, 1962), 422.

4. "Dadurch werden nun auch die poetischen Strophen länger, die sie denn unter sich einander gleich machen; weil man am Ende der einen, die Melodie wieder vom Anfange anheben mußte. Das Wort στροφη zeigt solches zur Gnüge, weil es von στρεφειν, oder vom Umkehren, seinen Ursprung hat, und also eine Wiederkehr bedeutet. Wenn man es also lateinisch einen Vers heißt, so ist es eben so viel; weil VERSUS von VERTERE hergleitet wird" (ibid.).

5. For a historical overview, see Belinda Cannone, *Philosophies de la musique (1752–1780)* (Paris: Klincksieck, 1990), 15–24.

6. Noël-Antoine Pluche, *Le spectacle de la nature*, 8 vols. (Paris: Estienne et Fils, 1749–56), 7.115.

7. Jean-Baptiste Dubos, *Réflexions critiques sur la poésie et la peinture* (Paris: Mariette, 1733), 426.

8. Condillac's *Essai sur l'origine des connaissances humaines* (Amsterdam: Mortier, 1746) posits music at the midpoint between the natural cries of emotion and the conventional sounds of language proper. In terms similar to Rousseau's, his famous myth of two abandoned children growing up without any outside contact illustrates how the natural accents of the moment eventually become fixed, by means of memory, into artificial signs capable of evoking what is no longer present. Like Rousseau, Condillac characterizes the first language as musical, but unlike in Rousseau, emphasis is placed entirely on need and use, as opposed to pure pleasure. In his essay *De l'analyse du discours*, he explains: "Given the necessity of asking for and giving assistance, the first men studied this [natural] language; they thus learned to use it with greater skill; and the accents, which for them were initially only natural signs, gradually became artificial signs which they modified with different articulations. This likely explains why the prosody of many languages was a kind of song" (cited in Downing Thomas, *Music and the Origins of Language: Theories from the French Enlightenment* [Cambridge: Cambridge University Press, 1995], 71).

9. "Ces deux termes [*aimez-moi, aidez-moi*], quoiqu'assés semblables, se prononcent d'un ton bien différent. On n'avoit rien à faire sentir, on avoit tout à faire entendre; il ne s'agissoit donc pas d'énergie mais de clarté. À l'accent que le cœur ne fournissoit pas, on substitua des articulations fortes et sensibles, et s'il y eut dans la forme du langage quelque impression naturelle, cette impression contribuoit encore à sa dureté" (*Essai sur l'origine des langues*, ROC 5.408).

10. I am referring of course to Derrida's sustained reading of Rousseau's *Essai* in *Of Grammatology*, trans. Gayatri C. Spivak (Baltimore: Johns Hopkins University Press, 1974).

11. In *Der Rhein*, Hölderlin names Rousseau as the speaker of "the language of the purest" ("die Sprache der Reinesten"), "from a holy fullness, foolishly divine and lawless, like the Wine-God" ("aus heiliger Fülle / Wie der Weingott, törig göttlich / Und gesetzlos").

12. See John T. Scott, "Rousseau and the Melodious Language of Freedom," *Journal of Politics*, no. 59 (1997): 803–29.

13. "C'est là ce qui s'appelle enchaîner des sons dont le succession fasse penser; savoir parler à l'âme et à l'oreille et connaître les sources du chant et de la mélodie, dont le vrai type est au fond du cœur" (Diderot, *Œuvres complètes*, 25 vols., ed. Jean Varloot [Paris: Hermann, 1975], 19.353).

14. *Entretiens sur le fils naturel*, in Diderot, *Œuvres*, ed. André Billy (Paris: Gallimard, Bibliothèque de la Pléiade, 1951), 1220–21.

15. Ernst Robert Curtius, *European Literature and the Latin Middle Ages*, trans. Willard Trask (New York: Pantheon, 1953), 573–83. Curtius essentially limits his interpretation to explaining how both Horace's and Diderot's texts elaborate the Stoic dictum "Only the wise man is free, and every fool is a slave."

16. See Yoichi Sumi, Le neveu de Rameau: *Caprices et logiques du jeu* (Tokyo: France Tosho, 1975), 117–18.

17. See Jean Starobinski, "L'accent de la verité," in *Diderot* (Paris: Comédie Française, 1984), 9–26.

18. Diderot, *Œuvres*, 1006

19. See Philippe Lacoue-Labarthe, "Diderot: Paradox and Mimesis," in *Typography: Mimesis, Philosophy, Politics*, ed. Christopher Fynsk (Cambridge: Harvard University Press, 1989), 248–66. My comparison of the actor and the nephew is highly indebted to Lacoue-Labarthe's reading.

20. Lacoue-Labarthe distinguishes the active mimesis of the actor (the willed ability to empty one's subjectivity) from the passive mimesis of the one possessed: "Possession . . . presupposes the supposit itself or the supporting medium, the matrix or malleable matter in which the imprint is stamped. . . . Possession, in other words, presupposes a subject; it is the monstrous, dangerous form of a *passive mimesis*, uncontrolled and unmanageable" (ibid., 264).

21. Rousseau, s.v. "Génie," *Dictionnaire de la musique*, in *Œuvres complètes*, 5 vols., ed. Bernard Gagnebin and Marcel Raymond (Paris: Gallimard, Bibliothèque de la Pléiade, 1959–95), 5.837.

22. For a full analysis on the history and problems concerning the "work-concept" in musicology, see Lydia Goehr, *The Imaginary Museum of Musical Works: An Essay in the Philosophy of Music* (Oxford: Clarendon, 1992).

23. The distinction between taking music either as performance or as composition bears significantly on theories of language and subjectivity. Susan Bernstein traces this theme from Saussure to Nancy by pressing the division between *langue* and *parole*. See *Virtuosity of the Nineteenth Century: Performing Music and Language in Heine, Liszt, and Baudelaire* (Stanford: Stanford University Press, 1998), 36–57.

24. Roland Barthes, "The Grain of the Voice," in *Image—Music—Text*, trans. Stephen Heath (New York: Hill and Wang, 1977), 182 and 188. Despite Barthes's claims—together with the linguistic analyses of Julia Kristeva, to whom Barthes refers—Susan Bernstein argues that a theory of expressivity is nonetheless re-installed, since expression remains implicit in the very theory of language employed by both Barthes and Kristeva: "Barthes wants to distance himself from an expressive theory based on the preexistence of a rational cogito. However, as for Kristeva, since the analysis is based on a linguistic model, it is hard to know how the suspension of signification attributed to music finally differs from a model of 'expression'" (*Virtuosity of the Nineteenth Century*, 49). In the end, Bernstein is right to detect a latent expressionism in these and other linguistically oriented theoreticians. In this regard, what Diderot allows to break through his text comes across as a far more radical insight into the irreducible, intractable qualities of the voice.

25. In Diderot, *Lettre sur les sourds et muets*, ed. Otis Fellows (Geneva: Droz, 1965), 52–53.

26. Louis-Bertrand Castel first presented his instrument in 1725, as a demonstration of the physical analogies between light and sound, which are concisely expressed in the term "chromatic" (from the Greek *"chrôma,"* "color"). For Castel, a Jesuit trained in mathematics and physics, the twelve-tone musical system corresponded exactly to the twelve partitions of the color wheel, as discussed in his essay *L'Optique des couleurs, fondée sur les simples observations, et tournée sur-tout à la pratique de la peinture, de la teinture et des autres arts coloristes* (Paris, 1740).

27. See Condillac, *Essai sur l'origine*, 234.

28. "Dès que l'homme se sentit entraîné par goût, par besoin & par plaisir à l'union de ses semblables, il lui étoit nécessaire de développer son ame à un autre, & lui en communiquer les situations" (s.v. "Langage," in Jean d'Alembert and Denis Diderot, *Encyclopédie; ou, Dictionnaire raisonné des sciences, des arts, et des métiers*, 17 vols. [Paris, 1751–72; facsimile reprint, New York: Pergamon, 1969], 9.242).

29. See also paragraphs 5.637, 5.na12, and 5.na15.

30. "Lui et Moi" was written in 1762, based on an encounter that Diderot later referred to in a letter to the sculptor Etienne Falconet (September 6, 1768). The text, including an excerpt from the letter to Falconet, may be found in Diderot, *Œuvres*, 713–15 and 1414–15. For a comparison of these texts with *Le neveu*, see Herbert Dieckmann, "The Relationship Between Diderot's Satire I and Satire II," *Romanic Review*, no. 43 (1952): 12–26; and Donal O'Gorman, *Diderot the Satirist:* Le Neveu de Rameau *and Related Works: An Analysis* (Toronto: University of Toronto Press, 1971).

31. Claude-Adrien Helvétius, *De l'esprit* (Paris: Durand, 1758; reprint, Paris: Fayard, 1988), 438.

32. *Réfutation suivie de l'ouvrage d'Helvétius intitulé* L'Homme, in Diderot, *Œuvres complètes*, 20 vols., ed. Jules Assézat and Maurice Tourneux (Paris: Garnier, 1875), 2.279.

33. Diderot, *Œuvres*, 899; English translation in Tancock's edition (1966): 181.

34. "Sovereignty cannot be represented, for the same reason that it cannot be alienated; its essence is the general will, and the will cannot be represented—either it is the general will or it is something else; there is no intermediate possibility" (Jean-Jacques Rousseau, *The Social Contract*, trans. Maurice Cranston [New York: Penguin, 1968], 141).

3. RESOUNDING SENSE

1. The autograph manuscript, now held at the Pierpont Morgan Library in New York, has since served as the basis for all subsequent editions For a complete account of the publication history, see Paul Vernière, "Histoire littéraire et papyrologie: À propos des autographes de Diderot," *Revue d'Histoire Littéraire de la France*, July–September 1966, 409–18. See also Vernière's *Diderot, ses manuscrits et ses copistes* (Paris: Klincksieck, 1967).

2. Here I am citing from Foucault's second edition, *Histoire de la folie à l'âge classique* (Paris: Gallimard, 1972), 443; English translation in *History of Madness*, trans. Jonathan Murphy and Jean Khalfa (London: Routledge, 2006), 353; translation slightly modified.

3. Ibid.

4. Silke-Maria Weineck, *The Abyss Above: Philosophy and Poetic Madness in Plato, Hölderlin, and Nietzsche* (Albany: State University of New York Press, 2002), 45; emphasis in original.

5. Foucault, *Histoire*, 437/*History*, 348; translation modified.

6. From Boileau's preface to the *Fragment d'un prologue d'opéra*, cited in William Brooks, "Mistrust and Misconception: Music and Literature in Seventeenth- and Eighteenth-Century France," in *Acta Musicologica*, no. 66 (1994): 23. Brooks proceeds to give a series of citations, which define what he names a "music-literary apartheid" (25).

7. Voltaire to Hénault, September 14, 1744, cited in Brooks, "Mistrust and Misconception," 25.

8. "L'usage qui est extrémement étendu depuis quelques siècles, de se passer de la musique vocale et de s'appliquer uniquement à amuser l'oreille sans présenter à l'esprit aucune pensée; en un mot de prétendre contenter l'homme par une longue suite de sons destitués de sens; ce qui est directement contraire à la nature même de la musique, qui est d'imiter, comme sont tous les beaux arts, l'image et le sentiment qui occupent l'esprit" (Noël-Antoine Pluche, *Le spectacle de la nature*, 8 vols. [Paris: Estienne et Fils, 1749–56], 7.111).

9. He is described as

> ein Erz-Taugenichts, der von den Schwächen andrer Leute lebte. Wenn er in einer Stadt die müßigen Music-Liebhaber durch sein Talent und die manntollen Weiber durch seine seelenlose Figur bezaubert hatte, nistete er sich auf eine Zeitlang ein und blieb dort, bis irgend ein verübtes Bubenstück ihn nöthigte, bey Nacht und Nebel fortzugehn, da ihm dann gewöhnlich die Flüche betrogner Gläubiger, mit Undank gelohnter Wohlthäter und verführter Mädchen nachfolgten. Dann trat er zwölf Meilen von da unter anderm Namen auf, hieß in St. Petersburg Monsieur Dubois, in Berlin Signor Carino, in Hamburg Herr Zarowsky und in Wien Herr Leuthammer; erschien bald in gestickten Fracks, mit zwey Uhren, bald im zerrißnen Überrocke, als blinder Passagier auf dem Postwagen.
>
> (ADOLF KNIGGE, *DIE REISE NACH BRAUNSCHWEIG*, ED. PAUL RAABE [KASSEL: WENDEROTH, 1972], CHAP. 5)

10. *Nachtwachten von Bonaventura*, ed. Raimund Steinert (Potsdam: Kiepenheuer, 1920), 11. Scholars now generally agree on attributing the text to Ernst August Klingemann.

11. *Anthropology from a Pragmatic Point of View*, trans. Victor L. Dowdell (Carbondale: Southern Illinois University Press, 1978), 111–12. For further discussion, see Theodore Ziolkowski, *German Romanticism and Its Institutions* (Princeton: Princeton University Press, 1990), 146ff.

12. Ibid., 117.

13. For the historical context, see Klaus Doerner, *Madmen and the Bourgeoisie: A Social History of Insanity and Psychiatry*, trans. Joachim Neugroschel and Jean Steinberg (Oxford: Blackwell, 1981), 198–207.

14. See Anke Bennoldt-Thomsen and Alfredo Guzzoni, "Der Irrenhausbesuch: Ein Topos in der Literatur um 1800," *Aurora*, no. 42 (1982): 82–110.

15. Friedrich Rochlitz, "Der Besuch im Irrenhause," in *Auswahl des Besten aus Friedrich Rochlitz' sämmtlichen Schriften*, 6 vols. (Züllichau: Darnmann, 1821–22). A fuller discussion of this text—so important to E. T. A. Hoffmann—is offered in chapter 6, below.

16. Herman Meyer, *Der Sonderling in der deutschen Dichtung* (Munich: Hanser, 1963), 101.

17. Ziolkowski, *German Romanticism*, 154.

18. *Traité du beau* (1715), cited in Georgia Cowart, "Sense and Sensibility in Eighteenth-Century Musical Thought," *Acta Musicologica*, no. 56 (1984): 254.

19. Cited in Hugo Goldschmidt, *Die Musikästhetik des 18. Jahrhunderts und ihre Beziehungen zu seinem Kunstschaffen* (Zurich, 1915; reprint, Hildesheim, 1968), 60.

20. Cited in Bellamy Hosler, *Changing Aesthetic Views of Instrumental Music in 18th-Century Germany* (Ann Arbor: UMI Research Press, 1981), 23.

21. René Descartes, *The Passions of the Soul*, trans. Stephen Voss (Indianapolis: Hackett, 1989), 59–60.

22. Johann Georg Sulzer, *Allgemeine Theorie der schönen Künste* (1771–74), 5 vols., 2d ed. (1792–95; reprint, Hildesheim: Georg Olms, 1967), 56. For a fuller discussion, see Cowart, "Sense and Sensibility," 263ff.

23. The best representative of this new monism in relation to music is Johann Nikolaus Forkel, *Allgemeine Geschichte der Musik* (Leipzig, 1788–1801). See Daniel Chua, *Absolute Music and the Construction of Meaning* (Cambridge: Cambridge University Press, 1999), 105–113.

24. Herder's contribution to the romantic overcoming of sentimentality in musical experience is discussed in the following chapter.

25. Johann Gottfried Herder, *Kalligone* (1800), in *Werke*, vol. 8, *Schriften zur Literatur und Philosophie, 1792–1800*, ed. H. D. Irmscher (Frankfurt: Deutscher Klassiker, 1998), 811–20.

26. Diderot, *Lettre sur les sourds et muets*, ed. Otis Fellows (Geneva: Droz, 1965), 101.

27. "In der gesamten Natur alle elastischen Körper auf einen Stoß oder Strich (uns hörbar oder minder hörbar) ihr *Inneres,* d. i . ihre erregten und sich wieder herstellenden Kräfte zu *erkennen geben*" (Herder, *Kalligone*, 811).

28. Goethe, *Die Leiden des jungen Werthers*, in *Werke* (Hamburger Ausgabe), 14 vols., ed. Erich Trunz and Benno von Wiese (Munich: Deutscher Taschenbuch, 1988), 6.26.

29. Ibid., 6.39.

30. Upon hearing the music of the angelic choir, Faust proclaims in frustration: "Was sucht ihr, mächtig und gelind, / Ihr Himmelstöne, mich am Staube?"

(I.762–63, in *Werke* [Weimarer Ausgabe], 4 sections in 152 vols. [Weimar: Böhlau, 1887–1919], 1.14.42). As for his *Novelle*, Goethe explains to Eckermann: "Zu zeigen, wie das Unbändige, Unüberwindliche oft besser durch Liebe und Frömmigkeit als durch Gewalt bezwungen werde, war die Aufgabe dieser Novelle, und dieses schöne Ziel, welches sich im Kinde und Löwen darstellt, reizt mich zur Ausführung" (January 15, 1827, *Goethes Gespräche mit Eckermann*, ed. Franz Deibel [Leipzig: Insel, 1908], 244–47).

31. For example, to Charlotte von Stein, Goethe explains how he turns to music "to soothe the soul and restore the spirits" (February 1779). This and further examples may be found in *Goethes Gedanken über Musik*, ed. Hedwig Walwei-Wiegelmann (Frankfurt: Insel, 1985), 83–96.

32. Goethe, *Wilhelm Meisters Lehrjahre*, in *Werke* (1998), 7.335; English: *Wilhelm Meister's Apprenticeship*, trans. Eric Blackall (Princeton: Princeton University Press, 1989), 203.

33. See Jack Stein, "Musical Settings of the Songs from *Wilhelm Meister*," *Comparative Literature*, no. 22 (1970): 125–46; and Lawrence Kramer, "Decadence and Desire: The *Wilhelm Meister* Songs of Wolf and Schubert," *Nineteenth-Century Music*, no. 10 (1987): 229–42.

34. On the circle gathered around Giebichenstein, see Walter Salmen, *Johann Friedrich Reichardt: Komponist, Schriftsteller, Kapellmeister und Verwaltungsbeamter der Goethezeit* (Freiburg im Breisgau: Atlantis, 1963), 75–147.

35. See Robert J. Richards, "Rhapsodies on a Cat-Piano; or, Johann Christian Reil and the Foundations of Romantic Psychiatry," *Critical Inquiry*, no. 24 (1998): 702.

36. Johann Christian Reil, *Rhapsodieen über die Anwendung der psychischen Curmethode auf Geisteszerrütungen* (Halle: Curt, 1803), 12.

37. Earlier, Hegel asserts: "Self-consciousness exists in and for itself when, and by the fact that, it so exists for another; that is, it exists only in being acknowledged" (*PG* 145/111).

38. See Suzanne Gearhart, "The Dialectic and Its Aesthetic Other: Hegel and Diderot," *Modern Language Notes*, no. 101 (1986): 1052–54. In his lectures on the *Phenomenology*, Jean Hyppolite remarks: "Diderot's description offered Hegel the satire of a world, a concrete example of human consciousness, and with regard to the dialectical development under discussion, the result of the culture in which the I is always alien to itself" (*Genesis and Structure of Hegel's "Phenomenology of the Spirit*," trans. Samuel Cherniak and John Heckaman (Evanston: Northwestern University Press, 1974), 412–13.

39. The compelling strength of Hegel's reading is evident among commentators who fail to realize that the philosopher interprets the nephew's statement in a way that contradicts the intention embedded in the dialogue's context. John Smith, for example, misses the nephew's point on innateness when he claims that Hegel and the nephew both share a scorn for the "type" (*espèce*), because such a person "falsely thinks he has an individual personality and thereby fails to recognize that he, like everyone else, must take his personality from the social roles at his disposal" (*The Spirit and Its Letter: Traces of Rhetoric in*

Hegel's Philosophy of Bildung [Ithaca: Cornell University Press, 1988], 210). Hans Robert Jauss more subtly takes the nephew's statement ironically and thereby aligns it with Hegel's interpretation. See *The Dialogical and the Dialectical* Neveu de Rameau: *How Diderot Adopted Socrates and Hegel Adopted Diderot* (Berkeley: Center for Hermeneutical Studies in Hellenistic and Modern Culture, 1983), 21. To my knowledge, the only one to argue for a complete contradiction is James Schmidt, "The Fool's Truth: Diderot, Goethe, and Hegel," *Journal of the History of Ideas*, no. 57 (1996): 634.

40. For a similar line of argumentation with different ramifications, see David W. Price, "Hegel's Intertextual Dialectic: Diderot's *Le Neveu de Rameau* in the *Phenomenology of Spirit*," *Clio*, no. 20 (1991): 223–33.

41. Goethe, "Anmerkungen über Personen und Gegenstände, deren in dem Dialog Rameau's Neffe erwähnt wird," in *Werke* (1887–1919), 1.45.184.

42. See Christine Lubkoll, *Mythos Musik: Poetische Entwürfe des Musikalischen in der Literatur um 1800* (Freiburg im Breisgau: Rombach, 1995), 28.

43. In his later lectures, Hegel consistently debases a "return to Nature"; see, for example, *Philosophy of Mind*, trans. William Wallace (Oxford: Clarendon, 2003), sec. 405, 94–96.

44. See Jean Starobinski, "Rousseau's Happy Days," trans. A. Tomarken, *New Literary History*, no. 11 (1979): 147.

45. Cited in Andrew Bowie, *Aesthetics and Subjectivity: From Kant to Nietzsche*, 2d ed. (Manchester: Manchester University Press, 2003), 157.

46. Cf. *Philosophy of Mind*, sec. 398, 69–70.

47. Ibid., sec. 406, 105–6.

48. In the supplemental note to sec. 398, reference is made to this "feeling of life" (*Gefühlsleben*) in terms highly reminiscent of Rousseau's *Fifth Promenade*: just as Rousseau was "cradled" ("berçoit" [ROC 1.1045]) by natural sounds, so Hegel's madman is tempted into unconscious "somnolence" by "the regular motion of the cradle, monotonous singing, the murmuring of a brook" (*Philosophy of Mind*, 69).

49. Georg W. F. Hegel, *Vorlesungen über die Ästhetik*, vols. 13–15 of *Werke*, 20 vols., ed. Eva Moldenhauer and Karl Markus Michel (Frankfurt: Suhrkamp, 1997), 15.133; English: *Aesthetics: Lectures on Fine Art*, 2 vols., trans. T. M. Knox (Oxford: Clarendon, 1988), 2.889.

50. Ibid., 15.154/2.906; emphasis in original:

> Expression in music has, as its *content*, the inner life itself, the inner sense of feeling and for the matter in hand, and, as its *form*, sound, which, in an art that least of all proceeds to spatial figures, is purely evanescent in its perceptible existence; the result is that music with its movements penetrates the arcanum of all the movements of the soul. Therefore it captivates the consciousness which is no longer confronted by an object and which in the loss of this freedom [of contemplation] is carried away itself by the ever-flowing stream of sounds.

51. *Philosophy of Mind*, sec. 408, 138.

4. THE MOST VIOLENT OF THE ARTS

1. In Johann Georg Sulzer, *Allgemeine Theorie der schönen Künste* (1771–74), 5 vols., 2d ed. (1792–95; reprint, Hildesheim: Georg Olms, 1967), 4.478.
2. For a good overview, see Carl Dahlhaus, "E. T. A. Hoffmanns Beethoven-Kritik und die Ästhetik des Erhabenen," *Archiv für Musikwissenschaft*, no. 38 (1981): 79–92.
3. Christian Friedrich Michaelis's essays have been conveniently collected in a recent edition: *Ueber den Geist der Tonkunst und andere Schriften*, ed. Lothar Schmidt (Chemnitz: Gudrun Schröder, 1997).
4. Jean-Jacques Rousseau, *Dictionnaire de musique*, s.v. "Sonate," ROC 5.1060.
5. (Pseudo-)Longinus, *On the Sublime*, trans. W. H. Fyfe, in *Aristotle: Poetics; Longinus: On the Sublime; Demetrius: On Style*, Loeb Classical Library (Cambridge: Harvard University Press, 1995), 1.1–4, 162–63 (slightly modified).
6. Heraclitus relies on this *figura etymologica* in fragment 48: τόξῳ ὄνομα βίος, ἔργον δὲ θάνατος (The bow's name is life, but its work is death).
7. Homer, *The Odyssey*, 2 vols., trans. A. T. Murray, Loeb Classical Library (Cambridge: Harvard University Press, 1919), 21.405–13.
8. "L'arc est la mort à distance: la mort inexplicable.... La lyre ou la cithare sont d'anciens arcs qui lancent des chants vers le dieu (des flèches vers la bête)" (Pascal Quignard, *La haine de la musique* [1996; reprint, Paris: Gallimard, 2002], 37).
9. The Grimms' dictionary, for example, explains: "Even now in the country one asks, for example, a child: 'To whom do you belong? ["wem gehörst du?") Who are your relatives [*angehörigen*]? More precisely: who are your parents? Who is your father? Really: whom must you obey [*gehorchen*]?" (Jacob Grimm and Wilhelm Grimm, *Deutsches Wörterbuch*, 33 vols. (Munich: Deutscher Taschenbuch Verlag, 1984), s.v. GEHÖREN, 5.2504–40.
10. The ramifications of this etymological network and its relation to maddening music are exploited by Heine in his novella *Die Florentinische Nächte*. See my article "*Sinneverwirrende Töne*: Musik und Wahnsinn in Heines *Florentinischen Nächten*," *Zeitschrift für Deutsche Philologie*, no. 126 (2007).
11. The opposition of vision and hearing motivated a rich and complex tradition of aesthetic theory throughout the eighteenth century. For an excellent investigation of the topic, see Joachim Gessinger, *Auge und Ohr: Studien zur Erforschung der Sprache am Menschen, 1700–1850* (Berlin: de Gruyter, 1994).
12. Edmund Burke, *A Philosophical Enquiry into the Origin of Our Ideas of the Sublime and Beautiful* (1757), ed. Adam Phillips (Oxford: Oxford University Press, 1990), 2.2, 53–54.
13. Burke ignores the emendation to "*aurem*."
14. This notion of passivity touches directly on a notion of selfhood that is irreducible to the concept or figure of subjectivity. The recent work of Timothy Reiss is particularly helpful in tracing the evolving formulations of this idea of a pre- or even nonsubjective self. To this end, he proposes the term "passibility" in contradistinction to "passivity" (which already implies the subject): "*Passibility* was

the fundamental nature of the human being *as* human. Its relation to the endlessly multiple matter, qualities and events of its surroundings—divine, animate, social, physical—was one of being always and constantly affected by simply being in them, more exactly, being of them. *Passibility* names the relation as *passivity* does not" (*Mirages of the Selfe: Patterns of Personhood in Ancient and Early Modern Europe* [Stanford: Stanford University Press, 2003], 97).

15. "The crescendo of motor activity in the trunk accentuates the functions expressive of our vital being at the expense of those which serve knowledge and practical action. . . . The 'I' of the awake, active person is centered in the region at the base of the nose, between the eyes; in the dance it descends into the trunk" (Erwin Straus, *Phenomenological Psychology*, trans. Erling Eng [New York: Basic Books, 1966], 26).

16. Alexandre Kojève, *Introduction to the Reading of Hegel*, ed. Alan Bloom, trans. James H. Nichols, Jr. (Ithaca: Cornell University Press, 1980), 141; emphasis in original.

17. On the concept of reason as a "counterviolence" (*Gegen-Gewalt*), see Corina Caduff, *Die Literarisierung von Musik und bildender Kunst um 1800* (Munich: Fink, 2003),122–23.

18. Jonathan Strauss comments succinctly on this course of sublimation: "It is through language, and writing, that we make manifest to ourselves the annihilating force of our own abstract faculties in relation to our sensuous ones" (*Subjects of Terror: Nerval, Hegel, and the Modern Self* [Stanford: Stanford University Press, 1998], 17).

19. As Kant explains, "It is the disposition of the mind resulting from a certain representation occupying the reflective judgment, but not the object, which is to be called sublime"; he concludes, "That is sublime which even to be able to think of demonstrates a faculty of the mind that surpasses every measure of the senses" (*KU* sec. 25, 250/134).

20. In sec. 7 Kant compares the beautiful with the agreeable, illustrating the latter with an example from music that strikingly recasts the Apollo-Marsyas battle beneath the rubric of "folly" (*Thorheit*): "One person loves the tone of wind instruments, another that of stringed instruments. It would be folly to dispute the judgment of another that is different from our own in such a matter" (*KU* 212/97).

21. It would be unfair to ascribe to Kant a fundamentally antimusical nature. Elsewhere, while maintaining music's power to spread its influence across distance, he emphasizes the pleasurable aspects of musical experience, for example, in the lectures on *Anthropology*: "Music is a communication of feelings in the distance to all present within the surrounding space, and it is a social pleasure which is not diminished by the fact that many people participate in it" ("On Hearing," sec. 18 of *Anthropology from a Pragmatic Point of View*, trans. Victor L. Dowdell [Carbondale: Southern Illinois University Press, 1978], 42–43).

22. See Winfried Menninghaus, "Zwischen Überwältigung und Widerstand: Macht und Gewalt in Longins und Kants Theorien des Erhabenen," *Poetica*, no. 23 (1991): 1–19.

23. Hence Nicola Gess concludes: "Only with Kant does this overpowering become existentially threatening. For here what is in play is the autonomy of the subject, for which the confrontation with the sublime becomes the touchstone" (*Gewalt der Musik: Literatur und Musikkritik um 1800* [Freiburg im Breisgau: Rombach, 2006], 245).

24. Immanuel Kant, *Critique of Practical Reason*, trans. Lewis W. Beck (New York: Macmillan, 1993), 36.

25. For a comparison of these varying philosophical uses of the voice metaphor, see Mladen Dolar, *A Voice and Nothing More* (Cambridge, Mass.: MIT Press, 2006), 83–103.

26. See Herman Parret, "Kant on Music and the Hierarchy of the Arts," *The Journal of Aesthetics and Art Criticism* 56 (1998), 251–164.

27. Johann Gottfried Herder, *Werke*, vol. 2, *Schriften zur Ästhetik und Literatur, 1767–1781*, ed. G. E. Grimm (Frankfurt: Deutscher Klassiker, 1993), 290.

28. Herder, *Werke*, vol. 8, *Schriften zur Literatur und Philosophie, 1792–1800*, ed. H. D. Irmscher (Frankfurt: Deutscher Klassiker, 1998), 862.

29. See Rafael Köhler, "Johann Gottfried Herder und die Überwindung der musikalischen Nachahmungsästhetik," *Archiv für Musikwissenschaft*, no. 52 (1995): 211.

30. For Herder's dual critique of Burke and Kant, see *Werke*, 8.861–74.

31. Herder, *Werke*, 8.890.

32. Rachel Zuckert, "Awe or Envy: Herder contra Kant on the Sublime," *Journal of Aesthetics and Art Criticism*, no. 61 (2003): 225.

33. Herder, *Werke*, 8.703; my emphasis.

34. Johann Gottfried Herder, *Sämmtliche Werke*, 33 vols., ed. Bernhard Suphan, (Berlin: Wiedmann, 1877–1913), 16.265. Subsequent citations from the *Cäcilia* essay are taken from this edition and marked by page number in the text.

35. Kant's analysis of the mathematical sublime, in the *Critique of the Power of Judgment*, may be understood as an essentially Protestant model for overcoming the threat to the imagination (see, e.g., sec. 26). His account of the process whereby reason provides a "counterforce" (*Gegen-Gewalt*) precisely where the imagination fails played an important role both in the development of the musical sublime and in the concomitant advance in formulating rules for composition and reception. See, for example, Christian Friedrich Michaelis, "Ueber das Erhabene in der Musik" (1801), in *Ueber den Geist der Tonkunst*, 168–74. For a useful discussion, see Gess, *Gewalt der Musik*, 243–312.

36. Jean-Luc Nancy, *The Inoperative Community*, ed. Peter Connor (Minneapolis: University of Minnesota Press, 1991), 7; emphasis in original.

37. Jean-Luc Nancy, "Vox Clamans in Deserto," in *Multiple Arts: The Muses II*, ed. Simon Sparks (Stanford: Stanford University Press, 2006), 38–41.

38. I am borrowing this last formulation from Adriana Cavarero, who turns to Nancy—together with Levinas and Arendt—to reflect on a "politics of voices." See *For More than One Voice: Toward a Philosophy of Vocal Expression*, trans. Paul A. Kottman (Stanford: Stanford University Press, 2005), 193–96.

39. Nancy, *The Inoperative Community*, 31.

40. See Carl Dahlhaus, *The Idea of Absolute Music*, trans. Roger Lustig (Chicago: University of Chicago Press, 1989), 54–55.

41. Tieck is reported to have described the father's reaction to his son's decision as extremely negative. See, for example, von Bülow's testimony in *WW* 2.419.

42. Goethe critically referred to the *Herzensergießungen* as exhibiting a "neu-katholische Sentimentalität" that he feared would have dangerous consequences for society at large (*Werke* [Weimarer Ausgabe], 4 sections in 152 vols. [Weimar: Böhlau, 1887–1919], 1.48.122).

43. See Michael Riffaterre, *La production du texte* (Paris: Seuil, 1979).

44. In general, scholarship has mostly been concerned with situating the *Berglinger* novella within contemporary currents of music aesthetics and history and has therefore barely recognized the darker implications of the story. For a critical overview, see Martin Bollacher, *Wackenroder und die Kunstauffassung der frühen Romantik* (Darmstadt: Wissenschaftliche Buchgesellschaft, 1983).

45. For a broader discussion of Wackenroder's contribution to early romantic theories of language and literature, see Barbara Naumann, *"Musikalisches Ideen-Instrument": Das Musikalische in Poetik und Sprachtheorie der Frühro-mantik* (Stuttgart: Metzler, 1990), 8–58.

46. See Jean Starobinski, *Words upon Words: The Anagrams of Ferdinand de Saussure*, trans. Olivia Emmet (New Haven: Yale University Press, 1979). For a good descriptive and critical account of Saussure's anagrammatism, see Samuel Kinser, "Saussure's Anagrams: Ideological Work," *Modern Language Notes*, no. 94 (1979): 1105–38.

47. See Starobinski, *Words upon Words*, 17–18.

5. WITH ARTS UNKNOWN BEFORE

1. Kleist to Wilhelmine von Zenge, September 19, 1800, in *KSW* 2.567; emphasis in original.

2. See Kleist's letter to Wilhelmine (November 18, 1800): "I myself have prepared a small repository of ideas [*Ideenmagazin*], which I would like to share with you one day and submit to your judgment" (*KSW* 2.597). For a reproduction of what this file may have contained, see Helmut Sembdner, *Heinrich von Kleist. Geschichte meiner Seele, Ideenmagazin: Das Lebenszeugnis der Briefe* (Bremen: Dieterich, 1959).

3. Kleist creates a pun on the words for "apart" or "by itself" (*für sich*) and "peach" (*Pfirsich*).

4. Goethe, *Wilhelm Meisters Lehrjahre*, in *Werke* (Hamburger Ausgabe), 14 vols., ed. Erich Trunz and Benno von Wiese (Munich: Deutscher Taschenbuch, 1988), 7.128.

5. Johann Gottfried Herder, *Cäcilia*, in *Sämmtliche Werke*, 33 vols., ed. Bernhard Suphan (Berlin: Weidmann, 1877–1913), 16.266.

6. Editors point out that Kleist did not return to Mainz until 1803, which hardly discounts his use of the name to evoke a particularly strong experience.

7. See Ilse Graham, *Heinrich von Kleist: Word into Flesh. A Poet's Quest for the Symbol* (Berlin: de Gruyter, 1977), 25–26.

8. The testimonies are taken from Helmut Sembdner, *Heinrich von Kleists Lebens- spuren: Dokumente und Berichte der Zeitgenossen* (Bremen: Schünemann, 1957), 8–11; and Helga Kraft, *Erhörtes und Unerhörtes: Die Welt des Klanges bei Heinrich von Kleist* (Munich: Fink, 1976), 34–47.

9. Paul de Man, "Aesthetic Formalization: Kleist's *Über das Marionettentheater*," in *The Rhetoric of Romanticism* (New York: Columbia University Press, 1984), 275.

10. "Ich kann, von zu viel Formen verwirrt, zu keiner Klarheit der innerlichen An- schauung kommen." (letter to Marie von Kleist, Summer 1811, *KSW* 2.873).

11. Carl Dahlhaus, "Kleists Wort über den Generalbass," *Kleist Jahrbuch* 5 (1984): 13–24.

12. All subsequent citations from *Die heilige Cäcilie* are from *KSW* 2.216–28, in- dicated by the first page number in the text. The second page number refers to the English translation in Heinrich von Kleist, *The Marquise of O—and Other Stories*, trans. David Luke and Nigel Reeves, trans. (New York: Penguin, 1978).

13. The most thorough discussions of the title's ambiguity remains Wolfgang Witt- kowski, "*Die heilige Cäcilie* und *Der Zweikampf*: Kleists Legenden und die ro- mantische Ironie," *Colloquia Germanica*, no. 6 (1972): 17–59. See also Rosemarie Puschmann, *Heinrich von Kleists Cäcilien-Erzählung* (Bielefeld: Aisthesis, 1988); and Dorothea von Mücke, "Der Fluch der Heiligen Cäcilie," *Poetica*, no. 26 (1994): 105–120.

14. See, for example, Robert Mühlner, "Heinrich von Kleist und seine Legende *Die heilige Cäcilie oder die Gewalt der Musik*," *Jahrbuch des Wiener Goethes-Vereins* 66 (1962): 149–56.

15. See Klaus Doerner, *Madmen and the Bourgeoisie: A Social History of Insanity and Psychiatry*, trans. Joachim Neugroschel and Jean Steinberg (Oxford: Blackwell, 1981), 153–55 and 250–59.

16. Augustine, *De Dialectica: English and Latin Selections*, trans. B. Darrell Jackson (Boston: Reidel, 1975), 86.

17. See von Mücke, "Der Fluch der Heiligen Cäcilie," 112–13.

18. See Gerhard Neumann, "Eselsgeschrhrei und Sphärenklang: Zeichensystem der Musik und Legitimation der Legende in Kleists Novelle *Die heilige Cäcilie oder die Gewalt der Musik*," in *Heinrich von Kleist: Kriegsfall—Rechtsfall—Sün- denfall*, ed. G. Neumann (Freiburg am Breisgau: Rombach, 1994), 370–74.

19. See Johann H. Kessel, "St. Veit, seine Geschichte, Verehrung und bildlichen Darstellungen," *Jahrbücher des Vereins für Altertumsfreunde im Rheinlande*, no. 43 (1867): 152–183.

20. In the year in which Kleist first worked on *Die heilige Cäcilie*, 1810, the Feast of Corpus Christi fell on June 14, the day before St. Vitus's. In 1809 the two feast days coincided.

21. See Puschmann, *Kleists Cäcilien-Erzählung*, 33–40.

22. On the multiple layers of the text's incongruities, see Donald Haase and Rachel Freudenburg, "Power, Truth, and Interpretation: The Hermeneutic Act and Kleist's *Die heilige Cäcilie*," *Deutsche Vierteljahrsschrift*, no. 60 (1986): 88–103;

and Michael Boehringer, "Of Meaning and Truth: Narrative Ambiguity in Kleist's 'Die heilige Cäcilie oder die Gewalt der Musik: Eine Legende,'" *Revue Frontenac*, no. 11 (1994): 103–28.

23. See Corina Caduff, *Die Literarisierung von Musik und bildender Kunst um 1800* (Munich: Fink, 2003), 142.

24. Bernhard Greiner reads the *Cäcilie* story in relation to Herder and the discourse on the musical sublime. See "'Das ganze Schrecken der Tonkunst': 'Die heilige Cäcilie oder Die Gewalt der Musik.' Kleists erzählender Entwurf des Erhabenen," *Zeitschrift für deutsche Philologie*, no. 115 (1996): 501–20.

25. For the historical details in this section, I have relied on David Bindman, "Roubiliac's Statue of Handel and the Keeping of Order in Vauxhall Gardens in the Early Eighteenth Century," *Sculpture Journal*, no. 1 (1997): 22–31.

26. Herder, *Cäcilia*, 16.253. Herder gives the Latin text from the *Acta Caeciliana* in a footnote.

27. Hans Maier, "Cäcilia unter den Deutschen: Herder, Goethe, Wackenroder, Kleist," *Kleist-Jahrbuch*, no. 15 (1994): 67–82; here 68ff.

28. See Christine Lubkoll, *Mythos Musik: Poetische Entwürfe des Musikalischen in der Literatur um 1800* (Freiburg im Breisgau: Rombach, 1995), 208.

29. Herder, *Cäcilia*, 16.254.

30. Goethe, *Italienische Reise*, in *Werke* (1998), 11.141.

6. BEFORE AND AFTER LANGUAGE

1. Charles Taylor, "Language and Human Nature," in *Human Agency and Language: Philosophical Papers* (Cambridge: Cambridge University Press, 1985), 215–47.

2. Andrew Bowie, *Aesthetics and Subjectivity: From Kant to Nietzsche*, 2d ed. (Manchester: Manchester University Press, 2003), 1. Bowie refers especially to the work of Hilary Putnam, Richard Rorty, and Donald Davidson. For his discussion of Taylor's designative/disclosive paradigms, see pp. 160ff.

3. Ibid., 160.

4. Compare the opening of Diderot's text: "Comment s'étaient-ils rencontrés? Par hasard, comme tout le monde. Comment s'appelaient-ils? Que vous importe? D'où venaient-ils? Du lieu le plus prochain. Où allaient-ils? Est-ce que l'on sait où l'on va?" (*Jacques le fataliste et son maître*, in *Œuvres*, ed. André Billy [Paris: Gallimard, Bibliothèque de la Pléiade, 1951], 475).

5. Johann Gottfried Herder, *Abhandlung über den Ursprung der Sprache*, in *Werke*, vol. 1, *Frühe Schriften, 1764–1772*, ed. Ulrich Gaier (Frankfurt: Deutscher Klassiker, 1995), 718–24.

6. Friedrich Schelling, *Die Philosophie der Kunst*, in *Sämtliche Werke*, ed. K. F. A. Schelling (Stuttgart: Cotta, 1856), 5.491.

7. Vladmir Jankélevitch, *Music and the Ineffable*, trans. Carolyn Abbate (Princeton: Princeton University Press, 2003), 25.

8. Frits Noske, "Forma formans," *International Review of the Aesthetics and Sociology of Music*, no. 7 (1976): 45.

9. See Daniel Chua, *Absolute Music and the Construction of Meaning* (Cambridge: Cambridge University Press, 1999), 98–113.

10. Schelling, *Philosophie der Kunst*, 491.

11. See Theodor Adorno, *Philosophy of Modern Music*, trans. A. G. Mitchell and W. V. Blomster (New York: Continuum, 2003), 5–24; and Max Paddison, *Adorno's Aesthetics of Music* (Cambridge: Cambridge University Press, 1993), 15–16.

12. Adorno, *Philosophy of Modern Music*, 39.

13. That is not to say that Hoffmann ignored the role of lyrical text in music production. Indeed, it is crucial to note that Hoffmann acknowledges the importance of words in a musical piece, if only because their lyrical form is subordinate to a music that is outside it. Thus his theories about music only become clear when posed in contradistinction to a particular understanding of rational language that strives to subordinate music to its formal rigor.

14. April 28, 1812, *HW* 1.244.

15. See Hartmut Steinecke, *Die Kunst der Fantasie: E. T. A. Hoffmanns Leben und Werk* (Frankfurt: Insel, 2004), 116–17.

16. The information about the Bamberg affair is taken from Kunz's *Erinnerungen*, cited in *HW* 2.1.690–94.

17. For a full discussion of the functioning of autobiographical elements in Hoffmann's literary work, see Wulf Segebrecht, *Autobiographie und Dichtung: Eine Studie zum Werk E. T. A. Hoffmanns* (Stuttgart: Metzler, 1967).

18. Letter to Rochlitz, January 12, 1809 (*HW* 1.204).

19. Friedrich Rochlitz, "Der Besuch im Irrenhause," in *Auswahl des Besten aus Friedrich Rochlitz' sämmtlichen Schriften*, 6 vols. (Züllichau: Darnmann, 1821–22), 6.5. Subsequent citations are from this edition, indicated with a page number in the text.

20. Tzvetan Todorov, *The Fantastic: A Structural Approach to a Literary Genre*, trans. Richard Howard (Ithaca: Cornell University Press, 1975).

21. The English translation is from *Selected Writings of E. T. A. Hoffmann*, vol. 1, *The Tales*, ed. and trans. Leonard J. Kent and Elizabeth C. Knight (Chicago: University of Chicago Press, 1969), 50. Subsequent translations, slightly modified, are from this edition and indicated in the text with a second page reference.

22. See Wolfgang Rüdiger, *Musik und Wirklichkeit bei E. T. A. Hoffmann: Zur Entstehung einer Musikanschauung der Romantik* (Pfaffenweiler: Centaurus, 1989), 24–26.

23. For a critical account of Schumann's cryptography, see John Daverio, *Crossing Paths: Schubert, Schumann, and Brahms* (Oxford: Oxford University Press, 2002), 65–102.

24. Thomas Mann, *Doktor Faustus: Das Leben des deutschen Tonsetzers Adrian Leverkühn, erzählt von einem Freunde* (Frankfurt: Fischer, 1998), 208; English: *Doctor Faustus: The Life of the German Composer Adrian Leverkühn as Told by a Friend*, trans. John E. Woods (New York: Vintage, 1999), 165.

25. See Walter Salmen, "Die Musik im Weltbild J. W. Ritters," in *Schlesien*, no. 2 (1957): 178–80.

26. In Goethe's translation: "Da fing er an die Stirne sich mit der Faust zu schlagen" (cf. Hoffmann's: "Eben habe ich . . . an die Stirne geklopft"). See *Rameau's Neffe*, in *Werke* (Weimarer Ausgabe), 144 vols. (Weimar: Böhlau, 1999), 45.34.

27. See George Schoolfield, *The Figure of the Musician in German Literature* (New York: AMS, 1966), 21–22.

28. Benno von Wiese, *Die deutsche Novelle von Goethe bis Kafka*, 2 vols. (Düsseldorf: Bagel, 1968), 2.87–103.

29. Carl Dahlhaus, *The Idea of Absolute Music*, trans. Roger Lustig (Chicago: University of Chicago Press, 1989), 7; see also 42.

30. Further on in the Beethoven essay, Kreisler remarks: "The master seems to be implying that the deeper mysteries can never be spoken of in ordinary words" (*HMW* 102).

31. Immanuel Kant, *Critique of Judgment*, trans. J. H. Bernard (New York: Hafner, 1951), 15.

32. For references, see the editors' note in *HW* 1.1042.

33. Letter to Julius Hitzig, January 8, 1821 (*HW* 6.202).

34. See Steven P. Scher, "Hoffmann and Sterne: Unmediated Parallels in Narrative Method," in *Comparative Literature*, no. 28 (1976): 309–25.

35. See Jean Paul's comments in *HW* 5.917.

36. Sarah Kofman pursues the ramifications of Hoffmann's gambit in *Autobiogriffures: Du chat Murr d'Hoffmann* (Paris: Galilée, 1984), 43–55.

37. See Claudia Liebrand's insightful discussion in *Aporie des Kunstmythos: Die Text E. T. A. Hoffmanns* (Freiburg im Breisgau: Rombach, 1996), 222–24.

HORS D'ŒUVRE II

1. Gilles Deleuze and Félix Guattari, *Kafka: Toward a Minor Literature*, trans. Dana Polan (Minneapolis: University of Minnesota Press, 1986), 19–20.

2. Friedrich Nietzsche, *Sämtliche Briefe: Kritische Studienausgabe*, 8 vols., ed. Giorgio Colli and Mazzino Montinari (Berlin: de Gruyter, 1975–84), 2.74.

3. Cited in Curt Paul Janz. *Friedrich Nietzsche: Biographie*, 3 vols. (Munich: Hanser, 1993), 3.33.

4. Thomas Mann, *Der Tod in Venedig und andere Erzählungen* (Frankfurt: Fischer, 1954), 79.

5. Ernst Bertram, *Nietzsche: Versuch einer Mythologie* (Berlin: Georg Bondi, 1929), 219.

6. Arthur Schopenhauer, "Über Lärm und Geräusch," in *Parerga und Paralipomena*, sec. 30, in *Sämtliche Werke*, 7 vols., ed. Arthur Hübscher (Wiesbaden: Brockhaus, 1972), 6.2.680.

7. Ferdinand von Saar, *Geschichte eines Wienerkindes*, in *Novellen aus Österreich*, 2 vols., ed. Karl Wagner (Vienna: Deuticke, 1998), 2.222. For the broader ideological context of this passage, see Marc A. Weiner, *Undertones of Insurrection: Music, Politics, and the Social Sphere in the Modern German Narrative* (Lincoln:

University of Nebraska Press, 1993), 12–15; the translation here is from p. 14, slightly modified.

8. See Georges Liébert, *Nietzsche and Music*, trans. David Pellauer and Graham Parkes (Chicago: University of Chicago Press, 2004), 151.

9. The English translation is from *The Birth of Tragedy and Other Writings*, trans. Ronald Speirs (Cambridge: Cambridge University Press, 1999), 100–101 (slightly modified).

10. Christoph Türcke, *Der tolle Mensch: Nietzsche und der Wahnsinn der Vernunft* (Frankfurt: Fischer, 1989), 8.

11. Jacques Derrida, *Otobiographies: The Teaching of Nietzsche and the Politics of the Proper Name*, trans. Avital Ronell, in *The Ear of the Other: Otobiograpy, Transference, Translation*, ed. Christie McDonald (Lincoln: University of Nebraska Press, 1988), 16.

12. *Birth of Tragedy*, 29–30.

Bibliography

PRIMARY SOURCES

Alighieri, Dante. *The Divine Comedy*. 3 vols. Trans. Charles S. Singleton, Princeton: Princeton University Press, 1973.

Apollodorus. *The Library*. Trans. J.G. Frazer. Loeb Classical Library. Cambridge: Harvard University Press, 1921.

Aristotle. *The Physics*. Trans. Philip H. Wicksteed and Francis M. Cornford. Loeb Classical Library. Cambridge: Harvard University Press, 1934.

———. *The Organon: The Categories; On Interpretation*. Trans. Harold P. Cooke. Loeb Classical Library. Cambridge: Harvard University Press, 1938.

Augustine. *De Dialectica: English and Latin Selections*. Trans. B. Darrell Jackson. Boston: Reidel, 1975.

Bertram, Ernst. *Nietzsche: Versuch einer Mythologie*. Berlin: Georg Bondi, 1929.

Burke, Edmund. *A Philosophical Enquiry into the Origin of Our Ideas of the Sublime and Beautiful* (1757). Ed. Adam Phillips. Oxford: Oxford University Press, 1990.

Castel, Louis-Bertrand. *L'Optique des couleurs, fondée sur les simples observations, et tournée sur-tout à la pratique de la peinture, de la teinture et des autres arts coloristes*. Paris, 1740.

Condillac, Étienne Bonnot de. *Essai sur l'origine des connaissances humaines*, Amsterdam: Mortier, 1746.

Cowley, Abraham. *Davideis: A Sacred Poem of the Troubles of David*. London, 1677.

d'Alembert, Jean, and Denis Diderot. *Encyclopédie; ou, Dictionnaire raisonné des sciences, des arts, et des métiers*. 17 vols. Paris, 1751–72. Facsimile reprint, New York: Pergamon, 1969.

Descartes, René. *Abrégé de musique (Compendium Musicae)* (1618). Ed. Frédéric de Buzon. Paris: Presses Universitaires de France, 1987.

———. *Discours de la méthode*. Ed. Laurence Renault. Paris: Flammarion, 2000. English: *Discourse on Method and the Meditations*. Trans. F.E. Sutcliffe. New York: Penguin, 1968.

———. *The Passions of the Soul*. Trans. Stephen Voss. Indianapolis: Hackett, 1989.

d'Étaples, Jacques Lefèvre. *Musica libris quatuor demonstrata*. 1496. Reprint, Paris: Cavellat, 1552.

Diderot, Denis. *Lettre sur les sourds et muets*. Ed. Otis Fellows. Geneva: Droz, 1965.

———. *Le neveu de Rameau*. Ed. Jean Fabre. Geneva: Droz, 1963. English: *Rameau's Nephew and D'Alembert's Dream*. Trans. Leonard Tancock. New York: Penguin, 1966.

———. *Œuvres*. Ed. André Billy. Paris: Gallimard, Bibliothèque de la Pléiade, 1951.

———. *Œuvres complètes*. 20 vols. Eds. Jules Assézat and Maurice Tourneux. Paris: Garnier, 1875.

———. *Œuvres complètes*. 25 vols. Ed. Jean Varloot. Paris: Hermann, 1975.

Dubos, Jean-Baptiste. *Réflexions critiques sur la poésie et sur la peinture*. Paris: Mariette, 1733.

Forkel, Johann Nikolaus. *Allgemeine Geschichte der Musik*. Leipzig, 1788–1801.

Goethe, Johann Wolfgang. *Goethes Gedanken über Musik*. Ed. Hedwig Walwei-Wiegelmann. Frankfurt: Insel, 1985.

———. *Goethes Gespräche mit Eckermann*. Ed. Franz Deibel. Leipzig: Insel, 1908.

———. *Werke* (Hamburger Ausgabe). 14 vols. Eds. Erich Trunz. Munich: Deutscher Taschenbuch, 1998.

———. *Werke* (Weimarer Ausgabe). 4 sections in 152 vols. Weimar: Böhlau, 1887–1919.

———. *Wilhelm Meister's Apprenticeship*. Trans. Eric Blackall. Princeton: Princeton University Press, 1989.

Gottsched, Johann Christoph. *Versuch einer Critischen Dichtkunst*. 1751. Facsimile reprint, Darmstadt: Wissenschaftliche Buchgesellschaft, 1962.

Grimm, Jacob, and Wilhelm Grimm. *Deutsches Wörterbuch*. 33 vols. Munich: Deutscher Taschenbuch, 1984.

Hegel, Georg W. F. *Phänomenologie des Geistes*. Vol. 3 of *Werke*, 20 vols. Ed. Eva Moldenhauer and Karl Markus Michel. Frankfurt: Suhrkamp, 1986. English: *Phenomenology of Spirit*. Trans. Andrew Miller. Oxford: Oxford University Press, 1977.

———. *Philosophy of Mind*. Trans. William Wallace. Oxford: Clarendon, 2003.

———. *Vorlesungen über die Ästhetik*. Vol. 13–15 of *Werke*, 20 vols. Ed. Eva Moldenhauer and Karl Markus Michel. Frankfurt: Suhrkamp, 1997. English: *Aesthetics: Lectures on Fine Art*. 2 vols. Trans. T. M. Knox. Oxford: Clarendon, 1988.

Helvétius, Claude-Adrien. *De l'esprit*. Paris: Durand, 1758. Reprint, Paris: Fayard, 1988.

Herder, Johann Gottfried. *Sämmtliche Werke*. 33 vols. Ed. Bernhard Suphan. Berlin: Weidmann, 1877–1913.

———. *Werke*. Vol. 1, *Frühe Schriften, 1764–1772*. Ed. Ulrich Gaier. Frankfurt: Deutscher Klassiker, 1995.

———. *Werke*. Vol. 2, *Schriften zur Ästhetik und Literatur, 1767–1781*. Ed. G. E. Grimm. Frankfurt: Deutscher Klassiker, 1993.

———. *Werke*. Vol. 8, *Schriften zur Literatur und Philosophie, 1792–1800*. Ed. H. D. Irmscher. Frankfurt: Deutscher Klassiker, 1998.

Hesiod—Homeric Hymns—Epic Cycle—Homerica. Trans. Hugh G. Evelyn-White. Loeb Classical Library. Cambridge: Harvard University Press, 1920.

Hoffmann, E. T. A. *E. T. A. Hoffmann's Musical Writings*. Ed. David Charlton. Cambridge: Cambridge University Press, 1989.

——. *The Life and Opinions of the Tomcat Murr*. Trans. Anthea Bell. New York: Penguin, 1999.

——. *Sämtliche Werke*. 6 vols. Ed. Hartmut Steinecke. Frankfurt am Main: Deutscher Klassiker, 1993.

——. *Selected Writings of E. T. A. Hoffmann*. Vol. 1, *The Tales*. Ed. and trans. Leonard J. Kent and Elizabeth C. Knight. Chicago: University of Chicago Press, 1969.

Homer. *The Odyssey*. 2 vols. Trans. A. T. Murray. Loeb Classical Library. Cambridge: Harvard University Press, 1919.

——. *The Iliad*. 2 vols. Trans. A. T. Murray. Loeb Classical Library. Cambridge: Harvard University Press, 1924.

Horace. *Q. Horati Flacci Opera*. Ed. Edward C. Wickham. Oxford: Clarendon, 1986.

Humboldt, Wilhelm von. *Werke*. 5 vols. Ed. Andreas Flitner and Klaus Giel. Darmstadt: Wissenschaftliche Buchgesellschaft, 1960–81.

Kant, Immanuel. *Anthropology from a Pragmatic Point of View*. Trans. Victor L. Dowdell. Carbondale: Southern Illinois University Press, 1978.

——. *Critique of Judgment*. Trans. J. H. Bernard. New York: Hafner, 1951.

——. *Critique of Practical Reason*. Trans. Lewis W. Beck. New York: Macmillan, 1993.

——. *Kritik der Urteilskraft*. Vol. 5 of *Gesammelte Schriften*, 24 vols. Ed. Royal Prussian Academy of Sciences. Berlin: de Gruyter, 1969. English: *Critique of the Power of Judgment*. Trans. Paul Guyer and Eric Matthews. Cambridge: Cambridge University Press, 2000.

Kierkegaard, Søren. *Either/Or* (1843). 2 vols. Trans. David F. Swenson and Lillian M. Swenson. Princeton: Princeton University Press, 1959.

Kleist, Heinrich von. *The Marquise of O—and Other Stories*. Trans. David Luke and Nigel Reeves. New York: Penguin, 1978.

——. *Sämtliche Werke und Briefe*. 2 vols. Ed. Helmut Sembdner. Munich: Deutscher Taschenbuch, 2001.

[Klingemann, Ernst August]. *Nachtwachten von Bonaventura*. Ed. Raimund Steinert. Potsdam: Kiepenheuer, 1920.

Knigge, Adolf. *Die Reise nach Braunschweig*. Ed. Paul Raabe. Kassel: Wenderoth, 1972.

(Pseudo-)Longinus. *On the Sublime*. Trans. W. H. Fyfe. In *Aristotle: Poetics; Longinus: On the Sublime; Demetrius: On Style*. Loeb Classical Library. Cambridge: Harvard University Press, 1995.

Mann, Thomas. *Doktor Faustus: Das Leben des deutschen Tonsetzers Adrian Leverkühn, erzählt von einem Freunde*. Frankfurt: Fischer, 1998. English: *Doctor Faustus: The Life of the German Composer Adrian Leverkühn as Told by a Friend*. Trans. John E. Woods. New York: Vintage, 1999.

——. *Der Tod in Venedig und andere Erzählungen*. Frankfurt: Fischer, 1954.

Michaelis, Christian Friedrich. 1997. *Ueber den Geist der Tonkunst und andere Schriften*. Ed. Lothar Schmidt. Chemnitz: Gudrun Schröder, 1997.

Nietzsche, Friedrich. *The Antichrist, Ecce Homo, Twilight of the Idols, and Other Writings*. Trans. Judith Norman. Cambridge: Cambridge University Press, 2005.

——. *The Birth of Tragedy and Other Writings*. Trans. Ronald Speirs. Cambridge: Cambridge University Press, 1999.

——. *Sämtliche Briefe: Kritische Studienausgabe*. 8 vols. Ed. Giorgio Colli and Mazzino Montinari. Berlin: de Gruyter, 1975–84.

Plato. *Complete Works*, Ed. John M. Cooper. Indianapolis: Hackett, 1997.

——. *Platonis Opera*, 5 vols. Ed. John Burnet. Oxford: Clarendon, 1972–76.

Pluche, Noël-Antoine. *Le spectacle de la nature*. 8 vols. Paris: Estienne et Fils, 1749–56.

Plutarch. *Moralia*. 16 vols. Vol. 14 (1086c—1147a). Trans. Benedict Einarson and Phillip H. De Lacy. Loeb Classical Library. Cambridge: Harvard University Press, 1986.

Reil, Johann Christian. *Rhapsodieen über die Anwendung der psychischen Curmethode auf Geisteszerrüttungen*. Halle: Curt, 1803.

Rochlitz, Friedrich. *Auswahl des Besten aus Friedrich Rochlitz' sämmtlichen Schriften*. 6 vols. Züllichau: Darnmann, 1821–22.

Rousseau, Jean-Jacques. *The Confessions*. Trans. J. M. Cohen. New York: Penguin, 1954.

——. *Œuvres complètes*. 5 vols. Ed. Bernard Gagnebin and Marcel Raymond. Paris: Gallimard, Bibliothèque de la Pléiade, 1959–95.

——. *The Social Contract*. Trans. Maurice Cranston. New York: Penguin, 1968.

Saar, Ferdinand von. *Novellen aus Österreich*. 2 vols. Ed. Karl Wagner, Vienna: Deuticke, 1998.

Schelling, Friedrich. *Sämtliche Werke*. Ed. K. F. A. Schelling. Stuttgart: Cotta, 1856.

Schlegel, Friedrich. *Kritische Friedrich Schlegel Ausgabe*. Vol. 13.2, *Philosophische Vorlesungen, 1800–1807*. Ed. Jean-Jacques Anstett. Munich: Schöningh, 1964.

Schopenhauer, Arthur. *Sämtliche Werke*. 7 vols. Ed. Arthur Hübscher. Wiesbaden: Brockhaus, 1972.

Sulzer, Johann Georg. *Allgemeine Theorie der schönen Künste* (1771–74). 5 vols. 2d ed. 1792–95. Reprint, Hildesheim: Georg Olms, 1967.

Vergil. *P. Vergili Maronis Opera*. Ed. R. A. B. Mynors. Oxford: Clarendon, 1969.

Wackenroder, Wilhelm Heinrich. *Sämtliche Werke und Briefe: Historisch-kritische Ausgabe*. 2 vols. Ed. Silvio Vietta and Richard Littlejohns. Heidelberg: Carl Winter, 1991. English: *Wilhelm Heinrich Wackenroder's Confessions and Fantasies*. Trans. Mary H. Schubert. University Park: Pennsylvania State University Press, 1971 (translations from the *Herzensergießungen* and the *Phantasien über die Kunst*).

SECONDARY SOURCES

Abbate, Carolyn. *Unsung Voices: Opera and Musical Narrative in the Nineteenth Century*. Princeton: Princeton University Press, 1991.

Adorno, Theodor. *Philosophy of Modern Music*. Trans. A. G. Mitchell and W. V. Blomster. New York: Continuum, 2003.

Albright, Daniel. *Untwisting the Serpent: Modernism in Music, Literature, and Other Arts*. Chicago: University of Chicago Press, 2000.

Andreasen, Nancy. *The Creating Brain: The Neuroscience of Genius*. New York: Dana, 2005.

Ashfield, Andrew, and Peter de Bolla, eds. *The Sublime: A Reader in British Eighteenth-Century Aesthetic Theory*. Cambridge: Cambridge University Press, 1996.

Barthes, Roland. *Image—Music—Text*. Trans. Stephen Heath. New York: Hill and Wang, 1977.

——. *The Pleasure of the Text*. Trans. Richard Miller. New York: Hill and Wang, 1975.

——. *The Responsibility of Forms: Critical Essays on Music, Art, and Representation*. Ed. Richard Howard. Berkeley: University of California Press, 1985.

——. *Writing Degree Zero*. Trans. A. Lavers and C. Smith. New York: Hill and Wang, 1968.

Becker, Otto. "Das Bild des Weges." *Hermes Einzelschriften*, no. 4 (1937): 160–64.

Benardete, Seth. *The Rhetoric of Morality and Philosophy: Plato's* Gorgias *and* Phaedrus. Chicago: University of Chicago Press, 1991.

Bennoldt-Thomsen, Anke, and Alfredo Guzzoni. "Der Irrenhausbesuch: Ein Topos in der Literatur um 1800." *Aurora*, no. 42 (1982): 82–110.

Bernstein, Susan. *Virtuosity of the Nineteenth Century: Performing Music and Language in Heine, Liszt, and Baudelaire*, Stanford: Stanford University Press, 1998.

Bindman, David. "Roubiliac's Statue of Handel and the Keeping of Order in Vauxhall Gardens in the Early Eighteenth Century." *Sculpture Journal*, no. 1 (1997): 22–31.

Blanchot, Maurice. *L'entretien infini*. Paris: Gallimard, 1969. English: *The Infinite Conversation*. Trans. Susan Hanson. Minneapolis: University of Minnesota Press, 1993.

——. *L'espace littéraire*. Paris: Gallimard, 1955. English: *The Space of Literature*. Trans. Ann Smock. Lincoln: University of Nebraska Press, 1982.

Boehringer, Michael. "Of Meaning and Truth: Narrative Ambiguity in Kleist's 'Die heilige Cäcilie oder die Gewalt der Musik: Eine Legende." *Revue Frontenac*, no. 11 (1994): 103–28.

Bollacher, Martin. *Wackenroder und die Kunstauffassung der frühen Romantik*. Darmstadt: Wissenschaftliche Buchgesellschaft, 1983.

Bowie, Andrew. *Aesthetics and Subjectivity: From Kant to Nietzsche*. 2d ed. Manchester: Manchester University Press, 2003.

Brandstetter, Gabriele, ed. *Ton—Sprache: Komponisten in der deutschen Literatur*. Bern: Paul Haupt, 1995.

Brenot, Philippe. *Le génie et la folie en peinture, musique, littérature*. Paris: Plon, 1997.

Brewer, Daniel. *The Discourse of Enlightenment in Eighteenth-Century France: Diderot and the Art of Philosophizing*. Cambridge: Cambridge University Press, 1993.

Brooks, William. "Mistrust and Misconception: Music and Literature in Seventeenth- and Eighteenth-Century France." *Acta Musicologica*, no. 66 (1994): 22–30.

Brown, Calvin. *Music and Literature: A Comparison of the Arts.* Athens: University of Georgia Press, 1948.

Caduff, Corina. *Die Literarisierung von Musik und bildender Kunst um 1800.* Munich: Fink, 2003.

Cannone, Belinda. *Philosophies de la musique (1752–1780).* Paris: Klincksieck, 1990.

Caplan, Jay. *Framed Narratives: Diderot's Genealogy of the Beholder.* Minneapolis: University of Minnesota Press, 1985.

Cavarero, Adriana. *For More than One Voice: Toward a Philosophy of Vocal Expression.* Trans. Paul A. Kottman. Stanford: Stanford University Press, 2005.

Christensen, Thomas. *Rameau and Musical Thought in the Enlightenment.* Cambridge: Cambridge University Press, 1993.

Chua, Daniel. *Absolute Music and the Construction of Meaning.* Cambridge: Cambridge University Press, 1999.

Cowart, Georgia. "Sense and Sensibility in Eighteenth-Century Musical Thought." *Acta Musicologica*, no. 56 (1984): 251–66.

Creech, James. *Diderot: Thresholds of Representation.* Columbus: Ohio State University Press, 1986.

——. "Diderot and the Pleasure of the Other: Friends, Readers, and Posterity." *Eighteenth-Century Studies*, no. 11 (1978): 439–56.

Curtius, Ernst Robert. *European Literature and the Latin Middle Ages.* Trans. Willard Trask. New York: Pantheon, 1953.

Dahlhaus, Carl. "E. T. A. Hoffmanns Beethoven-Kritik und die Ästhetik des Erhabenen." *Archiv für Musikwissenschaft*, no. 38 (1981): 79–92.

——. *The Idea of Absolute Music.* Trans. Roger Lustig. Chicago: University of Chicago Press, 1989.

——. "Kleists Wort über den Generalbaß." *Kleist-Jahrbuch* 5 (1984): 13–24.

Daverio, John. *Crossing Paths: Schubert, Schumann, and Brahms.* Oxford: Oxford University Press, 2002.

Deleuze, Gilles, and Félix Guattari. *Kafka: Toward a Minor Literature.* Trans. Dana Polan. Minneapolis: University of Minnesota Press, 1986.

de Man, Paul. *The Rhetoric of Romanticism.* New York: Columbia University Press, 1984.

Derrida, Jacques. *The Ear of the Other: Otobiography, Transference, Translation.* Ed. Christie McDonald. Lincoln: University of Nebraska Press, 1988.

——. *Of Grammatology.* Trans. Gayatri C. Spivak. Baltimore: Johns Hopkins University Press, 1974.

——. *Speech and Phenomena and Other Essays on Husserl's Theory of Signs.* Trans. D. B. Allison. Evanston: Northwestern University Press, 1973.

——. *Writing and Difference.* Trans. Alan Bass. New York: Routledge, 2001.

Diamond, Stephen. *Anger, Madness, and the Daimonic: The Psychological Genesis of Violence, Evil, and Creativity.* Albany: State University of New York Press, 1996.

Dieckmann, Herbert. "The Relationship Between Diderot's Satire I and Satire II." *Romanic Review*, no. 43 (1952): 12–26.

Doerner, Klaus. *Madmen and the Bourgeoisie: A Social History of Insanity and Psychiatry.* Trans. Joachim Neugroschel and Jean Steinberg. Oxford: Blackwell, 1981.

Dolar, Mladen. *A Voice and Nothing More.* Cambridge, Mass.: MIT Press, 2006.

Duchez, Marie-Elisabeth. "Principe de la mélodie et origine des langues: Un brouillon inédit de Jean-Jacques Rousseau sur l'origine de la mélodie." *Revue de Musicologie,* no. 60 (1974): 33–86.

Felman, Shoshona. *Writing and Madness: Literature/Philosophy/Psychoanalysis.* Stanford: Stanford University Press, 2003.

Fitzgerald, Michael. *Autism and Creativity: Is There a Link Between Autism in Men and Exceptional Ability?* New York: Routledge, 2004.

Foucault, Michel. *The Archaeology of Knowledge.* Trans. A. Sheridan Smith. New York: Pantheon, 1972.

——. *Histoire de la folie à l'âge classique.* Paris: Gallimard, 1972.

——. *History of Madness.* Trans. Jonathan Murphy and Jean Khalfa. London: Routledge, 2006.

——. *Language, Counter-Memory, Practice: Selected Essays and Interviews.* Ed. D. F. Bouchard. Ithaca: Cornell University Press, 1977.

Fournier, Pascal. *Der Teufelsvirtuose: Eine kulturhistorische Spurensuche.* Freiburg im Breisgau: Rombach, 2001.

Frank, Manfred. *Die Unhintergehbarkeit von Individualität: Reflexionen über Subjekt, Person und Individuum aus Anlaß ihrer "postmodernen" Toterklärung.* Frankfurt: Suhrkamp, 1986.

Franken, Franz. *Die Krankheiten grosser Komponisten.* 4 vols. Wilhelmshaven: Noetzel, 1986–97.

Fried, Michael. *Absorption and Theatricality: Painting and Beholder in the Age of Diderot.* Chicago: University of Chicago, 1988.

Gearhart, Suzanne. "The Dialectic and Its Aesthetic Other: Hegel and Diderot." *Modern Language Notes,* no. 101 (1986): 1042–66.

Gess, Nicola. *Gewalt der Musik: Literatur und Musikkritik um 1800.* Freiburg im Breisgau: Rombach, 2006.

Gessinger, Joachim. *Auge und Ohr: Studien zur Erforschung der Sprache am Menschen, 1700–1850.* Berlin: de Gruyter, 1994.

Ginzburg, Carlo. *I Benandanti.* Turin: Einaudi, 1966.

Goehr, Lydia. *The Imaginary Museum of Musical Works: An Essay in the Philosophy of Music.* Oxford: Clarendon, 1992.

Goldschmidt, Hugo. *Die Musikästhetik des 18. Jahrhunderts und ihre Beziehungen zu seinem Kunstschaffen.* 1915. Reprint, Zurich: Hildesheim, 1968.

Goodman, Nelson. *Languages of Art: An Approach to a Theory of Symbols.* Indianapolis: Bobbs-Merrill, 1968.

Graham, Ilse. *Heinrich von Kleist: Word into Flesh. A Poet's Quest for the Symbol,* Berlin: de Gruyter, 1977.

Greiner, Bernhard. "'Das ganze Schrecken der Tonkunst': 'Die heilige Cäcilie oder Die Gewalt der Musik.' Kleists erzählender Entwurf des Erhabenen." *Zeitschrift für deutsche Philologie,* no. 115 (1996): 501–20.

Haase, Donald, and Rachel Freudenburg. "Power, Truth, and Interpretation: The Hermeneutic Act and Kleist's *Die heilige Cäcilie*." *Deutsche Vierteljahrsschrift*, no. 60 (1986): 88–103.

Hamilton, John. "*Sinneverwirrende Töne*: Musik und Wahnsinn in Heines *Florentinischen Nächten*." *Zeitschrift für deutsche Philologie*, no. 126 (2007).

Hollander, John. *The Untuning of the Sky: Ideas of Music in English Poetry, 1500–1700*. Princeton: Princeton University Press, 1961.

Holz, Hans Heinz. *Macht und Ohnmacht der Sprache: Untersuchungen zum Sprachverständnis und Stil Heinrichs von Kleist*. Frankfurt, 1962.

Hosler, Bellamy. *Changing Aesthetic Views of Instrumental Music in 18th-Century Germany*. Ann Arbor: UMI Research Press, 1981.

Hyppolite, Jean. *Genesis and Structure of Hegel's "Phenomenology of the Spirit."* Trans. Samuel Cherniak and John Heckaman. Evanston: Northwestern University Press, 1974.

Jamison, Kay Redfield. *Touched by Fire: Manic-Depressive Illness and the Artistic Temperament*. New York: Free Press, 1993.

Jankélevitch, Vladmir. *Music and the Ineffable*. Trans. Carolyn Abbate. Princeton: Princeton University Press, 2003.

Janz, Curt Paul. *Friedrich Nietzsche: Biographie*. 3 vols. Munich: Hanser, 1993.

Jauss, Hans Robert. *The Dialogical and the Dialectical* Neveu de Rameau: *How Diderot Adopted Socrates and Hegel Adopted Diderot*. Berkeley: Center for Hermeneutical Studies in Hellenistic and Modern Culture, 1983.

Kessel, Johann H. "St. Veit, seine Geschichte, Verehrung und bildlichen Darstellungen." *Jahrbücher des Vereins für Altertumsfreunde im Rheinlande*, no. 43 (1867): 152–83.

Kinser, Samuel. "Saussure's Anagrams: Ideological Work." *Modern Language Notes*, no. 94 (1979): 1105–38.

Kofman, Sarah. *Autobiogriffures: Du chat Murr d'Hoffmann*. Paris: Galilée, 1984.

Köhler, Rafael. "Johann Gottfried Herder und die Überwindung der musikalischen Nachahmungsästhetik." *Archiv für Musikwissenschaft*, no. 52 (1995): 205–19.

Kojève, Alexandre. *Introduction to the Reading of Hegel*. Ed. Alan Bloom. Trans. James H. Nichols, Jr. Ithaca: Cornell University Press, 1980.

Kraft, Helga. *Erhörtes und Unerhörtes: Die Welt des Klanges bei Heinrich von Kleist*. Munich: Fink, 1976.

Kramer, Lawrence. "Decadence and Desire: The *Wilhelm Meister* Songs of Wolf and Schubert." *Nineteenth-Century Music*, no. 10 (1987): 229–42.

Kristeva, Julia. "La musique parlée; ou, Remarques sur la subjectivité dans la fiction à propos du 'Neveu de Rameau.'" In *Langue et Langages de Leibniz à L'encyclopédie*, ed. Michèle Duchet and Michèle Jalley, 153–206. Paris: Union Générale d'Éditions, 1977.

——. *La revolution du langage poétique: Avant-garde à la fin du XIXe siècle. Lautréamont et Mallarmé*. Paris: Seuil, 1974.

Lacoue-Labarthe, Philippe. *Musica Ficta (Figures of Wagner)*. Trans. Felicia McCarren. Stanford: Stanford University Press, 1994.

———. *Typography: Mimesis, Philosophy, Politics.* Ed. Christopher Fynsk. Cambridge: Harvard University Press, 1989.

Lacoue-Labarthe, Philippe, and Jean-Luc Nancy. *The Literary Absolute: The Theory of Literature in German Romanticism.* Trans. Philip Barnard and Cheryl Lester. Albany: State University of New York Press, 1988.

Laing, R. D. *The Divided Self: An Existential Study in Sanity and Madness.* 1960. Reprint, New York: Penguin, 1990.

Langer, Susanne. *Philosophy in a New Key: A Study in the Symbolism of Reason, Rite, and Art.* Cambridge: Harvard University Press, 1942.

Laplanche, Jean. *Hölderlin et la question du père.* Paris: Presses Universitaires de France, 1961.

Lejeune, Philippe. *Le pacte autobiographique.* Paris: Seuil, 1975.

Liébert, Georges. *Nietzsche and Music.* Trans. David Pellauer and Graham Parkes. Chicago: University of Chicago Press, 2004.

Liebrand, Claudia. *Aporie des Kunstmythos: Die Texte E. T. A. Hoffmanns.* Freiburg im Breisgau: Rombach, 1996.

Lippmann, Edward. *Musical Thought in Ancient Greece.* New York: Columbia University Press, 1964.

Loquai, Franz. *Künstler und Melancholie in der Romantik.* Frankfurt: Peter Lang, 1984.

Lubkoll, Christine. *Mythos Musik: Poetische Entwürfe des Musikalischen in der Literatur um 1800.* Freiburg im Breisgau: Rombach, 1995.

Ludwig, Arnold. *The Price of Greatness: Resolving the Creativity and Madness Controversy.* New York: Guilford, 1995.

Mathiesen, Thomas. *Apollo's Lyre: Greek Music and Music Theory in Antiquity and the Middle Ages.* Lincoln: University of Nebraska Press, 1999.

Maier, Hans. "Cäcilia unter den Deutschen: Herder, Goethe, Wackenroder, Kleist." *Kleist-Jahrbuch* 15 (1994): 67–82.

Menninghaus, Winfried. "Zwischen Überwältigung und Widerstand: Macht und Gewalt in Longins und Kants Theorien des Erhabenen." *Poetica,* no. 23 (1991): 1–19.

Meyer, Herman. *Der Sonderling in der deutschen Dichtung.* Munich: Hanser, 1963.

Monelle, Raymond. *The Sense of Music: Semiotic Essays.* Princeton: Princeton University Press, 2000.

Morrow, Mary Sue. *German Music Criticism in the Late Eighteenth Century: Aesthetic Issues in Instrumental Music.* Cambridge: Cambridge University Press, 1997.

Mücke, Dorothea von. "Der Fluch der heiligen Cäcilie." *Poetica,* no. 26 (1994): 105–20.

Mühlner, Robert. "Heinrich von Kleist und seine Legende *Die heilige Cäcilie oder die Gewalt der Musik.*" *Jahrbuch des Wiener Goethes-Vereins* 66 (1962): 149–56.

Nancy, Jean-Luc. *La communauté désœuvrée.* Paris: Bourgois, 1986. English: *The Inoperative Community.* Ed. Peter Connor. Minneapolis: University of Minnesota Press, 1991.

————. *Multiple Arts: The Muses II.* Ed. Simon Sparks, Stanford: Stanford University Press, 2006.

Naumann, Barbara. *"Musikalisches Ideen-Instrument": Das Musikalische in Poetik und Sprachtheorie der Frühromantik.* Stuttgart: Metzler, 1990.

Navratil, Leo. *Manisch-depressiv: Zur Psychodynamik des Künstlers.* Vienna: Brandstätter, 1999.

Neubaurer, John. *The Emancipation of Music from Language: Departure from Mimesis in Eighteenth-Century Aesthetics.* New Haven: Yale University Press, 1986.

Neumann, Gerhard. "Eselgeschrei und Sphärenklang: Zeichensystem der Musik und Legitimation der Legende in Kleists Novelle *Die heilige Cäcilie oder die Gewalt der Musik.*" In *Heinrich von Kleist: Kriegsfall—Rechtsfall—Sündenfall,* ed. G. Neumann, 365–89. Freiburg am Breisgau: Rombach, 1994.

Noske, Frits. "Forma formans." *International Review of the Aesthetics and Sociology of Music,* no. 7 (1976): 43–62.

O'Gorman, Donal. *Diderot the Satirist: Le Neveu de Rameau and Related Works: An Analysis.* Toronto: University of Toronto Press, 1971.

Paddison, Max. *Adorno's Aesthetics of Music.* Cambridge: Cambridge University Press, 1993.

Padel, Ruth. *Whom Gods Destroy: Elements of Greek and Tragic Madness.* Princeton: Princeton University Press, 1995.

Palisca, Claude. "The Alterati of Florence, Pioneers in the Theory of Dramatic Music." In *New Looks at Italian Opera: Essays in Honor of Donald J. Grout,* ed. W. Austin, 9–38. Ithaca: Cornell University Press, 1968.

Parret, Herman. "Kant on Music and the Hierarchy of the Arts." *Journal of Aesthetics and Art Criticism,* no. 56 (1998): 251–64.

Poizat, Michel. *The Angel's Cry: Beyond the Pleasure Principle in Opera.* Trans. Arthur Denner. Ithaca: Cornell University Press, 1992.

Potter, Pamela, ed. *Most German of the Arts: Musicology and Society from the Weimar Republic to the End of Hitler's Reich.* New Haven: Yale University Press, 1998.

Price, David W. "Hegel's Intertextual Dialectic: Diderot's *Le Neveu de Rameau* in the *Phenomenology of Spirit.*" *Clio,* no. 20 (1991): 223–33.

Prieto, Eric. *Listening In: Music, Mind, and the Modernist Narrative.* Lincoln: University of Nebraska Press, 2002.

Promies, Wolfgang. *Die Bürger und der Narr; oder, Das Risiko der Phantasie.* Munich: Hanser, 1966.

Puschmann, Rosemarie. *Heinrich von Kleists Cäcilien-Erzählung.* Bielefeld: Aisthesis, 1988.

Quignard, Pascal. *La haine de la musique.* 1996. Reprint, Paris: Gallimard, 2002.

Reiss, Timothy J. *Knowledge, Discovery and Imagination in Early Modern Europe: The Rise of Aesthetic Rationalism.* Cambridge: Cambridge University Press, 1997.

————. *Mirages of the Selfe: Patterns of Personhood in Ancient and Early Modern Europe.* Stanford: Stanford University Press, 2003.

Richards, Robert J. "Rhapsodies on a Cat-Piano; or, Johann Christian Reil and the Foundations of Romantic Psychiatry." *Critical Inquiry*, no. 24 (1998): 700–36.

Riffaterre, Michael. *La production du texte*. Paris: Seuil, 1979.

Rigoli, Juan. *Lire et délire: Aliénisme, rhétorique, et littérature en France au XIXe siècle*. Paris: Fayard, 2001.

Ronell, Avital. *Finitude's Score: Essays for the End of the Millennium*. Lincoln: University of Nebraska Press, 1994.

Rouget, Gilbert. *La musique et la transe: Esquisse d'une théorie générale des relations de la musique et de la possession*. Paris: Gallimard, 1980.

Rüdiger, Wolfgang. *Musik und Wirklichkeit bei E. T. A. Hoffmann: Zur Entstehung einer Musikanschauung der Romantik*. Pfaffenweiler: Centaurus, 1989.

Saint-Amand, Pierre. *Diderot: Le labyrinthe de la relation*. Paris: Vrin, 1984.

Salmen, Walter. *Johann Friedrich Reichardt: Komponist, Schriftsteller, Kapellmeister und Verwaltungsbeamter der Goethezeit*. Freiburg im Breisgau: Atlantis, 1963.

——. "Die Musik im Weltbild J. W. Ritters." *Schlesien*, no. 2 (1957): 178–80.

Sève, Bernard. *L'altération musicale*. Paris: Seuil, 2002.

Scher, Steven P. "Hoffmann and Sterne: Unmediated Parallels in Narrative Method." *Comparative Literature*, no. 28 (1976): 309–25.

Scheuffelen, Thomas and Angela Wagner-Gnan, eds. *"—die Winter-Tage bringt er meistens am Forte Piano zu—" aus der Nürtinger Pflegschaftsakte: Zwölf Briefe Ernst Zimmers aus den Jahren 1828–1832 über Hölderlin im Tübinger Turm*. Nürtingen: Zimmermann, 1989.

Schmidt, James. "The Fool's Truth: Diderot, Goethe, and Hegel." *Journal of the History of Ideas*, no. 57 (1996): 625–44.

Schoolfield, George. *The Figure of the Musician in German Literature*. New York: AMS, 1966.

Scott, John T. "Rousseau and the Melodious Language of Freedom." *Journal of Politics*, no. 59 (1997): 803–29.

Segebrecht, Wulf. *Autobiographie und Dichtung: Eine Studie zum Werk E. T. A. Hoffmanns*. Stuttgart: Metzler, 1967.

Sembdner, Helmut. *Heinrich von Kleist, Geschichte meiner Seele, Ideenmagazin: Das Lebenszeugnis der Briefe*. Bremen: Dieterich, 1959.

——. *Heinrich von Kleists Lebensspuren: Dokumente und Berichte der Zeitgenossen*. Bremen: Schünemann, 1957.

Smith, John. *The Spirit and Its Letter: Traces of Rhetoric in Hegel's Philosophy of Bildung*. Ithaca: Cornell University Press, 1988.

Starobinski, Jean. "L'accent de la verité." In *Diderot*, 9–26. Paris: Comédie Française, 1984.

——. "Diderot et la parole des autres." *Critique*, no. 296 (1972): 3–22.

——. "Rousseau's Happy Days." Trans. A. Tomarken. *New Literary History*, no. 11 (1979): 147–66.

——. *Words upon Words: The Anagrams of Ferdinand de Saussure*. Trans. Olivia Emmet, New Haven: Yale University Press, 1979.

Stein, Jack. "Musical Settings of the Songs from *Wilhelm Meister*." *Comparative Literature*, no. 22 (1970): 125–46.

Steinecke, Hartmut. *Die Kunst der Fantasie: E. T. A. Hoffmanns Leben und Werk.* Frankfurt: Insel, 2004.

Steiner, George. *Language and Silence: Essays on Language, Literature, and the Inhuman.* New York: Atheneum, 1967.

Straus, Erwin. *Phenomenological Psychology.* Trans. Erling Eng. New York: Basic Books, 1966.

Strauss, Jonathan. *Subjects of Terror: Nerval, Hegel, and the Modern Self,* Stanford: Stanford University Press, 1998.

Sumi, Yoichi. Le neveu de Rameau: *Caprices et logiques du jeu.* Tokyo: France Tosho, 1975.

Taylor, Charles. *Human Agency and Language: Philosophical Papers.* Cambridge: Cambridge University Press, 1985.

Thomas, Downing. *Music and the Origins of Language: Theories from the French Enlightenment.* Cambridge: Cambridge University Press, 1995.

Todorov, Tzvetan. *The Fantastic: A Structural Approach to a Literary Genre.* Trans. Richard Howard. Ithaca: Cornell University Press, 1975.

Tomlinson, Gary. *Music in Renaissance Magic: Toward a Historiography of Others.* Chicago: University of Chicago Press, 1993.

Türcke, Christoph. *Der tolle Mensch: Nietzsche und der Wahnsinn der Vernunft.* Frankfurt: Fischer, 1989.

Vernière, Paul. *Diderot, ses manuscrits et ses copistes.* Paris: Klincksieck, 1967.

——. "Histoire littéraire et papyrologie: À propos des autographes de Diderot." *Revue d'Histoire Littéraire de la France,* July–September 1966, 409–18.

Weineck, Silke-Maria. *The Abyss Above: Philosophy and Poetic Madness in Plato, Hölderlin, and Nietzsche.* Albany: State University of New York Press, 2002.

Weiner, Marc A. *Undertones of Insurrection: Music, Politics, and the Social Sphere in the Modern German Narrative.* Lincoln: University of Nebraska Press, 1993.

Wiese, Benno von. *Die deutsche Novelle von Goethe bis Kafka.* 2 vols. Düsseldorf: Bagel, 1968.

Wilson, Arthur M. *Diderot.* New York: Oxford University Press, 1972.

Wittkowski, Wolfgang. "*Die heilige Cäcilie* und *Der Zweikampf*: Kleists Legenden und die romantische Ironie." *Colloquia Germanica,* no. 6 (1972): 17–59.

Wyss, Edith. *The Myth of Apollo and Marsyas in the Art of the Italian Renaissance: An Inquiry into the Meaning of Images.* Newark: University of Delaware Press, 1996.

Ziolkowski, Theodore. *German Romanticism and Its Institutions.* Princeton: Princeton University Press, 1990.

Žižek, Slavoj, and Mladen Dolar. *Opera's Second Death.* New York: Routledge, 2002.

Zuckert, Rachel. "Awe or Envy: Herder contra Kant on the Sublime." *Journal of Aesthetics and Art Criticism,* no. 61 (2003): 217–32.

Index